Driven

DRIVEN

How the Bathurst Tragedy
Ignited a Crusade for Change

RICHARD FOOT

Edited by John Sweet.
Cover and page design by Julie Scriver and Chris Tompkins.
Image of students from REUTERS/Paul Darrow.
Tire Tracks in Snow image from Rochelle Hartman (www.flickr.com/photos/tinfoilraccoon).
Printed in Canada.
10 9 8 7 6 5 4 3 2 1

Library and Archives Canada Cataloguing in Publication

Foot, Richard, author
  Driven: how the Bathurst tragedy ignited a crusade for change / Richard Foot.

Includes index.
Issued in print and electronic formats.
ISBN 978-0-86492-916-7 (pbk.). — ISBN 978-0-86492-785-9 (epub)

1. Acevedo, Ana. 2. Hains, Isabelle. 3. Acevedo, Ana — Family. 4. Hains, Isabelle — Family. 5. Traffic accidents — New Brunswick — Bathurst. 6. Traffic fatalities — New Brunswick — Bathurst. 7. School children — Transportation — New Brunswick — Safety measures. 8. Community activists — New Brunswick — Bathurst — Biography.
I. Title

LB2864.F66 2013   363.1259   C2013-903044-1   C2013-903045-X

Goose Lane Editions acknowledges the generous support of the Canada Council for the Arts, the Government of Canada through the Canada Book Fund (CBF), and the Government of New Brunswick through the Department of Tourism, Heritage, and Culture.

Goose Lane Editions
500 Beaverbrook Court, Suite 330
Fredericton, New Brunswick
CANADA E3B 5X4
www.gooselane.com

For Julia and Jeremy

* * *

and in memory of the Boys in Red

Contents

"Our government doesn't listen to its citizens. You defend, you deny, you delay. And we lost our children because of it, because your government didn't put children's safety first. And you continued to do it after their deaths. And it's a shame. So who's going to get reprimanded for this? Nobody. Just like when our children died. Nobody. Everybody just walked away."

—Isabelle Hains

"That winter morning when I picked up the paper and read about this terrible event in a small town upstate, with all those kids lost, I knew instantly what the story was; I knew at once that it wasn't an "accident" at all. There are no accidents. I don't even know what the word means, and I never trust anyone who says he does."

—Russell Banks, *The Sweet Hereafter*

Introduction

ON THE MORNING of January 12, 2008, my news editor in Ottawa called, asking me to go immediately to northern New Brunswick. There'd been a highway tragedy involving a high school basketball team. Seven kids and a teacher were dead. Would I drive up to the town of Bathurst to cover the story?

My heart sank, not because of the awful crash, but at this sudden, unwanted assignment. It was a Saturday morning in Halifax. I had groceries to buy, kids of my own to ferry around to weekend activities, and other family obligations. On top of all that, as a newspaper reporter for the previous fourteen years, I'd covered many fatal tragedies before, from plane crashes and marine disasters to deadly hurricanes, and none of them were easy subjects. Editors always wanted reporters to knock on the doors of perfect strangers, heartbroken families in the throes of tears and mourning, and ask for interviews, which was a horrible chore for most journalists; I certainly hated doing it. I also didn't see much depth or texture to the Bathurst story beyond the fact of a simple highway accident. Of course, the death of nearly an entire team of students was an appalling, sensational event, but there didn't seem to be any more to this than a straightforward highway collision.

I was a staff writer for Canwest News Service, a national chain of newspapers later known as the Postmedia News Network. My boss wanted a story from Bathurst, and as Canwest's only available reporter on the East Coast, I could hardly say no. So I quickly packed a bag, rented a car, and made the long, snowy, five-hour drive from Halifax.

I spent the whole week in Bathurst, along with a large crew of colleagues from other news outlets, searching for relatives of the victims, knocking on doors of the families whose sons had miraculously survived the crash, and interviewing townspeople, students, and municipal and school officials. It wasn't easy finding family members who wanted to talk — a few did, but most simply shook their heads and shut their doors. Yet there was so much emotion flowing around the small, isolated community that the stories just wrote themselves anyway. The accident had ignited a tidal wave of shock and heartbreak, which swept through Bathurst in those early days and culminated in the extraordinary spectacle of the huge public funeral service for the seven boys at the city's hockey arena. Despite my initial reservations, I was glad to have covered the story. It was big national news, and being in Bathurst that week was a moving and poignant experience.

When the funeral was over, the media all left town, as I did, assuming there was little left to say about the tragedy. The story faded quickly from the headlines, especially the national headlines, and I think it's fair to say most reporters who covered the event were surprised, months later, to hear about two mothers speaking out, asking questions about the crash, and knocking heads with the government.

As the months and years went by, I wrote about developments in the story. I became intrigued by the way Isabelle Hains and Ana Acevedo, two ordinary working-class moms who had lost their sons in the tragedy, were managing not only to force their agenda upon school and government authorities, but were doing so with verve, skill, and spirit. It is no easy thing to take on the powers of government, at any level, yet these mothers were somehow demanding action and change — and quite often winning. They even had a no-holds-barred online blog, which read at times like the raw copy of an investigative reporter's notebook. The moms were digging up challenging documents, and getting comments and correspondence from government officials, all of which they published online, making for some fascinating and extraordinary reading. They had become citizen journalists, holding public officials to account, and sniffing out the truth behind the circumstances of their sons' deaths. The tragedy wasn't, it turns out, as straightforward or excusable as it first seemed. There were serious questions of accountability and responsibility, not to mention concerns about the future safety of school travel — questions that wouldn't have come to light if Ana and Isabelle hadn't had the courage to ask them. These moms were doing the work that journalists ought to have done, if we hadn't been so quick to accept the conventional wisdom that the death of eight people was just a random accident no one could have prevented. Instead we descended on Bathurst, wrote a few stories about sorrow and heartbreak, then lost interest and drifted away.

· · ·

What interests me most about Ana and Isabelle's story is the light they bravely shone on the fallibility of the status quo, the *accepted way of doing things* — and on the folly of trusting leaders too set in their ways, or too self-assured, to break out of their inertia.

Everywhere we rely on experts and people in authority to guide us in our affairs — in science, business, sports, politics, and, as Bathurst showed us, in our schools. We are also guided by custom and tradition, and we often casually accept that our systems and institutions work the way they do simply because, well, things have always worked that way, or because we trust the people in charge to know best.

The crash of Western financial markets in the fall of 2008 offers a spectacular example of the mistake of blindly following the supposed good guidance of establishment leaders and so-called experts, in this case the sophisticated minds of high finance in business and government who ran and regulated the economy. The powerful, wealthy princes of Wall Street and elsewhere, who controlled the world's biggest banks, and their über-smart bond traders who devised the madcap assets known as mortgage-backed derivatives would end up bringing down their own banks in addition to others, jeopardizing the world economy and causing hardship to millions of families and homeowners. They had done all this with the blessing of equally smart government experts whose job was to regulate the market and protect the economy. American author Michael Lewis, among others, has documented much of this, and as he shows in his 2010 book *The Big Short*, it wasn't a random, unavoidable accident. There was a small, vocal band of financial players—naysayers—who could see what was coming and who tried to warn the government and the banking bosses that the financial system would one day collapse unless it changed course. But their voices were ignored, partly because the money of the game was too good, but also because of hubris and complacency, a belief that the banks simply couldn't fail, and anyway, a bunch of very clever, very respected people were running and regulating the system, so why should we challenge or question them?

Change is hardest when it forces institutions, or the people in them, to embrace new ideas, new ways of thinking, new practices, because it often threatens their worldview or the comfortable place they've carved out for themselves in the establishment of those institutions. In 2003, Lewis examined this phenomenon in another book, *Moneyball*, in which he showed the way a radical new system of analyzing baseball talent had helped an uncompetitive team, the Oakland Athletics, become a playoff contender without the deep pockets of richer teams in big-market cities. Sabermetrics, as Oakland's new talent-spotting system was called, revealed flaws in the way professional baseball scouts had spotted talent for more than a century. Ultimately it transformed Major League Baseball's thinking on the issue, but its first serious proponent, Oakland's general manager Billy Beane, was ridiculed by many in the baseball world, even people on his own team, when he dared to impose the idea of sabermetrics on this tradition-bound game. A few, however, recognized the genius of the new system and the fearlessness of Beane in embracing it. *Moneyball* was eventually made into a Hollywood movie, with Brad Pitt starring as Beane. In the movie, the owner of the Boston Red Sox encourages Pitt's character not to lose heart, not to give in to the critics and skeptics, and he receives a lesson in why pioneers of change who seek to alter the status quo are so often scorned.

"I know you're taking it in the teeth out there," the Red Sox owner says. "But the first guy through the wall, he always gets bloodied. Always. Because it's threatening, not just to the way they do business, but in their minds it's threatening the game. But really what it's threatening is their livelihoods, their jobs. It's threatening the way that they *do* things. And every time that happens, whether it's a government, or a way of doing business, or whatever it is, the people who are holding the reins, who have their hands on the switch, they go batshit crazy."

Isabelle and Ana challenged the people holding the reins in their sons' school, their town, and their province. They asked the establishment to wake up. They confronted a complacent, hidebound system and shocked it with some new, though hardly radical, ideas:

Maybe our kids shouldn't be travelling at night in snowstorms.

Maybe there should be laws governing after-school travel, and those laws should be enforced.

Maybe someone should stand up and take responsibility for the deaths of our sons.

At first glance, Ana and Isabelle were powerless figures in a community of deep loyalties and carefully protected interests. When their sons died, they did what no one expected them to, not even their own families. They questioned the way things were. They stood up to leaders who wanted them to be silent. They urged change on institutions reluctant to consider anything new, or to even conceive that mistakes might have been made.

It would be wrong to call these moms "heroes." They made their own mistakes, they didn't succeed in all their battles, and their crusade took some wrong turns. Sometimes the crusaders became so focused on their mission that it clouded their judgment. In their minds the issues were always black-and-white, when sometimes things were more grey. But people who strike out against conventional wisdom, who lead lonely struggles against established orthodoxy, are never orthodox themselves. Their eccentricity is often born out of a deep personal trauma. They can be obsessive, abrasive, and immune to public censure. In this respect, Ana and Isabelle weren't perfect either. They turned out to be profoundly human. Yet in spite of their flaws, Ana and Isabelle showed in their own small way what a pair of uncommonly determined individuals can accomplish in a society lulled by lassitude and comforted by the status quo. That the mothers did this in the midst of terrible heartache is even more remarkable. Ana and Isabelle struggled with grief, but they were never consumed by it. Instead they were inspired by it to rise up and honour the memory of their sons. After all, this is not the story of a tragedy; it's the tale of two women transformed by loss into unlikely agents of courage and change.

Prologue
SNOW ANGEL

HEAVY SNOW WAS falling, yet again, along the North Shore of New Brunswick. It was a Friday afternoon in late March, and the deep icy layers that had accumulated all winter, obscuring front steps and wooden decks and backyard barbeques, wrapping the town of Beresford under what looked like a crusty mantle of baker's fondant, had turned soft and silky again with the fresh snow. Beside the town, the Bay of Chaleur was still frozen over, still speckled in places with the colourful shacks of ice fishermen, tempting their fate on the frigid sea. The great white frozen bay reached inland from the open waters of the Gulf of St. Lawrence like a huge icicle thrust sideways into the body of the continent, dividing the distant grey hills of Quebec's Gaspé Peninsula from the frostbitten coast of the Maritimes.

Inside her home, besieged amid this glacial landscape, Ana Acevedo was feeling the cold. A mother of five, Ana had lived in northern New Brunswick for twenty years, but she had never grown accustomed to its endless winters. Most of her life had been spent in the subtropics of Central America, where life hadn't been easy, but at least the climate was hospitable. Before coming to New Brunswick she had heard incredible stories about how the snow lay so thick and heavy upon the rooftops that men would climb up and shovel it off. Or how sometimes the white drifts grew so high you couldn't even open the front door to your house. The stories turned out to be true, at least in towns like Beresford, where Ana owned a small house in a plain but well-kept neighbourhood of clapboard bungalows and split-levels.

Today she was home alone, except for her husband Francisco who was outside, shovelling his way through the drifts in the driveway, digging out Ana's Honda CR-V. Inside the house, the central heating was on, but Ana couldn't get warm. On days like this the winter seemed to penetrate the very walls of her house, tendrils of frost reaching through the insulation and the drywall and wrapping themselves around Ana's bones. She climbed into bed and pulled the covers up to her neck. She closed her eyes. The house was empty and silent, the only sounds being the tapping of icy, windblown snow-flakes against the windows, and the muffled scrape...scrape...scrape...of Francisco's shovel on the asphalt driveway.

Ana lay inside her blankets, shivering and lonely, listening to the storm, until she felt the weight of a body sit down on the end of her bed. Francisco had not come inside; she could still hear him working in the driveway. But someone was on the end of her bed. Their warm hands were underneath the covers now, rubbing her bare feet — teenage hands, too small for an adult but too large for a child, gently caressing her feet. Then a voice whispered softly, right beside her ear.

"Mom."

Ana listened. The familiar voice spoke again.

"Mom... *Mom*."

"Javi?" Ana said quietly. "I knew you were not gone. I knew you were coming back."

Ana felt the hands of Javier, her seventeen-year-old son, warming her feet. She heard his voice and felt his presence in her bedroom. But when she opened her eyes and looked around, the house was still silent and cold and empty.

Of course it was. Ana's four older children had all left home. Some lived across town, others across the country. Her youngest child, Javier, the lovely, handsome boy she so deeply treasured, was gone too, killed only three months ago along with six of his friends on an ice-covered highway not far from home.

One

HIGHWAY 8

THE DRIVE BETWEEN Bathurst and Moncton takes roughly two-and-a-half hours, along a highway that sometimes seems to have no end. For much of the way a straight, single-lane strip of asphalt cuts through mile after flat mile of fir and maple woodland, interrupted now and again by a lonely house or a patch of farmland carved out of the bush. The monotony is broken only occasionally, when the road darts across a series of majestic rivers draining into the Gulf of St. Lawrence—the Bouctouche, the Richibucto, and the grandest of all, the Miramichi, with its impressive bridge spanning the river under the trusses of a high, steel archway. In midwinter this journey between the small, isolated city of Bathurst in northern New Brunswick and the province's more populous southeast is not only a long and tedious slog, but a treacherous one. The ditches beside the road are often thick with snow, much of the old highway is narrow and sometimes notched with frost heaves, and driving the route in darkness, especially during winter storms, can be a taxing experience.

So when Isabelle Hains began hearing weather reports of a snowstorm forecast to hit the region on Friday, January 11—the night that her second son Daniel and his high school basketball team, the Bathurst High Phantoms, were scheduled to drive to Moncton for their first road game of 2008—she immediately began to worry.

"They're forecasting snow and freezing rain tonight, Dan," she told her son after waking him up for school on Friday morning, five days after the end of the Christmas break. "I don't know if it's a good idea to be going to Moncton."

"Don't worry, Mom. If the weather's bad they'll just cancel the game. Or we'll stay in a hotel."

Isabelle wasn't convinced. "Dan doesn't know what he's talking about," she thought to herself. "It's his first year playing basketball, and he's never played a winter road game before in bad weather. He's just assuming they'll stay in a Moncton hotel."

She went back to the kitchen with her worries, and made Daniel his lunch and also a shake for his breakfast. Daniel never took long to get ready for school. Minutes later he was dressed and sitting in the car gulping down his shake, a seventeen-year-old giant of a kid, dwarfing his mother as she drove him downtown to the school. On the way they talked about Daniel's dreams of busking his way through Europe after graduating from high school in the spring. Isabelle tried to convince him to go to trades college instead, but Daniel had his heart set on taking a year off, with his guitar and his backpack and some of his buddies from school.

Bathurst High started each day at 8:35 a.m., but this morning they arrived a few minutes late.

"I guess you'll have to go to the office and get a late slip," she told him as they pulled up to the front doors. "Dan," she said, "the weather's going to be bad tonight —"

Daniel cut her off. "Don't worry, Mom. We'll stay in Moncton," he said, grabbing his bag from the car and waving goodbye.

Isabelle watched her son charge through the doors of the school, then drove herself to work under a grey and gloomy January sky.

• • •

Out in Beresford, a seaside bedroom community next to Bathurst, Ana Acevedo and her son Javier had watched The Weather Network Thursday night before bed. Environment Canada, the federal government's weather service, had issued a "Winter Storm Watch" for Friday. The official forecast was calling for a mix of heavy snow and gusting winds beginning late in the afternoon in Bathurst. The snow would later turn to ice pellets and freezing rain, then turn to rain overnight as temperatures rose above zero Celsius. The forecast was much the same for Moncton, only with less snow: two to four centimetres compared to ten to fifteen for Bathurst. Whatever the snowfall amounts, it was going to be messy.

Javier was a friend and teammate of Daniel Hains and was also due to travel on Friday with the Phantoms. "Mom, look at the weather," Javier said. "I don't feel like going to Moncton tomorrow night."

"Well, if you don't feel like going, don't go," Ana told him.

It wasn't just the impending storm that bothered Javier. None of the Phantoms liked playing Friday night games out of town. They'd far rather spend their weekend nights in Bathurst, hanging out with friends or going to the movies, than playing ball for their school in another city. The only opportunity the bad weather offered was the remote chance of a night at a Moncton hotel, where the boys could have fun, swim in the hotel pool, and maybe meet some girls also stranded overnight.

The next morning, Javier woke Ana, as he did each day, gave her a bear hug, and climbed into the shower. Ana made them each a cheese omelette, ate hers alone in the kitchen, and left Javier's on the stove. Her cooking shift at nearby Danny's Inn, Restaurant, and Conference Centre started at eight a.m., so she left the house ahead of Javier, but not before ironing a dress shirt he would need to wear that morning. BHS ball players all had to wear good shirts and ties to school on game days.

"Javi, I've ironed your shirt, I have to go now," she told him through the bathroom door.

"OK Mom, bye."

"Love you."

"Love you too, Mom."

"If you don't want to go to Moncton, don't go," she shouted as she went out the front door.

...

A third basketball mom, Marcella Kelly, was also pondering the weather that morning. Would her son Nikki and the rest of the team really travel to Moncton on a storm day? When Nikki left the house for school, Marcella felt certain she'd be seeing him, not at midnight as originally planned after the game, but later that afternoon at the end of school.

Still, when Nikki shouted goodbye and headed out the door that morning, Kelly was overcome by a sense of disquiet, compelling her to do something she'd never done before. She walked down the hallway into Nikki's room and climbed into his bed, grabbing the covers and pulling them snugly around her. She lay there, alone in the quiet house, her head on her son's pillow, looking around the bedroom—at Nikki's sports trophies and medals, and at the pictures of him and his girlfriend. He was a successful student, a gifted athlete, and a leader among his peers. Everything was going so well in her son's life; how could Marcella not feel anything but happiness that morning? Yet something troubling nagged at her, something she couldn't quite put her finger on. Her "mother's intuition," she would later call it, was making her uneasy.

Nick Quinn was one of Nikki Kelly's best friends. They'd known each other since kindergarten, attended Cubs and Scouts together, and played every kind of sport together. As little boys they used to say they had "Nick Power." Nick's sixteenth birthday was coming up on Saturday. Although they were only now in grade ten, both had been pulled up above their age level to play with the senior kids on Bathurst High's top-tier, varsity basketball squad. Like Nikki, Nick Quinn was a natural athlete and an easy-going, highly coachable kid.

Nick's parents, Chris and Krista, were both lab technologists at the Bathurst hospital. As the family was getting ready for work and school that morning, Krista asked Nick about the impending storm. Would the team still be travelling to Moncton?

"He told me if the weather was bad, they would stay over in Moncton," remembers Krista. "They'd been told to bring money and extra clothes in case they stayed over. And I thought this was reasonable, so I gave him money and he took along a bag of extra clothes to school with him that morning."

• • •

The snow started falling around two p.m., even earlier than Environment Canada said it would. At 2:30, a waitress arriving for her evening shift at Danny's Restaurant announced to Ana and the other kitchen staff that Highway 8, the road up from Moncton, was slippery and getting worse.

"Oh my gosh, don't tell me that," said Ana.

She tried to reach Javier on his cellphone. She knew her son was teased at school for being a "mama's boy," but she called him anyway, wanting to know if the school had cancelled the game. There was no answer. "There's no way they're going to go in this weather," she told herself. But at four p.m., when Ana still hadn't heard from Javier—she knew he would have called if the game had been cancelled—she realized the road trip was under way.

Carol Ann Cormier, who worked in the office at Danny's and whose seventeen-year-old son Justin also played basketball with the Phantoms, came into the kitchen that afternoon. Ana told her how bad the roads were and how scared she was, but Cormier tried to reassure her.

"They'll be back late tonight," she said, "and then we'll be in peace."

Leaving the restaurant at the end of the day, Ana slipped and fell on the snowy sidewalk on the way to her car. She drove home through the falling snow, took a bath, and ate some supper, all the while fretting about Javier and the other boys and the weather.

At 9:30 p.m. she went to bed but she couldn't sleep. By 11:30 there was still no word from Javier, so she called his cellphone. No response. She figured he might not be answering because he was embarrassed, surrounded by his friends, to have to talk to his mother.

Five minutes later she called again and this time he answered.

"Javi, where are you? Which hotel are you in?"

"Oh Mom, I'm almost home. We passed Miramichi already," he said, sitting with the rest of his team in the school van, on the highway heading north towards Bathurst.

Ana couldn't believe the team was driving back to the city in such lousy conditions. Javier's own car was waiting for him in the parking lot outside Bathurst High, and Ana warned him the roads were bad and that he should be careful.

"Javi, when you arrive at the school, make sure you clean that car really good and just drive a little first in the parking lot. If you find it too slippery, call me back and I'll come and get you."

"Mom, I won't call you. I'll just take a taxi."

"OK."

"See you soon, Mom."

"OK. Love you, babe."

"Love you too, Mom."

Ana was too nervous to sleep. She ate a bowl of cereal and watched the clock, wishing her son was already home. She wasn't friends with any other parents of Javier's teammates, so she sat alone in her snowbound house, waiting and worrying, and eventually drifting off to sleep.

The telephone rang at 2:20 a.m., startling Ana awake.

"Mrs. Acevedo?" a woman's voice said. "This is the hospital calling. There's been an accident with the school van."

"My son's OK? Javi's OK, yeah?" said Ana.

"Ma'am, you need to come to the hospital."

• • •

When he arrived at Bathurst High on Friday morning, Phantoms coach Wayne Lord was well aware of the storm warnings. But this was Bathurst in January; serious winter storms were a fact of life here, and hardly unusual. As coach, the decision to stay or go to Moncton was unofficially his to make, at least that's how things had always worked at BHS since he started coaching the boys basketball team in 1992. If school classes were cancelled because of bad weather, the game would automatically be called off. But that hadn't happened on Friday. Lord briefly discussed the forecast with Vice-Principal Don McKay that morning; as he always did, McKay let Lord make the call.

Lord was a man of few words, a quiet-spoken, businesslike coach, and a popular one. He had spent years juggling both teaching duties and the extracurricular coaching that was his passion as an educator. He'd driven school vehicles filled with kids across New Brunswick dozens and dozens of times. His main concern today wasn't getting to Moncton before the snow started, it was getting home during the treacherous changeover to rain. If the rain didn't come soon enough, they might be caught driving home during the changeover itself, in that period of heightened hazard, when the thermometer hovers at zero Celsius and the snow turns to freezing rain, rattling off windshields and covering the highway with a deceptive film of ice and slush, before finally turning to actual rain.

"I was hoping that it would already be turned to rain before I came home, and thinking that the roads would be okay at that point," Lord would later explain.

Lord was a grade nine math teacher. He taught his classes that morning and then left Bathurst with the Phantoms just after two p.m., just as the snow was starting to fall. They stopped briefly after crossing the big river at Miramichi, so the boys could pick up a slice of pizza and something to drink at the Irving gas station just outside town, then continued south on the highway. The snow fell steadily, but not hard, for most of the journey and the team arrived without incident at Moncton High School, in time for its 6:30 p.m. game.

Bathurst High had three Ford vans to carry its students to sporting events around the province: an eleven-year-old white van, due to be replaced in the coming months with a newer model; a ten-year-old red van; and a seven-year-old red van. This time the Phantoms were travelling in the old white van, a decision made by another teacher at the school who was responsible for assigning vans to the various school teams and clubs for extracurricular travel. Lord had driven all the vans on numerous trips, and neither he nor his players gave much thought to, or had any hang-ups about, which van they travelled in (although the white van smelled the worst, thanks to years of carrying student athletes and their sweaty gear bags around the province). On this trip, like most others, the boys piled into the middle and rear seats, leaving the front-most bench seat filled with game gear and equipment.

The white van, a 1997 E-350 Ford Club Wagon, was designed to carry fourteen passengers and a driver, but only nine boys were on board for the game in Moncton. At least two other boys who were regular Phantoms players didn't make the trip that night, because of illness or other conflicts. The team played a lacklustre game against the Moncton High Purple Knights, losing 75-65, an embarrassing result for Bathurst considering they'd trounced Moncton earlier in the season. After tonight's loss, the boys were hungry. They changed out of their uniforms, climbed back into the white van, and drove a short distance to Moncton's Champlain Place mall, a sprawling retail complex on the edge of the city's downtown, where they ate a regular, post-game meal at the food court. There, Lord met up with his teenage daughter Katie and his wife, Beth, a fifty-one-year-old elementary school math and music teacher who had driven the Lords' eldest daughter to Moncton that day to meet her fiancé. The Lords' car would stay with their older daughter in Moncton, and Beth and Katie would catch a ride home with Wayne in the van.

It was nine p.m. when the team finished eating. Outside, the snow had about an hour earlier turned to rain. Lord examined the parking lot pavement. It looked clear and free of ice. So everyone piled into the van and headed out onto the highway for the long drive home. The storm appeared to have petered out. Lord, sitting behind the wheel, with his wife in the front passenger seat and his daughter Katie and the nine boys behind them, figured he'd have wet but clear roads on the dark highway back to Bathurst.

By the time they reached the City of Miramichi almost two hours later, however, conditions had worsened. As the van crossed the Miramichi River and pressed north towards Bathurst, wet snow and freezing rain began to fall, covering the tarmac in icy slush. In the back seats of the van, surrounded by darkness, Javier spoke to his mom on his cellphone, as did one or two other players, assuring their parents they'd be home soon. As Lord drove on, the painted line markings on the road disappeared and, eventually, so did the previous tire tracks of other vehicles.

At midnight, Lord and his passengers were only about fifteen minutes away from the outskirts of Bathurst. They all sang "Happy Birthday" to Nick Quinn, who had just turned sixteen.

Eight minutes later, just four kilometres south of the Bathurst exit, the bright headlights of a fifty-three-foot tractor-trailer appeared in the southbound lane at the top of a blind crest. Peering through his wipers and the freezing rain, Lord moved the van slightly to the right to give the big truck a wide berth. Lord couldn't clearly see the edge of the asphalt; the van's right wheels dropped off the pavement and hit the slush-covered shoulder of the road. Lord quickly corrected, turning the steering wheel left to get the van back onto the road. The van jumped back on the highway but then, to Lord's horror, kept moving leftwards despite his efforts to straighten the wheels. There was no response from the steering wheel or the brakes, and the van crossed the yellow line and headed directly into the floodlit path of the oncoming truck.

• • •

Austin Ward was a sixty-something trucker who had been delivering freight almost all his life. He was driving a large Mack transport that night, on his way to the Loblaws grocery store depot in Moncton with a load of empty wooden pallets, having spent the evening dropping off grocery supplies at stores in northeast New Brunswick. The freezing rain — "dirty weather" he called it — wasn't a serious problem for big rigs like his, but it made the driving more difficult. As he crested the hill outside Bathurst, he watched in disbelief as the oncoming Ford van careened inexplicably into his lane. Ward had only seconds to react. He cranked his wheel to the right and touched his brakes, but it was no use.

"There was just a flash, and then something hit my windshield," he recalled later, "and then everything went black."

Ward's rig barrelled off the right-hand side of the road and came to a standstill in the sharp ditch between the highway and the forest, having carved a muddy track through the snow. The big trailer was stretched perpendicular across almost the width of Highway 8. Rattled, but unhurt, Ward climbed out of his cab, noticed the hood had been ripped off his engine, and then wandered in the pitch black and the freezing rain back up the highway towards the crest of the hill. He wasn't sure what to expect. He heard voices in the distance and walked towards them. Wayne Lord came up to him, looking frantic and peering through the darkness.

"Did you see my kids anywhere?"

Ward stared at Lord for a moment, digesting the news. "You had kids with you?"

As the two men began searching the snowy ditch, a young couple, Sebastien Morrison and his girlfriend Julie Chiasson, came upon the scene as they were driving south on their way to Morrison's home in the nearby village of Saint-Sauveur. Morrison immediately pulled over and was approached by Lord, who shouted at the couple through their window to call 911. As Chiasson dialed for help on her cellphone, Morrison parked his Suzuki Grand Vitara 4x4 facing the ditch. He turned on his high beams to illuminate the crash site and was confronted with a harrowing scene: the white van was a crumpled mess of steel and glass. Its rear doors and the entire right side of the vehicle had been ripped clean away, like the top of a sardine can, along with many of the passenger bench seats in the back. Those benches and most of the boys who'd been sitting in them only minutes ago, laughing and talking and singing "Happy Birthday," were scattered like pieces of flotsam in the snow around the crash site.

Morrison scrambled down the embankment towards the van. Inside, Beth Lord was dead in the front passenger seat, but her daughter Katie and players Tim Daley and Bradd Arseneau were alive. Arseneau and Daley had been sitting together near the front of the van, sharing the earpieces to Arseneau's iPod, when the collision occurred. Daley had been watching the slush-covered road, feeling a little nervous about the drive, when he suddenly felt the back end of the van swing wide.

"I grabbed the seat," he explained afterwards, "and then we slipped over the other side of the road, and I saw the lights coming. And then it was over.

"I was lying in the ditch. My shoe was off and I noticed my wrist was broken. Bradd was reaching out to me, asking me for help and telling me he loves me. I put my hand there and I grabbed him, and Katie was sitting and sobbing in front, asking what happened."

Morrison and Chiasson found Katie and the two boys in shock, and shivering in the cold. Katie was strong enough to walk over to the shelter of the Suzuki, and eventually, despite the pain shooting through his broken pelvis, Daley limped over to the jeep too. Arseneau wasn't able to move, so Morrison ripped open a gear bag, covered him with spare clothes, and went to help Wayne Lord and Austin Ward search for other survivors.

They were soon joined by Corporal Mario Dupuis, a long-time cop and a dog handler with the Bathurst detachment of the Royal Canadian Mounted Police, who was returning from an out-of-town call when he happened upon the accident. Dupuis switched on his flashing police lights and radioed dispatchers to send another officer to direct traffic around what he thought was merely a transport truck that had slid off the road. But as he drove his unmarked SUV around the rear of the tractor-trailer, he saw the mangled van and the full horror of what had happened. He immediately called the dispatch centre again. "I need a lot of members, a lot of vehicles — all the ambulances, all the firefighters you can send. I've probably got seven to eight dead here at the scene," he shouted into his radio.

After quickly checking on the survivors, Dupuis worked frantically at the site with Lord, Ward, and Morrison to locate the other passengers. The remains of six boys were found lying in various parts of the ditch, amid patches of bloodstained snow. A seventh was missing, until Dupuis found him buried by snow in front of the engine of the big transport. In the chaos and the darkness, Dupuis hadn't realized that the victims he was dealing with were mostly kids. Each one was tall and well built and appeared to be an adult. It wasn't until he found the body of Codey Branch, a seventeen-year-old whom Dupuis recognized by the large basketball tattoo on one of his legs — the same young man who worked at the Canadian Tire in Bathurst, who had helped Dupuis during a recent visit to the store — that he realized the victims were all from the high school. Only then did the awful truth of the tragedy overcome him.

Also lying in the snow, along with Codey Branch, were the remains of Javier Acevedo, Daniel Hains, Nathan Cleland, Justin Cormier — all seventeen — Nikki Kelly, fifteen, and Nick Quinn, who died in the opening minutes of his sixteenth birthday.

About twenty minutes after his arrival at the crash site, Dupuis was joined by an RCMP collision expert and a stream of ambulances, municipal police officers, and firefighters. Lord told Dupuis that many of the boys' parents would be waiting for their children at the McDonald's restaurant in town, a regular rendezvous spot where Lord often dropped some of the boys off after road games. Despite the deadly trauma of the crash, including the loss of his wife, Lord had acted with purpose and professionalism since the collision, focused on locating each of the boys in his care. But now he was becoming distraught, agitated about facing the other families. "I should have stayed there overnight," he told Dupuis. "What will I do with the parents? How are the parents going to look at me?"

Dupuis tried to reassure him. "It's an accident," he said.

Dupuis then told the Bathurst police to find the parents at McDonald's and tell them not to come out to the crash site, but to go immediately to the city hospital. "One more thing," he told the other cops. "Make sure there's a priest waiting for the families at Emergency."

Amid the carnage stood the most surreal and unfortunate backdrop: the big trailer stretched across the highway was emblazoned along the full length of its sides with a giant, cheery, sky-blue Loblaws advertisement, lit up in the dark like a carnival sign by a multitude of headlights and the flashing, red-and-blue warning lights of emergency vehicles. It was an ad for the grocery chain's "President's Choice Children's Charity," that showed a stick-figure drawing of a happy-faced child perched in a wheelchair, along with the awkward slogan, in big, bold letters, "Making difficult lives a little easier."

...

Ginette Emond didn't normally worry when her son Codey travelled for out-of-town games. He'd grown up playing hockey and basketball all his life, so being on the road at night, even in snowstorms, was nothing unusual. But on this night, for reasons she's never understood, Emond began to feel anxious. She and Dale Branch, Codey's father, no longer lived together. And because Codey was staying the weekend at his dad's place, Emond was waiting up, as she routinely did on Friday game nights, for a phone call from Codey to hear that he was home safely from Moncton.

"At about 11:30 p.m. I started to get this feeling that they should be home by now," Emond says. "So I called Dale and said, 'I'm concerned. Don't you think the team should be home by now?' He said, 'Don't worry, he's okay, he can take care of himself.'"

Emond wasn't satisfied. She called Wayne Lord's house, but there was no answer. "Then I started getting really anxious, which normally never happened when my kids were travelling."

Before midnight, Dale Branch drove himself to the McDonald's on St. Peter Avenue, the city's main retail strip, to wait for the school van. Krista Quinn was also there in her car in the parking lot, along with Bruno Blanchard, Nikki Kelly's dad, and John Cleland, Nathan's dad. The parents knew each other well and sometimes socialized together. Only Branch was a stranger to the group because Codey was a newcomer at BHS. He had transferred there at the beginning of his grade twelve year from a francophone high school in the area, for the purpose of playing varsity-level basketball with the Phantoms.

The four parents sat in their cars in the snowy lot, as the time ticked by and the van never showed. By one a.m. nobody had heard anything, and their boys weren't answering their cellphones. So Bruno Blanchard knocked on the window of Krista Quinn's car.

"It doesn't make sense," he said. "They should be here by now."

"Let's go talk to John," she said. "He'll know what to do."

John Cleland, a long-time teacher at BHS, was widely respected by all the kids, some of whom called him "Magistrate Cleland." Cleland suggested they start calling other team families, including Bradd Arseneau's mother, Peggy, who was also a teacher at Bathurst High. The Arseneaus didn't know why the van wasn't back either, so on a hunch, Quinn called the hospital, using a private line she knew because she worked there in the lab. Over the telephone, the hospital sounded like a hive of activity, which Krista considered highly unusual for that time of night. After several attempts, she finally found someone there she knew, who told her there'd been an accident on the highway involving one of the teams from the high school.

"They're just bringing the kids in on ambulances now."

Krista was shocked and worried. But still, it seemed inconceivable that anyone had been seriously injured. She passed on the upsetting news to the other three parents in the parking lot, and the four of them drove in convoy through the snow-covered streets to the hospital, where they imagined ambulances would be bringing in their sons with cuts and bruises, and maybe, at worst, some broken bones.

● ● ●

Isabelle Hains hadn't gone to McDonald's. She was at home, waiting for Daniel to be dropped off by Javier Acevedo, who usually collected his car at the school and gave Daniel a drive home. She learned something horrible had happened, not from the police, but from a group of Daniel's friends. They had called her after midnight to say they were listening to an emergency dispatch scanner, which was crackling with police radio chatter about an accident on Highway 8. Isabelle telephoned Sandra Cleland, one of the few BHS basketball parents she knew well enough to call late at night, and told her about police scanner conversations of an accident on the highway.

"It can't be our boys," Cleland told her. "I just heard from Nathan on his cellphone a few minutes ago. He was in the van with the rest of them. John is down at McDonald's waiting to pick him up."

After Isabelle hung up, Daniel's buddies called her again, to say the accident chatter on the scanner involved a basketball team. "I don't want to worry you, Mrs. Hains, but they're talking about a transport hitting a van full of kids."

Isabelle immediately called the hospital, asking if they knew anything about an accident on the highway. She told them her son's name was Daniel Hains. The nurse on the other end told her they had no one by that name in the hospital. The nurse paused for a minute and then a second nurse came on the line: "Mrs. Hains, I think you'd better come down here right away."

Before leaving the house, Isabelle called her husband, Allan, in Alberta, where he had gone only weeks earlier to begin a new job in the Fort McMurray oil sands. Isabelle told her hsusband there had been a highway crash involving Daniel and his team, and she'd call him again with more news once she got to the hospital. She didn't want to go alone, so she picked up her mother on the way. Isabelle was distraught, and in tears.

"Mom," she said, crying uncontrollably. "Dan's gone, my baby's gone."

"Don't say that. You don't know that," her mother replied. "Wait till we get there, it might not be that bad."

• • •

The Chaleur Regional Hospital is a bleak, concrete, four-storey complex off Sunset Drive, in a residential neighbourhood on the northwest side of town. A long, tree-lined driveway leads from the street up to the building, where on the right-hand side, the place is illuminated at night by a large lit EMERGENCY sign that casts a gloomy, lime-green glow over the entrance. By the time Isabelle and her mother had arrived, many of the other parents were already inside. Word of the crash was now spreading quickly around Bathurst, and students from the high school were milling about in knots near the green-glow entrance. Bathurst High Principal Coleen Ramsay was also there with a handful of other teachers, as well as their boss, super-intendent of area schools John McLaughlin. He knew Isabelle and many of the other parents because, years ago, they'd all attended school together as students themselves. Isabelle was met at the entrance by her best friend, Sheila Doucet, whom Allan had contacted from Alberta, asking her to go to the hospital. Doucet was also Bradd Arseneau's aunt.

Inside, there was a state of confusion, with phones ringing, nurses and emergency workers rushing around, and worried parents demanding to know why more ambulances hadn't been dispatched to the highway to collect all the remaining boys. Isabelle, her mother, and Doucet were taken into a room where the parents who had come from McDonald's were now waiting. On their way in, they walked past Bradd Arseneau, sitting up on an ambulance stretcher with his mother and father at his side. The injured boy and Isabelle watched each other in silence as she walked past. At that moment she had no doubt; she knew for certain that Daniel was dead.

The parents of five boys were sitting silently and nervously in an Outpatients room, when Isabelle walked in. One of the last to arrive was Ginette Emond. After trying and failing to reach Wayne Lord on the phone, Emond had gone to bed with a set of Velcro curlers in her hair. At one a.m. Codey's dad had called, telling her to come to the hospital. Emond leapt out of bed and began frantically, and with difficulty, pulling the curlers off her head, ripping out clumps of hair as she grappled with the stubborn Velcro, until she finally got into her car and drove, as fast as she could through the ongoing storm, to Emergency.

Emond was ushered into the room with the other parents, and it wasn't long before a small, nervous doctor walked in, his hands visibly shaking as he read aloud from a piece of paper: "This is the list of names of the students who didn't survive the crash," he said. "Javier Acevedo, Codey Branch, Nathan Cleland, Justin Cormier, Daniel Hains, Nick Kelly, and Nick Quinn." As each name was announced, so followed the anguished screams of parents. Only Javier's name was greeted with silence, because his mother and father weren't at the hospital. No one had yet contacted them.

Devastated, Isabelle left the room to find a pay phone to call Allan in Alberta. Although he was now working in Fort McMurray, he was spending the weekend with his sister Bev in the town of Cold Lake, a large air force station in northern Alberta. Isabelle was relieved to know he'd have family nearby to comfort him. The nurses escorted Isabelle away from the pay phones to a private room with a telephone. At first, the line to Alberta was busy, but she finally got through. "Dan's gone," she told her husband through her tears. At the other end of the line, and on the far side of the country, Allan roared out in pain. Isabelle had never heard her husband cry so hard.

There were counsellors and priests at the hospital, waiting to help the parents, but Isabelle just wanted to escape the place and go home. As she walked with her mother across the parking lot towards her minivan, Daniel's school friends, waiting outside the entrance, surrounded her and peppered her with questions.

A few weeks later, Isabelle would record her memories of that night in a detailed personal journal. "I went outside [the hospital]," the journal says. "The kids were there. I saw Gina and I fell into her arms and told her 'Dan is gone.' She fell to her knees, and I hugged Kailan and Jason Vienneau, Jason Comeau, Jordan [and] Chipper. I told them to come to the house."

Some of the kids climbed into Isabelle's van to go home with her. As they were leaving, Superintendent John McLaughlin opened Isabelle's door.

"All the other parents are in the hospital, come inside," he asked her. "We have some people there to help you, to talk with you."

"I don't want to talk to you or anybody," she said, pulling her door closed. "I just want to be with my family."

At her home on Lakeside Avenue, Isabelle telephoned her sisters and brothers, Daniel's aunts and uncles in Bathurst — "Auntie Linda, Auntie Claudette, Uncle Steve, Uncle David" — and she was soon surrounded by family members and a crowd of high school kids, all shedding tears as they sat in shock and disbelief around the Hains living room. Isabelle's older son, Clark, lived in Moncton, but she was too terrified to call him with the awful news. The two brothers had always been close; how on earth would she tell him? Then, at two a.m., there was a phone call from the police.

"Mrs. Hains, your son was in an accident tonight, and he passed away."

"I already know that," Isabelle snapped back.

"Well, we need you to come back to the hospital to identify the body."

At 5:30 a.m., Isabelle was driven to the hospital morgue by her brothers and sisters. They had to hold her upright; her legs felt so weak, she could barely walk. There were doctors and nurses and a priest in the morgue. Daniel's body was laid out on a table, cleaned up as much as was possible. His bearded face had cuts and scrapes, and his body was held together by a blanket, wrapped tightly around him from his feet to his shoulders.

"Oh Daniel my baby all I could do was hug you and kiss you and smooth your hair," Isabelle would later write in her journal, talking directly to her son. "I remember asking the nurses if you suffered and they said you didn't. I don't know how long I stayed there with you. I told everyone in the room you were a good boy. Beautiful boy. My gentle giant.

"I didn't want to leave you all alone on that table, and kept kissing you and saying I am going to miss you so much. I remember the nurses giving me a wet cloth because there was blood on my hands and face but I didn't care. All I wanted to do was to keep kissing you and rubbing your eyebrows. The priest got us to say a prayer. Our Father. O Dan, I still can't believe that you are gone."

● ● ●

Corporal Mario Dupuis had also come to the hospital. The crash site was now in the formal care of a team of RCMP fatality and collision investigators. Other police officers were also on scene directing highway traffic around the site. Dupuis was no longer needed there, so he climbed in his SUV and drove to the hospital to see if he could be of some use to the grieving parents. "I thought I could help, maybe answer a couple of questions of the parents, being the first officer at the scene, and being a parent myself, and a grand-parent." He walked through the hospital's green-glow entrance into a crush of emergency personnel — paramedics, doctors, nurses, police officers, plus a small crowd of civilians in different states of tears and distress. Dupuis was a tough and experienced Mountie. He'd worked in cities and in small towns across Canada, and had seen his share of ugly crime scenes and traumatic accidents. But inside the hospital, surrounded by so much sorrow, the un-expected horror of the past hour and the images of Beth Lord and of those seven boys lying dead in the snow suddenly overwhelmed him. He found the sergeant in charge and asked if he could be of any help. "No, you've done enough," the sergeant told him. So Dupuis went into the hospital washroom, locked himself inside a cubicle, and wept.

• • •

For reasons she has never understood, Ana Acevedo wasn't contacted by the hospital until 2:20 a.m., roughly two hours later than the other families. "It has always bothered me why they didn't call me earlier," she says now. "Was there a chance that Javi was still alive immediately after the accident? Did they try to save him?"

Ana has never found the definitive answer to that question. When the hospital did finally call and tell her to come to Emergency, Ana telephoned her friend Lydia, waking her and asking her to meet Ana at the hospital. Before heading out, she tried Javier's cellphone one more time, but there was no answer.

It was no easy feat getting to the hospital that night from Beresford. With her heart racing and her legs weak, she pulled a winter coat over her pajamas and had to spend the next ten minutes scraping the snow and ice off her Honda in her driveway. It then took her forty-five minutes to navigate the ice-bound streets into Bathurst and Chaleur Regional. "I'll probably find him in a wheelchair," she thought. Her precious Javi. "He probably has some broken bones. He might be all banged up."

Lydia arrived at the hospital first and already knew the truth when she met Ana outside the doors to Emergency. "I was so worried about you, it's so slippery. Come on," she said, grabbing Ana's hand. "Let's go inside."

"He's OK, huh?" Ana asked.

"Let's go inside."

By this time, most of the other parents had gone home. The two women were escorted by a nurse down a hallway, past the X-ray room, to an empty outpatient clinic. Ana, wondering where Javi was waiting for them, was handed a glass of water and a plastic medicine cup with pills in it. A doctor greeted her and said, "I'm very sorry, but your son didn't make it."

"What?" said Ana. "Didn't make it where? He's still outside?"

"No. I'm sorry, Mrs. Acevedo. Your son is dead."

Ana stared at the doctor. "You're crazy."

"Yes, Ana," said Lydia. "Javi passed away."

Ana's body suddenly went soft. She collapsed onto the floor and started screaming, hoping to wake herself from what seemed like the worst kind of dream. Lydia and the doctor helped her up and asked her to take the medication, but she pushed it away. She was taken to a downstairs room where Ginette Emond and Carol Ann Cormier, whom Ana knew from Danny's Restaurant, were waiting to meet with a funeral director. "It's not true, huh?" said Ana to the other grief-stricken mothers as she walked into the room, but they simply looked away.

Ana was in no condition to make decisions about whether Javier should be buried or cremated, so she left the hospital and went to Lydia's house, where she called Danny's to say she wouldn't be coming to work that day. She then tried calling her husband, Francisco, from whom she was separated. After she had made several tries, he finally picked up the phone; he was in a foul mood.

"What do you want?"

"I'm calling . . . because Javi died," Ana cried over the phone.

Francisco hung up and drove to Lydia's house. Standing outside the front door, he was ugly at first, yelling at Ana for failing to take care of their son. But eventually he came inside, collapsed on Lydia's kitchen floor, and was overcome with tears.

Soon the hospital was calling, asking Ana to come back to Chaleur Regional to formally identify Javier's body. She returned with Francisco, just as dawn was starting to break, casting its dull light over the fresh snow and ice that blanketed the sleeping city. Inside the morgue, Javier's body was lying on a stretcher. Aside from a few scrapes, there was hardly a bandage on it. He looked peaceful. Ana, a small woman, leapt on top of the stretcher and started giving her son's body CPR, pumping up and down on the chest. "Come on, you can't go, you can't leave me," she shouted at the boy through her tears. She kept pushing frantically on his chest. "Wake up. Come on, Javi, I know you can do it. Wake up!"

With Francisco's help, the hospital staff pulled Ana off the body. "He's going to be okay, he's going to be okay," she pleaded with them as they tugged her into a wheelchair.

"No, Mrs. Acevedo. He's passed away."

"No he didn't! He just needs to wake up. He's stable, he's stable!"

Ana was wheeled away by Francisco, and the two then drove back to Beresford, sobbing in grief and hardly saying a word. Outside Ana's house, Francisco lit a cigarette and poured out his pain and anger at the world, yelling at the sky and waking up the neighbours.

• • •

Saturday morning arrived, and with it came the news broadcasts of a horrific highway tragedy on the east coast that had virtually wiped out a school's basketball team and devastated eight families, news that would soon spread shock waves across the country. By Saturday afternoon all of Bathurst was in mourning. Flags flew at half-mast on both public and private buildings, and commercial signs across the city expressed their sorrow. "God Bless our BHS Phantoms Angels," said one sign outside the Home Hardware store downtown. As news of the tragedy rippled across Canada — it was the top story, throughout the day, on radio and television broadcasts from coast to coast — Prime Minister Stephen Harper sent his condolences, and hundreds of miles away, the Toronto Raptors held a minute of silence for the dead boys in their arena Saturday night before their National Basketball Association game against the Portland Blazers. Canada's high school coaching community was especially hard hit by the news. Many coaches were all too familiar with the demands of driving teams of students across their provinces in vehicles large and small, in winter weather. Stephen O'Rourke, the athletic director at Fredericton High, one of New Brunswick's largest high schools, was stunned by the news reports on Saturday morning. He was shaken by thoughts of how easily such a tragedy might have happened on his watch. "There are countless coaches in this country, who have driven passenger vans or other vehicles in not always perfect weather conditions," he would say later. "We all just shuddered to think about the same thing happening to us. It would be the worst possible nightmare."

Ana spent the weekend in a sleepless, dream-like state of shock. On Saturday morning she called her sister, her friends, and her three adult daughters—Maria, Elmy, and Carla, who was pregnant—to tell them the terrible news. The days were a blur of ashen-faced visitors coming and going from the small house on Aimeé Crescent in Beresford, empty now of Javier's boisterous presence. On Sunday, Maria arrived from Ottawa. After days of dark skies and stormy winter weather, it was finally clear and sunny, but bitterly cold. Ana wanted to go out to the highway, to see the crash site for the first time. She drove south from the city on Highway 8 with Maria, Lydia, and Tanya, another close friend, until they reached the top of a blind crest. Just below, a gaggle of cars was parked on both sides of the road, and people were standing on the shoulder, staring down at the ditch between the asphalt and the trees.

There was no sign of the van or the big transport, only a set of deep, muddy tire tracks scarring the ditch, some broken tree limbs, and a few patches of blood on the snow. By now, of course, there were also bouquets of flowers at the site, small photos of the boys, plus candles and greeting cards, many brought by kids from the high school. Pilgrims came all weekend to see where the tragedy had happened, appalled that eight lives could have been so easily snuffed out on their city's doorstep. Among them was Ann Arseneau, who stood in the crisp sunshine overlooking the site, marvelling at the miracle that had saved her grandson Bradd.

"Oh my God, we won the lotto we did," she said, wiping away tears. "No money can buy the life we got yesterday. But then you think of the others, and you're sick to your soul. Those poor little boys. God wanted them. They're all angels now."

Soon there would be a pair of portable basketball nets erected in the ditch as the centrepieces of a growing, makeshift shrine—a memorial that remains today—as well as a collection of basketballs, and rugby and soccer balls, scrawled over in black ink with farewell notes from the grief-stricken

The day after the tragedy, students from Bathurst High School
place flowers at a basketball net erected as a makeshift shrine
at the scene of the crash beside Highway 8. A net remains today
at the site, a permanent memorial to the crash victims.
(The Canadian Press/Andrew Vaughan)

to the dead. Before the crash, Ana and Javier had made a habit of going to Tim Hortons together on Sundays for hot chocolate and Danishes or cheese croissants. Tanya had paid a visit to the coffee shop just before going to the crash site with Ana and Lydia. She walked down into the ditch and placed a cup of hot chocolate and a neatly folded paper bag with a Danish and a croissant inside, among the flowers and photos and other mementos in the snow. There was a brief tribute handwritten on the paper bag: "Javi — we love you and we miss you. Love, your family."

Two

ANA AND ISABELLE

ANA LEIVA, AS she was known before she married, was born into hardship. Her family lived in the city of Quezaltepeque, El Salvador. She never knew her father, who died when she was only five. Her mother struggled to make a living, selling soup to farmworkers. The family grew up poor.

By the time Ana was eighteen she had two children, a son named Gabriele and a baby daughter named Maria. It was the early 1980s and El Salvador's civil war was in full swing, bringing death squads, fear, and turmoil to the country. Ana fled the violence, leaving her son at home in the care of family members, and taking herself and her baby Maria to Honduras; but life was little better there. Four years later she followed her older sister Marta into Texas, joining the underground pipeline of illegal immigrants streaming north out of war-torn Central America into the United States.

Ana now had two daughters, Maria and Carla, whom she left in the care of a woman in Honduras, before placing her own life and her money into the hands of human smugglers. Travelling by day and night, the smugglers brought her into Guatemala, then Mexico, and eventually across the Rio Grande, swimming the treacherous river along with other "mojados" stealing their way into the Texas desert.

Ana was reunited with her sister in Houston, where she spent more than a year living among an underground community of Latin American refugees.

There, she gave birth to a third daughter, Elmy, whom she had carried in her womb across the Rio Grande. In Houston, Ana also met and married Francisco Acevedo, another illegal alien, who worked as a cook in a Chinese restaurant. Ana worked at odd jobs herself, sending money whenever she could to her daughters in Honduras, hoping they'd receive it.

"Now when I think about going to the States, I laugh," says Ana. "Imagine, a person with no education, not speaking the language, not even there legally. How did I think I was going to go there and live a good life? But that was the mentality back home. Going to the U.S. was like going to heaven."

In the mid-1980s, Canada opened its doors to El Salvadoran political refugees, accepting and resettling thousands of them in designated cities across the country, especially in regions crying out for new immigrants. Ana's sister Marta had already applied under the program and been accepted, and had left Houston for a new life in the small city of Bathurst, New Brunswick, a faraway place Ana had never heard of. Eventually Ana, Francisco, and Elmy were accepted into Canada too. In the summer of 1988 they boarded an airplane in Houston for a long series of flights via Chicago, Toronto, and Montreal, before they finally arrived at a quiet little airport set among the fresh air and the green, forested expanse of northern New Brunswick.

"I had no idea where I was," says Ana. "I'd never heard of New Brunswick. But I was happy because I had come as a landed immigrant. My papers had been stamped at the airport. And I had come on a plane, sitting down! I didn't have to run across the border.

"I knew Canada was cold. I was a little uneasy about the upcoming winter. But still, I thought I had come to the best place on Earth."

The government provided Ana and her family with their airline tickets, the first month's rent at a subsidized apartment complex in Bathurst, and tuition for a twenty-week English-speaking course at the New Brunswick Community College. But nothing was free and everything had to be paid back to the government eventually. Francisco found a job at a local restaurant and, despite his limited English, enrolled in an apprenticeship program where he soon obtained his chef's papers.

Meanwhile Ana worked with Canadian authorities to bring her other daughters—Maria, who was eight, and Carla, two—from Honduras to New Brunswick. They arrived in October, only a few months after Ana. She hadn't seen her girls for more than two years, had hardly known Carla since she was a newborn.

"When I went to pick my girls up at the airport, it broke my heart because my poor kids, they looked like refugees," she says. "I'd sent money to buy them a suitcase and decent clothes for the plane. You know what they sent them with? A garbage bag and a couple of rags. My poor babies, their ears were full of dirt. And Carla didn't know me. She cried because she wanted to go back to her 'Mama' in Honduras.

"I remember that first night they were with us in Bathurst. Francisco had cooked some store-bought chicken cutlets for supper. Oh my gosh, now I wouldn't even eat that. But it was a luxury for us then, especially my girls. And they ate a whole bunch of slices of bread with ketchup. Maria said, 'Oh, this is so good.' Back home we only had food like that for special occasions. But I said to them, 'Don't worry. Here you can eat that every day—every, every day, not just today.'"

Eventually Ana also managed to bring her son Gabriele to New Brunswick from El Salvador, and the family began a new life together, six Spanish-speaking immigrants finding their way in a small, working-class, French–English city unaccustomed in the 1980s to outsiders settling in its midst. Bathurst was isolated, its climate was harsh, and its culture was foreign to the Acevedos, but it was a quiet, peaceful place, and it promised them a new chance at a decent life.

Francisco worked nights as a chef, while Ana found a job during the day, cleaning rooms at Danny's Inn and Conference Centre, a busy motel and restaurant just down the shore from Bathurst in the town of Beresford. Without telling Francisco, she religiously put money aside from her small paycheques in the hope of one day having enough savings to buy a house. She didn't want her kids growing up in the low-rent apartment building they shared with dozens of other poor families.

On December 30, 1990, Ana and Francisco had their first child together, a chubby, ten-pound baby they named Javier. Even though she was an experienced mother, Javier represented something entirely new for Ana. For years as a young woman in Latin America, she had given birth to children in a climate of poverty, violence, and political turmoil. She loved those children and devoted herself to them as any mother would.

But Javier was different. He was the first child Ana had ever had inside a marriage, and the first born in the safety and security of her new homeland, Canada, with all the opportunity it offered. Life had been hard for her other children, especially Gabriele, Maria, and Carla. But Javier's childhood, Ana vowed, would be better. This was her chance to give at least one of her kids, from the very beginning of their young lives, the normal, happy upbringing she herself had been denied, and which for so many years she had been unable to provide her previous children. Ana had high hopes for Javier, and into him she poured her love, her protective instincts, and her promises to be the best mother she could be.

Javier turned out to be a sickly toddler. Allergic to antibiotics, he was often ill and in the hospital. Ana worried terribly for him and breastfed "Papie," as she nicknamed her little son, until he was three-years-old. He and Ana even shared a bed until Javier finished grade eight. He only stopped sleeping with his mother because Carla would embarrass him at school, calling him a "mama's boy."

"We were close, close, all the time," says Ana. "As he grew up, he became my best friend. He was my everything, everything I could ask for."

The sleeping arrangements between Ana and Javier angered Francisco, or Frank as he became known in New Brunswick. But there were other more serious pressures in the marriage, including Francisco's drinking, and eventually the relationship collapsed. "We'd married each other in Houston because we needed each other's help," Ana says. "By the time Javi came, things were not good between us anymore."

Still, they managed within a few years to save enough money to leave their public housing apartment and buy a small home of their own on Aimeé Crescent, a quiet street in Beresford, not far from where Ana cleaned rooms at Danny's motel. Javier grew up in the family's new house, adored not just by his mother, but by his older sisters, especially Maria, who also treated him like a son. She helped him with his homework, and they called each other "Tunki," chubby little pig.

Eager to supplement her wages at Danny's, Ana also started cleaning houses in Bathurst. The city had a growing community of Latin American and Asian immigrants, some of whom were physicians who'd been recruited in the 1990s to fill the many hospital vacancies in northern New Brunswick. As Canadian-trained doctors flocked to jobs in the bigger cities, smaller hospitals in isolated towns like Bathurst solved their doctor shortages by bringing in physicians from other countries. Among these was a plastic surgeon from Colombia, as well as a Filipino doctor. Ana cleaned houses for some of the doctors, and became friends with their families too. Javier and his sisters grew up socializing with the doctors's kids, enjoying their fancy homes and their pools, and often spending Christmas together.

"We made good friends, but mingling with all these rich people wasn't always easy for me," says Ana. "There were a lot of gifts at Christmas parties; there would be trees filled with presents underneath, but I didn't buy them.

"At Christmas time, when the doctors's kids got lots of toys, I remember telling Javi: 'There is no such thing as Santa. *I'm* Santa, and *I* have to buy the toys if you want them.' He cried when he heard this. He was only in grade one. I said, 'What do you prefer, all those toys and no food in the fridge, or do you want your food?'

"My kids, they never starved. But they never had luxurious things, because I couldn't afford it. I dressed my kids at a second-hand store where I'd go to buy my clothes and theirs. They were always well dressed, but mine didn't have designer clothes."

Javier was well aware of the class differences around him, and it bothered him how hard his mother toiled for other people.

"He would tell me, 'Mom, I'm going to be successful, I'm going to be a plastic surgeon. And when I become a doctor, you won't have to be washing any more toilets. Somebody's going to wash your toilets for you.'"

Eventually Ana had several jobs on the go. She cleaned homes during the day, as well as a branch of the Bank of Montreal and a dentist's clinic, and worked in the evenings at Danny's; by now she was no longer a housemaid at the motel, but a cook in its restaurant. And her cooking was good. She brought a Latin American flair to the kitchen, always trying to jazz up the bland Canadian food that filled the motel menu, adding a dash of spice here, a sprinkle of fresh cilantro or jalapeño there.

When the young dentist couple whose clinic she cleaned got married and started a family, they asked Ana to quit all her other jobs and become a nanny for their young child. They promised to pay her whatever she needed to make up the wages from her other jobs. Ana agreed; however, her bosses at Danny's didn't let her go so easily, convincing her to at least cook at the restaurant on the weekends.

"My gosh, to me it was like I hit the jackpot," says Ana. "I worked for the dentists from Monday to Thursday, looking after their baby. And because I got tired of sitting on my butt and watching TV while the baby was sleeping, I started cooking and cleaning and ironing for them too, so they even gave me extra money! Working for them was not like working. They became like a second family. As he got older, Javi would play with their kids. And when my kids needed dental work, they just said, 'Come into the clinic, no charge, nothing.' Those people really treated me well."

After so many years of hardship and insecurity, Ana was finally hitting her stride. She made enough money to buy her first new car, a Honda SUV. "I thought it was a dream," she marvels. "No consignment, no husband's income, nothing. I did it all myself. That really boosted me up. I said, 'I can do it by myself.'

"Life was good. I had a home, a car, and good kids."

Her marriage, of course, had broken down, and Francisco had moved out of the house. But their separation had the positive result of offering Javier some occasional space from his mother and siblings, and bringing him closer to his father. They spent time alone together on weekends and evenings, playing sports, watching movies, and going for drives in Francisco's

Javier and his mother, Ana, in a picture reproduced on Javier's granite
tombstone, where this photo was taken. (Richard Foot)

car. Ana worried that Francisco's drinking might rub off on her teenage
son, and she developed a bad habit of calling to check up on him whenever
he was with his dad.

"Hey Javi, what are you doing?" Ana would say over the phone, speaking
to her son, as usual, in her heavily accented English: "Hey Hah-vee, what
are joo doing?"

"It's OK Mom, I'm with Dad."

"Ya, but what are joo doing?"

"We're watching a movie. OK? Love you Mom."

"I love joo too babe."

A couple of hours later: "Hey Hah-vee, ees Mom. What are joo doing?"

Javier was fiercely loyal to both his parents. He often helped Ana with
her cleaning jobs when he wasn't in school. And one day when he was
sixteen, he scolded her for badmouthing Francisco. "'Mom, I don't want
you saying bad things about my Dad. He's my Dad and I love him, and he
doesn't say those things about you.'

"Whoa, that was a wake-up call," says Ana. "I said, 'Well Javi, I'm sorry. It's just that I'm afraid. Promise me that if he offers you a beer or something, you'll never take it. Can you promise me that?'"

Ana had little reason to worry. Javier was a responsible kid, and a fine student in school. He was popular with his peers, even though many found it strange that the boy with the olive brown skin and the exotic name spent so much time at home with his mother, or at his father's house, rather than hanging out at the mall or going to the movies with his buddies.

Sports were Javier's passion. He was a natural athlete and wanted to play in every organized sporting league he could find. Although he loved hockey, Ana couldn't afford to enrol him in the game, so he played soccer and baseball instead, and pickup basketball on outdoor courts in the neighbourhood. He called himself "Latino Heat." Ana drove him all over New Brunswick for soccer games, to Saint John, Fredericton, Miramichi, and elsewhere. She'd rub shoulders with the other soccer moms and dads at the fields, but she never felt accepted by them. For one thing, she spoke hardly any French, and her English was shaky. For another, she was cook and a cleaner; most of the Canadian parents had better jobs than she did.

Perhaps Ana's protective ways played a part too. She was determined that Javier would socialize with only the right people, the right friends. Her fears that he and his siblings might get caught up in drugs, or hang around with what she calls "uncouth people" is partly what motivated her to move her family, as soon as possible, out of the government housing complex that was their home during their early years in Bathurst.

"I wanted to get out of the low-rentals because I wanted my kids to be different than that," she says. "Some people were not good enough to come around my kids. Not money-wise, but their behaviour, their influence. I was a lion like that. My kids knew. They'd say, 'If my friend didn't pass the "Mom Test," my friend was not coming to my house.'"

By the time Javier reached high school, he and Ana were the only ones left in the house in Beresford. Francisco had his own place, and Ana's four other children had grown up and moved out: Gabriele and Maria lived in Ontario, Carla had children of her own and was living with her partner, and Elmy was away at university in Newfoundland. Living alone with Ana, Javier was equally as protective of his mother as she was of him. Every night, Javier would say good night to his Mom by closing her door and saying he loved her, and each weekday morning he would wake her up at 6:30 a.m. They ate breakfast together before going their separate ways, but kept in touch on cellphones through the day while Javier was at school. And while Ana vetted Javier's friends, so he kept close tabs on hers.

"I think he felt he had to take responsibility. He was the man of the house," she says. "If I went somewhere, he'd call."

"Mom, where are you?"

"Well, I went for a drive with my friend."

"Yeah? You didn't tell me. What time are you coming home, Mom?"

"Soon."

"Well, how long?"

"Maybe twenty minutes."

Twenty minutes later, Javier would call back. "Mom, you're not here yet. I'm worried, where are you?"

When Ana fell sick with the flu or a migraine, Javier would warm up soup for her, then ask his father to drive him to the dentists' clinic so Javier could get the cleaning done.

Francisco gave Javier his own car in high school, a second-hand Chevy Cavalier, and taught him how to drive.

"I told his dad," says Ana, "'If you give that car to him, it has to have winter tires, it has to have its checkups, and you have to pay the insurance too.' He said that he would. I was afraid that he might have an accident. I was afraid to lose the best I have."

Some nights Javier would sneak out of the house after Ana was in bed. He had girlfriends — after all he was good looking, and he had a car — but he didn't tell his mother much about the girls in his life, worried perhaps that she wouldn't like them.

One of the high school friends she did know about was Daniel Hains, a big, strapping buddy of Javier's, who was a teammate on the Bathurst High School basketball squad, the Phantoms. Daniel and Javier had been schoolmates, off and on, since the elementary grades, but their friendship cemented itself in grade twelve when they played high school basketball together. Javier had played soccer for Bathurst High for years, but he never tried out for senior basketball until his final year. After making the team, he asked his mother for the $250 basketball registration fee.

"Babe, I don't have money for that," said Ana. In fact, Ana was better off financially than she had ever been. Her main concern was not the money, but the fact that joining yet another team meant Javier would be away more often, travelling on nights and weekends to basketball games around the province. Wasn't he playing enough sports, and wasn't he busy enough already? In the end Ana relented, and Javier joined the Phantoms.

The team took its name from an old Bathurst legend about a pirate ship, the "Fire Ship," whose flaming apparition appears on the Bay of Chaleur whenever an ocean storm threatens and meteorological conditions are just right. The phenomenon has allegedly been witnessed by dozens of local residents. Some attribute the illusion to St. Elmo's fire, others say it's the result of natural gas bubbling to the surface from underwater seams in the seabed; still others believe it's the ghost ship of a notorious pirate who once haunted the Chaleur coasts centuries ago, raiding Indian villages for pelts and furs.

As Phantoms teammates, Javier and Daniel became good friends, and they developed a routine: when their team returned in the school van from an out-of-town ball game, often getting back to the high school late at night, the two boys would climb into Javier's Cavalier waiting in the BHS parking lot, and Javier would drive Daniel to his house on Lakeside Avenue, on the west side of Bathurst harbour. Javier would then head home to Beresford where Ana was usually waiting up for him in her pajamas, happy to see her son safely home after a long day of school and sports.

. . .

Daniel Hains was a seventeen-year-old giant. He was tall — six-foot-three — but also strong and burly. One of his favourite things was to take the girls he knew in high school, who flocked to his side, and twirl them around his shoulders while they shrieked and laughed like children. On his broad, smiling face he sported a scruffy, Quaker-style beard that, with his size, made him look mature beyond his years. As a friend once said, "It took a body that big to hold a spirit like Dan's."

His large body didn't slow him down. He was a nimble athlete, excelling in soccer, badminton, and rugby. In fact, he was fearsome on the rugby pitch, and after skipping the basketball program at Bathurst High through grades nine to eleven, he decided to join the team in grade twelve because he figured playing basketball would keep him in shape through the winter until rugby season started in the spring. And anyway, focusing on sports was more fun than getting serious about academics. High school was a blast for the sports and the social scene, but classes just weren't that interesting.

"Daniel, I don't think he ever opened up a book," says his mother, Isabelle. "It didn't really matter because he had a photographic memory; whatever he heard in class he'd just remember it later and put it down on paper. And he was excellent in math. Daniel was an honours student most of the way through school. But once he got to grade nine he just wanted to play sports and have fun."

A generation earlier, Daniel's mother had also gone to Bathurst High before settling down and starting a family. Isabelle Christie, as she was known then, was a quintessential small-town girl: she'd grown up in Bathurst, found a job there, met her husband there, and would raise a family there, neither wanting nor expecting to live anywhere else. While many New Brunswickers, especially those in the province's southern cities, considered Bathurst a suffocatingly small, industrial outpost on the remote North Shore, Isabelle was perfectly content there. The uncomplicated life of a wife and mother, raising a family in a small quiet city, suited her just fine.

Isabelle grew up in a large, French–English family, the second-oldest of five children and the oldest girl among all her siblings. Her parents had little money; even by working-class standards, they were poor. Her father, also named Daniel, was a francophone lumberjack who'd been working in the woods since he was a child. Unable to read or write, he toiled at one of the toughest jobs ever conceived — a self-employed logger, working outdoors amid the bad weather and the stinging flies, cutting spruce and fir with a chainsaw from dawn to dusk, then hauling it out of the thick forest to the Bathurst pulp and paper mill for sale. As time went on, Isabelle's dad bought himself a mechanized Timberjack tree harvester. The work of felling trees became easier, but the long hours, the clouds of blackflies, and the unpredictable price vagaries of the pulpwood market remained.

Isabelle's English-speaking mother, Gertrude, worked hard too — at a corner store during the day and for a janitorial service at night. The family lived in a tiny, two-bedroom house in central Bathurst, the parents in one room and five children crammed into another, until they moved to a larger home when the kids were older. When Isabelle was seven years old, her mother had given birth to a sixth child, Alice, but the baby died of double pneumonia three months after she was born.

As the oldest daughter it was Isabelle's job, as soon as she was able, to look after her siblings while her parents were working. "I was like a mother hen," she says. "I always took care of the younger ones when my mother was busy.

"We were a poor family, but we were all happy kids. We played a lot of sports. I was a tomboy. I always played with the boys — baseball, hockey, and all that — and I took care of my younger brothers and sisters."

Isabelle and her brothers and sisters all spoke French at home when they were young, but their French faded after they started attending school, the nearest one being an English elementary school in their neighbourhood. High school followed, and Isabelle graduated from Bathurst High in 1977. She worked as a waitress in restaurants for a while before taking a secretarial course at the local college. She then found work as a data entry clerk at the Bathurst mine before landing a job with the federal government, which operated a large office in town — now called Service Canada — that processed applications and cheques for Employment Insurance, pensions, and other public social programs.

In 1984, a year after getting hired by the government, Isabelle married Allan Hains, another Bathurst High graduate whom she had known casually in school but hadn't been close to. Isabelle was quiet, shy, and unadventurous. She never smoked, rarely touched a drink, and avoided parties. Allan, however, had run with the popular crowd in school, the kids who liked to party. After high school he got a job at the Bathurst pulp and paper mill, the massive, industrial complex on the town's waterfront. Allan worked as a technician there, testing water quality and effluent levels. He became an active member of the mill's union and for years chaired the committee in charge of the Labour Day celebrations — the meet-and-greet, the supper-and-dance, and the always-popular Monday Labour Day parade, for which the mill's union contributed a large float — and Isabelle always dressed up as a clown and entertained the kids.

What Isabelle wanted most in life, however, was to become a mother.

"I wanted children and I wanted boys," she says. "I didn't want to have girls. I'm a girl, and I know what girls can be like, and I find boys are not as difficult as girls. I would still have loved a girl if I'd had one. But I really wanted boys."

Isabelle had become pregnant when she and Allan first started going out, but the baby, a boy they named Derek, was born two months premature, weighing only two pounds, four ounces. His lungs weren't fully developed, and he died after three days. They buried him in a peaceful little hilltop cemetery named Holy Rosary, overlooking the town. Isabelle and Allan then married, but she struggled to get pregnant again. After four years of trying, they finally had another son, Clark, and two years after that they had Daniel.

"I loved being a mom," Isabelle says. "Bringing up my boys was the happiest time in my life. I didn't want to do anything, just be a stay-at-home mom. Nothing else interested me but my boys."

For nine years Isabelle worked on a seasonal basis for the federal government so she could spend more time at home. They lived together in what had once been Allan's family home, a simple but spacious, two-storey house on Lakeside

Avenue, beside a trailer park on the western shore of Bathurst harbour. Clark and Daniel were close growing up. Daniel followed his older brother everywhere, imitating everything he did and trying hard to compete. He also grew fast. He was taller than Clark by the time he was nine, and by the age of thirteen he was even towering over his father. In fact, Daniel grew so quickly that in kindergarten he was already wearing a regular size three shoe, while his classmates were still in kiddie sizes.

"In kindergarten he already knew how to tie his shoes, so when recess came all the other kids would go to Daniel and he'd tie all their shoes for them, zip up their coats, and hurry up and get them all outside," says Isabelle. "Everybody wanted help and they just picked Daniel as their favourite friend. Nobody ever picked on him. They just loved him."

Allan and Isabelle made sure their boys knew from a young age that there was a bigger world outside their small town. When Daniel was six the family took a bus tour to Florida. Three years later they all piled into the family car and spent the summer driving across Canada, all the way to the Pacific and back.

Allan and Isabelle were also generous to other kids, and frequently opened up their home to children in the community who had lost their way, teenagers who had left home under difficult circumstances, or who didn't have homes for one reason or another. When it came to children, Isabelle's love and patience knew no bounds. She took them in, fed them, and bought them clothes and books for school. The house was always filled with kids playing and partying in the basement, where Clark and Daniel, plus the kids that Isabelle took in and all their many friends, had the run of a full basement apartment, downstairs from the main living area. Isabelle liked the sounds of the kids' voices downstairs, and she was happier to have them hanging out and making noise at her house than roaming about on the streets or at the mall.

And make noise they did. When Daniel was thirteen he had asked for a guitar, and he taught himself to play by following guitar courses over the Internet. He played until his fingers bled, and Isabelle taped them up with Band-Aids until they toughened up. Two years later, he taught himself to

Clockwise from left: Daniel, Clark, Allan, and Isabelle Hains in a
family portrait taken fifteen days before Daniel's death.
(Isabelle Hains)

play the drums, too, and started a band that practiced on weekends in the basement. Suddenly, sports weren't his only passion; music was too.

"The kids made a whole bunch of noise before it turned into actual music," says Isabelle. "We were always upstairs, and they were always downstairs playing their instruments and singing. By the time Dan was sixteen, they began playing very well. I would listen to them playing and singing along. It was great."

Daniel eventually owned a handful of electric and acoustic guitars, and he earned a reputation in high school as a competent musician. Sometimes he brought his acoustic guitar to school, where at lunch hour he'd sit on the floor with the guitar case open beside him, busking for cash in the Bathurst High hallways. He was a lovable, larger-than-life boy, and girls were drawn to him like honeybees to nectar. There were always groups of teenage girls in the Hains basement on the weekends until their midnight curfews kicked in, at which point Daniel and his male buddies would walk the girls to the front door of the house and everyone would hug each other goodnight. "Bye Dan. We love you. See you tomorrow," the girls would shout as they headed out to their cars parked on the street. Isabelle says the friendships were mostly platonic as far as she could tell. The girls called Daniel "Teddy Bear," while the boys called him "Big D." His friends looked up to him, not just literally, but also for his optimistic advice and wisdom. When someone was having trouble, he would tell them, "Look, tomorrow's going to be a better day, it's not all that bad."

"He was a happy kid," says his mom. "He always had to have people around him, he didn't like being alone."

In grade twelve, Daniel wrote in the journal that he kept on his computer: "Being the social person I am, friends play a major role in my life. Having a person or group of people to count on, leads to nothing but happiness. Every weekend that I spend with my friends, exchanging thoughts or experiences I encountered throughout the week, is a weekend I will remember throughout my life."

Like any teenager, Daniel also butted heads with his parents. For years, Allan and Isabelle had put money aside for their sons to go to university or community college after high school. In grade twelve, Daniel announced he wanted to become an underwater welder, a good career if he could get fully qualified. Isabelle was pleased with his plans, but she was horrified to learn that he first planned to take a year off, perhaps with a school buddy, and travel around the world with his backpack and his guitar, busking his way through Europe and then who knows where. Isabelle was a protective mother, wildly protective at times.

"I didn't want him to go because I was afraid that someone would kidnap him and take his body parts and sell them for money," she says. "I'd watched this movie on TV one time, and it had happened to a bunch of kids. I guess my imagination had gotten away with me.

"Anyway, he wanted to take a year off and travel, and I would have worried the whole time."

There were, however, more realistic reasons for worry in the Hains household and elsewhere by the time Daniel reached grade twelve. The paper mill where his father had worked for years had shut down in 2005, throwing Allan and about 275 other people out of work, and casting a pall over the town's future.

Bathurst was a blue-collar town, and for most of its history the pulp mill had been the beating heart of the community. Founded during the First World War, the mill had fuelled the area's economy and lured workers and new residents there for nearly a century. In the Crown-owned forests of Gloucester County, truckloads of softwood were cut on vast timber leases, some taken to local sawmills, but most of it hauled to the big pulp mill where the wood was turned into corrugated cardboard and other paper products and shipped out to the world through Bathurst harbour and the Bay of Chaleur. Good-quality lead and zinc was also mined nearby in one of the biggest underground zinc mines in the world, another source of jobs and prosperity. In the 1970s the mill and the Brunswick Mine had boosted Bathurst's population to more than sixteen thousand, making it the largest town on the North Shore.

But the good times didn't last. By the late 1990s, the town's economy was in steady decline, and everyone knew it. The zinc was running out and the mine was slated to close in 2012 (it did eventually close in the spring of 2013). Meanwhile the glory days and the easy profits of the North American forest industry were over. There was global competition, consolidation, and recession, and the economic pressures on old pulp and paper mills like the one in Bathurst simply piled up. By 2005, after a series of different corporate owners, the mill shut down for good. As Bathurst's industrial base slipped away, so did its population. Stores, restaurants, and businesses closed, particularly in the small, historic downtown core along the harbour. Those who remained worked mainly for the government and the local service industries it supported.

"When we lost the mill, we thought it was the end of the world," remembers Bathurst's long-time mayor, Stephen Brunet, who, despite the losses of the last decade, has refused to give in; to this day he maintains a steadfast optimism, a common trait on the North Shore.

"We still have two sawmills," says Brunet. "We just had a new dealership go up, a new hearing clinic, a new dental clinic, two new restaurants, and a new bank. The jobs aren't forty-dollar-an-hour jobs, they're in the service sector. But we've also got the fly-in/fly-out workers" — a burgeoning remittance economy that is funded by skilled North Shore tradesmen who keep their families in the area while commuting to the oilfields of Alberta or to the iron and nickel mines of Labrador.

In 2007, as these changes were underway Bathurst High remained a bustling-enough place, still running a full athletic program of which Daniel Hains was a big part. By December the basketball season had begun, and the BHS Phantoms were at the beginning of a busy winter hoops season in New Brunswick's top-tier high school league. The game schedule would kick into full gear in January. Thankfully, the team — with its heavy roster of new players, including Daniel — was finally starting to gel and show some promise under the leadership of Wayne Lord, a widely loved high school coach.

But first there was Christmas to enjoy. This would be Allan's last Christmas at home on Lakeside Avenue before packing his bags and heading west. Like so many other workers in the area, he had also found employment in the oil sands of northern Alberta; he was leaving for his new job in the new year. Clark had by now completed school and left home, and Isabelle was making plans to join Allan in Alberta once Daniel had graduated in the spring and figured out what he wanted to do. She and Daniel were planning to spend the first half of 2008 alone in Bathurst, before Isabelle would leave New Brunswick, at least temporarily.

But that was still months away. For now the whole family was gathered one last time in Bathurst for Christmas. Two weeks before the school break, Isabelle had taken Daniel shopping for good clothes, including a pair of size thirteen dress shoes for the BHS Christmas dance. Daniel hadn't been shy about shopping with his mom; he'd even put his arm around her as they walked through the shopping mall.

On the night of the big event, a handful of Daniel's friends gathered at his house with their female dates, to have their pictures taken before the dance. Among them was Javier Acevedo, the tall, handsome boy whom Isabelle liked immensely because he was always so polite, always addressing her as "Mrs. Hains."

Sure, times were tough in Bathurst, and now her husband was getting ready to leave home for a strange, new job on the other side of the country. But at that moment in mid-December inside her home on the cusp of Christmas holidays—surrounded by her happy son and his boisterous friends, the boys looking sharp in their dress shirts and jackets, the girls preening in their party dresses and their fancy hairdos, and everyone laughing as they had their photos snapped beside the twinkling lights of the Christmas tree—Isabelle felt like the luckiest mom in the world.

Three
KINDRED SPIRITS

THE SUBLIME PLEASURES of Christmas and the New Year were quickly forgotten, replaced suddenly and shockingly on January 12 by the tragedy on Highway 8. Disbelief and sadness enveloped Bathurst and much of the North Shore, and for eight families, life would never be the same again.

Two days after losing his son, Dale Branch walked into the parking lot outside Bathurst High, clutching a yellow photo album hastily but lovingly assembled over the weekend with pictures of Codey, the boy RCMP Corporal Mario Dupuis had identified in the snowy ditch on Highway 8 by the basketball tattoo on his leg. It was Monday, and although the imposing, grey-stone school building in the city's downtown was opening officially for the first time since the tragedy, there would be no classes, only a chance for students to enter the hallways, meet with friends and with counsellors if necessary, and continue digesting the awful fate of Beth Lord and the "Boys in Red," a collective name for the seven young victims, inspired by their team's colours.

Branch, a postal worker, was the only parent among the seven grieving families to show up outside the school that morning. He stood in the parking lot in the cold, winter sunshine, a stoic figure of sorrow, opening his album for anyone who cared to gaze at the pictures of Codey, seventeen, and his brother Patrick, fifteen, both tall, strapping basketball fanatics.

"Those are my boys," said Branch, struggling to hold back tears. "They loved playing basketball to the utmost.

"Sitting at home is not going to help me," he said when asked why he had come down to the school grounds that morning. "Being with friends and hugging and talking, that's the right way to do it."

News reporters and photographers had converged on Bathurst from across New Brunswick and elsewhere in Canada, and many were now in the school parking lot hoping to interview students on their way into the building. Branch's unlikely appearance was a stroke of luck for the reporters, and he was soon surrounded by a small gaggle of TV cameras and news people, asking him about his son and his thoughts on the crash.

"How do you feel towards Wayne Lord?" "What did you say to the coach after seeing him at the hospital on Saturday?"

Branch quickly made it clear that in spite of his pain and sorrow, he carried no ill will towards Lord. In his eyes, the crash was an accident, pure and simple.

"There's no blame on anybody," he said. "Wayne Lord was a volunteer. My son loved him and respected him, and I wouldn't have it any other way. It's a freak accident. That's all it is.

"I met Wayne at the hospital that night," continued Branch. "He came up to me and said he was sorry. I said, 'No, no.' And he hugged me."

Branch wasn't alone in this view. Acceptance was the prevailing attitude among the parents, the students, the people of Bathurst, and even among the professional skeptics, the news reporters, who'd come to cover the event. In the immediate aftermath of the tragedy, almost no one raised questions that it could have been anything but a terrible, unavoidable accident.

• • •

Beyond the school parking lot, however, across the white, frozen expanse of Bathurst Harbour at the Hains home on Lakeside Avenue, a very different outlook was taking shape. Isabelle was accustomed to having a house full of people, but in the days after the tragedy there were no longer crowds of happy kids making music in her basement, but rather a steady stream of mourners, young and old, filling the house. Allan had come home immediately from Alberta. All of Isabelle's brothers and sisters, plus family friends and high school mates of Daniel's, were parked in chairs around the kitchen and sprawled through the basement and the living room. Isabelle was in too much shock to follow their conversations, too numb to yet be forming her own opinions. But the talk among her family wasn't about acceptance, or of coming to grips with a freak accident. Instead, people were asking questions: *What the heck happened here anyway?*

Her father had examined the crash site on the highway and wanted to know how the collision could have occurred there, on such a straight stretch of road. One of Isabelle's brothers happened to know the local mechanic hired by the RCMP to do the collision inspection of the crumpled school van, and word was seeping out that the van's tires had not been in good shape, and were badly worn prior to the crash. *How could they put kids in a van with bald tires?*

Three days after the crash, Canadian newspapers also began carrying reports, fuelled by phone calls and emails to the press from an American lawyer, that the vehicle-type in question, a 15-seat van, had been involved in similar deadly accidents across the United States and was the subject of official safety warnings and advisories issued by the U.S. government. In fact, so controversial were 15-seat vans that several U.S. states had even made it illegal for schools, daycares, and service clubs to transport children in them. The province of Nova Scotia had also banned schools from transporting students in 15-seat vans following the deaths of three young hockey players in a van-truck highway collision in 1986. Within days the Canada Safety Council, an independent, Ottawa-based watchdog, was recommending a nation-wide ban on the use of 15-seat vans for children. The New Brunswick government suspended use of the vans by its schools on January 17 and launched a review of the situation for a possible permanent ban.

As friends and relatives of the Hains family began to arrive in Bathurst from outside New Brunswick, they brought newspapers with them — the

Globe and Mail, the *Toronto Star*, the *Vancouver Sun*, the *Calgary Herald*—and those papers, with front-page stories about the Bathurst tragedy and the van's questionable safety record, were now spread across the coffee table in Isabelle's living room, adding to the family's skepticism.

The questioning spirit that manifested itself so early inside the Hains household—the sense that Daniel's death was not merely the result of a random accident and that someone, somewhere, owed the family some honest answers to its questions—would take root deep inside Isabelle in the days to come, and never leave her. What those in positions of power and authority at Bathurst High and the wider political system didn't know at the time was that among the heartbroken parents in Bathurst, there was a singularly determined mother who would soon embark on an unwavering quest to find answers and seek accountability for her son's death.

…

For now Isabelle was trying to cope with her shock and disbelief. She shuffled through these early days like a wounded ghost, ashen-faced, exhausted from lack of sleep, her days and nights a hazy blur of visitors and well-wishers coming and going from her house. News reporters and cameramen who found the address and knocked on the door were turned away by Isabelle's sisters and her friend, Sheila Doucet—who had accompanied her to the hospital early Saturday morning—and who was now answering the door and the phone, and looking after Isabelle's affairs in the midst of all the mourners.

Two visitors for whom the door was opened on Monday were Coleen Ramsay, the high school principal, and John McLaughlin, the superintendent of School District 15, who together were making a series of difficult courtesy calls to all the grieving families. The two stood in Isabelle's crowded kitchen, expressing their condolences and trying to make polite conversation. McLaughlin, a large, genial man with the down-home demeanour of a kindly uncle, had himself attended Bathurst High with Isabelle when the two were teenagers, and now he had risen to become the top English-language education bureaucrat in Bathurst.

"Oh, Isabelle and I go way back," he said after introducing himself to the family. But Isabelle was in no mood for what she considered false sincerity.

"No," she curtly replied. "We were never friends in school." Then, after a few minutes of awkward silences and small talk, McLaughlin and Ramsay left the house to continue their other family visits.

The two school officials were dealing with an unprecedented crisis. Few educators could have imagined that a disaster of such proportions would ever confront them during their careers. Not only was their school community in shock; no one yet knew what the police investigation would reveal about the tragedy, or how the parents of the dead boys might react. Would anyone take legal action against the school or its staff?

Most immediately, they also had a major funeral to organize. They were joined in this task by Bathurst Mayor Stephen Brunet, himself a former teacher at BHS. Brunet had been mayor since 2004 (and would be handily re-elected in 2008 and 2012). He was a small, soft-spoken, yet highly confident man; like any mayor, he was a great promoter of his own city. And he became a ubiquitous figure in the weeks after the tragedy. Although it wasn't officially his role, Brunet had jumped into the fray, becoming a media spokesman for the wider school community, and helping to plan a series of public events to honour the dead. Brunet, McLaughlin, and other officials had decided, in consultation with the undertakers at Elhatton's Funeral Home, that a large public wake and subsequent funeral should be held jointly for all seven boys at the K.C. Irving Regional Centre, the three-thousand-seat hockey arena that was normally the home of the Acadie-Bathurst Titan of the Quebec Major Junior Hockey League. Beth Lord would be honoured at a separate, private, family funeral. But the dead teens would be remembered together, the doors to the event thrown open to the media, political bigwigs, the community, and anyone else who wished to attend. It seemed like a fitting way to honour the victims of such a high-profile and momentous tragedy. On Monday, the parents of the seven boys had been invited to a downtown church hall to discuss the matter and give their consent to the funeral plans, although Isabelle says she didn't understand at the time that the events would take place in the main hockey arena among thousands of onlookers. She assumed it would be a quieter affair for only the families and their guests, inside a smaller room at the arena.

By Monday night the family of each of the seven boys had also had the chance to visit the funeral home — a large, red-brick complex in the heart of the downtown, not far from City Hall — to say goodbye to their sons and brothers in more private fashion. Coach Wayne Lord was there, paying his respects, when Isabelle and Allan showed up to see Daniel laid out in his open casket in a shirt and tie.

"I saw Wayne Lord for the first time at the funeral home," Isabelle remembers. "I was on my way out of the building when I saw him. I went up to him and said, 'I wish you would have stayed in Moncton that night.' He said, 'Yes.' I never said another word to him. That was the last conversation we ever had."

...

Two days later, Isabelle and her family arrived at the K.C. Irving Centre, greeted by an astonishing sight: another winter storm was under way, and thousands of people, most of them strangers with no connection to the grieving families other than their shared community, were standing patiently in the cold and falling snow in a long line that snaked through the parking lot and around the building, everyone waiting to enter for the publicly advertised wake. Inside, the hockey arena had been turned into a hushed house of sorrow. Where noisy fans normally cheered for the Bathurst Titan, the lights were now turned down low, and a red carpet led onto the arena floor where seven open caskets were on display against the boards on one side of the rink. Inside each one lay the remains of a teenage boy, eyes closed, faces heavily dusted with embalming makeup. There were prized possessions laid out on tables beside some of the boys — a Montreal Canadiens teddy bear, a clutch of athletic medals, and, for Daniel, a guitar.

It was January 15, Daniel's eighteenth birthday. Isabelle and Allan hovered near their son's casket, like the other parents standing beside their sons, greeting a relentless stream of people who shuffled by the row of caskets, gazing in sadness and silence and curiosity at the dead.

"What a way to spend your birthday," Allan muttered to one family friend.

Isabelle tried to escape the tide of mourners to meet some of the other parents, and laid eyes on Ana Acevedo for the first time, a petite, Latin American woman, walking slowly among the caskets, her face red with tears.

"The boys were all laid out there, one after another," says Ana. "Javi had his suit and his blue shirt. Codey had a red shirt. I couldn't believe what I was seeing; it seemed like something from a movie, something not real. I kept on going from one boy to another. I didn't know personally any of the parents. Even Carol Ann Cormier, I worked with her but I didn't know her well. So I walked to each of them, and finally I saw Daniel. And I remember this tall lady, Isabelle. She was saying, 'This is my Daniel. This is my Daniel.'"

Ana kept reaching into her own son's coffin to touch Javier's face, but the funeral home staff asked her, much to her irritation, to keep her hands off the boy "…because it was going to ruin the makeup."

She also remembers a lot of girls from the high school coming by, in tears, to see Javier. "One told me, 'Did you know I'm his girlfriend? Did you know I was going to go to the prom with him? I'm his date.' Okay," says Ana. "I didn't know Javier had a girlfriend."

After several hours, the wake was over, the public and the families were ushered out, and the seven coffins were closed and sealed and placed together at one end of the arena for the funeral the next day, with large photos of each boy placed beside their respective caskets.

"That wake was horrible," recalls Krista Quinn. "We were on our feet forever. And people came by and shook our hands, people who we didn't recognize, because we were not totally functional. I could easily have done without that big wake. It felt like we were on show. But the joint funeral the next day, I think the boys' funerals had to be together. I don't think the city could have gone through eight separate funerals. It would have been the same people having to go over and over, eight times, because everybody knew everyone."

Athletes from Bathurst High place roses on the stage at the mass funeral
for the seven boys inside the K.C. Irving Regional Centre on January
16, 2008. A picture of Daniel Hains, behind his casket, sits in the
foreground. (The Canadian Press/Andrew Vaughan)

Once again, more than five thousand people descended on the building
for the big funeral service, many of them wearing red. Among those in the
crowd were Shawn Graham, the premier of New Brunswick, who met privately with each of the families before the service started, as well as the
Moncton Purple Knights, the basketball team from Moncton High School
whose members had played the Phantoms only hours before the tragedy. But
most people in the audience were strangers who had come simply to share
their sorrow with the families, and stand in solidarity with the dead boys.

"I'm here because these kids are in my heart," Geannette Plourde, one
of the mourners, told a reporter as she stood in line outside the building,
clutching seven red roses. "I've got kids the same age as them, and I feel the
families need our encouragement."

People who couldn't find seats in the main arena watched the proceedings on a big screen inside a smaller hockey rink next door. The event was also broadcast live on television across Canada. There were brief, poignant eulogies for each boy delivered by friends and relatives, as well as a speech by Stephen Brunet, decked out in his mayor's chain of office.

"We have received thousands of phone calls from across the province, the region, the Maritimes, Canada, and the world," Brunet said. "Bathurst thanks all who have sent your sympathies and expressions of sorrow."

Brunet also remembered Wayne Lord, who was sitting in the crowd. "Our hearts go out to Wayne today. Wayne, we're here for you."

Messages were read from Pope Benedict XVI, as well as from the Governor General, Michaëlle Jean. "Our nation grieves with you," Jean wrote. "On behalf of all Canadians, I offer our deepest sympathies."

When it was over, the seven caskets were taken back to the funeral home, where they would stay until the spring when the ground had thawed sufficiently to allow for cemetery burials.

Isabelle and her family went home, accompanied by dozens of friends, young and old, many of whom remained in the house until the wee hours of the next morning. Isabelle told Daniel's friends to take anything of his they wanted as keepsakes to remember him by, except his computer. The kids also filled a big chalkboard in the house with messages; where once it said "Dentist at three p.m.," now it was filled with "Dan the Man," and "Daniel I love you." Allan was introduced by a friend of the family to the Facebook page that had been created a few days earlier in honour of the Boys in Red. Four days after the crash there were already more than forty-five thousand "friends" on the site, plus thousands of messages of support.

Ana and her family were also up late the night of the funeral. Javier's sister Carla was nearly nine months pregnant with her second child, and although the due date was still a couple of weeks away, she began having contractions during the funeral service. They took her straight to the hospital when the funeral was over, the same hospital where Ana had gone only four days earlier to identify Javier's body, but the baby didn't come that night. The doctors said Carla's contractions had probably been brought on by stress. Ana was relieved. A few years earlier, there had been medical complications when Carla had given birth to her first child. Both the baby and the mother survived the ordeal, but doctors had advised Carla not to have any more children. When she became pregnant again, neither Ana nor Javier were pleased.

"Mom, I don't want Carla to have this baby," Javier had told Ana back in December. "I don't want to lose my sister."

Four days after her false alarm during the funeral, Carla returned to the hospital with her husband and safely gave birth to a healthy baby girl, her second daughter. Carla was visited in the maternity ward by her sisters, Maria and Elmy, who were still home following Javier's death. Ana was also there, beset by a conflicting ball of emotions including both sorrow and happiness. Carla wanted to name her new daughter Javier, but Ana wouldn't allow it, so she called the baby Havana instead—Javi-and-Ana—Havana.

"When I held the baby," says Ana, "she stared and stared and stared at me, like she knew me already.

"There's something really, really different about that child. Some people tell me they think Javi came back in her. I don't know. But as she grew older, she began to do things that left me speechless, things just like Javi used to do. She loves blueberries like him. She has the same mannerisms. And she plays soccer like she's played it many times before."

•••

In February, Allan Hains departed Bathurst for the second time to return to work in northern Alberta. He left behind his devastated wife and his surviving son, Clark, who would soon return to his own apartment in Moncton. Isabelle's sister Linda, the head cashier at a grocery store chain, moved into the house along with her teenage daughter, to support Isabelle and help with meals and housework. Before Allan left they had been visited by the mayor, Stephen Brunet, and the school principal, Coleen Ramsay, who had come to the house with a pamphlet on how to heal from emotional wounds. They also wanted to talk about money. There was insurance money, about fifty thousand dollars per child, for the families of each of the dead boys. And there was also a growing sum of money accumulating at a local branch of the Canadian Imperial Bank of Commerce, the result of donations, large and small, sent in from sympathetic schools, corporations, and individuals across Canada, contributions to an account set up after the tragedy to help the grieving families. In the end, more than one hundred thousand dollars was raised in this way, and Brunet and school officials were suggesting that some of it be used to build a monument to the Boys in Red in downtown Bathurst. The families agreed, and a memorial was eventually built with a share of the money, although construction only began on the project in the summer of 2012. The remainder of the donated money was distributed among seven families, after Wayne Lord opted not to receive any, and the families in turn put some of the cash toward a series of student scholarships.

In the first weeks following the crash, however, all of this was still undecided. And when Brunet and Ramsay arrived at Isabelle's house in January to discuss these issues and offer the Hains family some resources on healing, Isabelle was in no mood to talk about either money or healing. Sitting around her kitchen table, Isabelle, Allan, and their son Clark hit the visitors instead with some blunt questions:

"What happened?" Isabelle asked. "Why was my son out in bad weather that night? Why didn't they stay in Moncton? Was there not money for a motel?

"The principal said, 'Yes, there was money for motels.' So I said, 'Then why didn't they stay there?'

"The mayor didn't say anything. But Ramsay just kept saying, 'It was an accident. It was an accident.' They began to get nervous, because they didn't have the answers to our questions."

Ramsay wasn't the only person telling Isabelle to accept the tragedy as an accident, to find a way to heal. Friends and co-workers who dropped by her house to offer their sympathies also encouraged her to resolve Daniel's death in her heart and move on. A common refrain was, "Their time was up" or "There's a reason why God took Daniel from you." Even some of the other parents who'd lost sons were finding comfort in sentiments such as, "The boys all played together and died together, doing what they wanted to be doing." Almost all the grieving families believed their sons had died in a random, unavoidable accident.

"I'm not an overly religious person," says Krista Quinn, "but I honestly believe that God took those boys. Whether he was going to take seven at once, or one at a time, I believe that was their destiny. Whether it happened that day in that van, or whether it would happen on the way to a soccer trip, together or individually, I believe that for whatever reason, God wanted those boys and he took them. That is the best way I can cope with things."

Isabelle found no solace in such thoughts, and steadfastly refused to believe that Daniel's death was in any way part of God's plan, or that it was a simple accident no one could have prevented.

"*I just couldn't accept that,*" she insists. "When people told me that my son's time was up, that used to make me really angry. If there's a God, he wouldn't put me through this torture. Why would he do something like that? God is there to protect us, not to take a life.

"Our boys' deaths could have been prevented. The reason their lives were taken wasn't because of God's plan; it was because people didn't do their jobs. That was my son, and I wasn't going to accept anything from anybody that just said, 'It was an accident.'"

Two meetings were called in the following weeks at Bathurst City Hall between town officials, the CIBC account manager, and all the parents, to talk about the insurance money and the family fund. Allan attended the first one, where the families heard that an anonymous donor had given Bathurst High a new school bus, considered a safer vehicle than the 15-seat vans.

"Yeah, but who's going to drive it? The same people?" asked Allan, making the point that perhaps professional school bus drivers, rather than coaches and teachers, should be driving sports teams to out-of-town events. Allan told the other parents that they should all hire a lawyer to help them deal with the insurance and other matters with the school.

Allan was away in Alberta when the second City Hall meeting took place in February, so Isabelle went instead. Emotionally frail and still physically exhausted, she was accompanied by her other sister, Claudette. It was her first encounter with all the families since the funeral.

"Wayne Lord was there and I couldn't keep my eyes off him," she says. "It was the first time I'd seen him since the funeral, and I was very angry with him. He looked very uncomfortable."

The mood among many of the other families, however, seemed cheerful and buoyant, at least on the surface, something that amazed Isabelle. Their sons had been dead less than a month, yet many of the parents were chatting amiably, and laughing and joking. Some had already gone back to work. Others were going ahead with plans to take winter holidays in Cuba and Florida.

"I couldn't believe what I was hearing," says Isabelle. "They were going on vacation, and here I was at the very bottom, I wasn't even sleeping yet. None of these people were okay; they were hurting just like me but they were handling it very differently. When they say people handle grief differently, they really do."

As Isabelle quietly surveyed the group, she noticed that two other mothers were in a similar zombie-like state as she was. Marcella Kelly and Ana Acevedo were the only other parents around the table that day who appeared numb, unable to smile, engage in small talk, or show any desire to discuss money matters.

"I remember Ana saying at the meeting, 'Can we just stop talking about the money? Can we talk about something else instead?' I felt a different connection with her than with most of the families, I felt like she was at my level," says Isabelle.

As they were leaving the meeting, Isabelle approached Ana and introduced herself.

"You're Javier's mom, aren't you? Javier used to come to my house to see Daniel. Would you like to come over and visit with me some time?"

Ana had also felt a disconnect between herself and most of the other parents, but she had noticed this tall, sad, quiet woman — "Was that Daniel's mother?" — who seemed equally out of place among the group.

"I liked her," says Ana. "It was like we had something in common. What, I don't know...but there was something that attracted me to her."

The two mothers exchanged hugs and phone numbers, planting the seeds of a friendship, and an alliance that would grow and deepen in the months to come, taking them on an extraordinary journey, down pathways neither one could have predicted that winter morning at City Hall.

...

On extended leave from work, and with no sons or husband to care for at home, Isabelle had time to ponder the circumstances of the crash when she wasn't hosting well-wishers in her kitchen, or coping with her tears. She sat down at the computer in the basement of her house and poured her energy into the Internet. She'd never spent much time on the computer at home, it had mostly been used by Daniel and his mates. But now it became a lifeline for Isabelle, a place where she could try searching for some of the answers to the questions that troubled her and kept her awake at night. She didn't know exactly what she was looking for, what she might find, or where to begin. So with the help of her sister Linda, she opened up the Web site of Bathurst High School and found a section on policies, which seemed like a good place to start.

The school had a mandate that focused on ensuring the safety and security of its students. There were also links there to the provincial Department of Education, which in turn led Isabelle and Linda to a series of policies and guidelines under the authority of the Education Act. Most important were Guidelines 512 and 513, which contained detailed recommendations for how schools should acquire and maintain their own vehicles, such as vans and minibuses, for off-site sports and extracurricular travel, as well as the rules for how students should be transported to such events. The guidelines weren't hard and fast requirements, they were only best practice recommendations. But they were provincial government guidelines, nonetheless.

Isabelle and Linda read carefully through each document. Guideline 512 said that responsibility for student travel rested with the principal, saying he or she "should not permit students to be transported . . . to an off-site school-related activity unless all the requirements of this guideline, and Guideline 513 . . . are met."

It said schools should have a designated teacher responsible for looking after the registration, insurance, and maintenance of all extracurricular vehicles, that vehicles should be properly maintained and inspected, and that all drivers should have defensive driving courses. It also said snow tires should be used during winter months.

Guideline 512 also said students should not be driven to or from off-site activities "through the night," and that "groups traveling out of town should be prepared to stay overnight if weather or road conditions present a hazard."

The guideline also said no driver should be behind the wheel after being on duty for more than fourteen hours in a day: "For example," the document said, "if an individual came in to work at eight a.m., worked until four p.m., and then drove a sports team to another area, coached behind the bench, and then drove back home at 1:05 a.m., that individual would have more than fourteen hours 'on duty' time."

The guideline said school drivers should maintain vehicle logbooks and should conduct detailed safety inspections of their vehicles before setting out on the road.

Isabelle was astounded. Right before her, in black-and-white, in the Department of Education's own documents, were the very safety standards that might possibly have saved the lives of Daniel and six other boys, as well as Beth Lord. She had no way of knowing whether Bathurst High followed the guidelines or not, whether Wayne Lord had worked more than fourteen hours the day of the crash, or whether he had filled out a logbook or con-ducted a pre-trip safety inspection. But she did know the team had driven home during a winter storm, late at night, perhaps with or without the principal's blessing—all contrary to the Education guideline. She also knew from her brother, a friend of the mechanic inspecting the van for the RCMP, that the BHS van was equipped with badly worn tires, again contrary to the guidelines.

No one from the school had ever mentioned the existence of these standards to her before, not even when the principal and the superintendent were themselves standing in her kitchen, expressing their sorrow, deflecting her questions, and telling her to accept Daniel's death as a freak accident. How seriously did the officials and their coaches take these guidelines? Did they even know the guidelines *existed*? As Isabelle thought the matter over, her shock and anger began to grow.

"When Daniel signed up to play basketball, he had to sign a code of conduct governing his behaviour. They expected children to follow a code of conduct, but they couldn't follow any of their own codes or rules," she says.

What upset her most is that she herself had always been very careful how her sons travelled to sporting events.

"I was very particular about my boys," she says. "I didn't let them drive with anybody. I always drove them. When they were in city league they weren't allowed to drive with another parent. I took them to the games because I had winter tires on my vehicle, and I wouldn't let them drive during the winter without snow tires."

She trusted the school system to take the same basic precautions. As Isabelle now began to realize, there were no policies forcing schools to transport kids in the safest possible fashion; but there were certainly guidelines, a long list of sensible, recommended practices made under the authority of the Education Act, available for any principal or school official to read and enforce for the students in their care.

Isabelle's discovery prompted her to dig deeper. In the ensuing weeks, she and her sister Linda spent countless hours together, searching the Web, often late into the night, scouring through government policies and legislation. They examined the Motor Vehicle Act and became familiar with the different classes of driving licences, particularly for school bus drivers and for anyone licenced to drive school vans and minibuses. They found the Pupil Transportation Act and read through its myriad clauses and requirements. They learned to distinguish between the stricter and more comprehensive regulations governing unionized school bus drivers versus the relatively looser system for coaches, teachers, and volunteers who drive kids, not to daily classes, but to off-site sporting events. They read page after page of legalese and regulations and guidelines, all buried—but publicly available—in the online hinterlands of the provincial government.

"We were trying to piece together the legal framework which was supposed to protect our children and keep them safe," says Isabelle. "Instead, what we found was a legal framework which failed our children at every turn, because the people whose job it was to know these guidelines, regulations, policies, and acts, didn't do their job."

Isabelle wasn't a highly educated person. She had no specific skills as a lawyer, a researcher, or an investigative journalist. She had never researched a university paper before. She had only a high school diploma and her career experience processing applications for Service Canada—but none of that really mattered. What mattered is that she could *read*, and that she was fuelled by a burning desire to find answers to Daniel's death. While other families worked to acknowledge the loss of their sons and resolve their grief, Isabelle transformed her own sorrow into a mission to find the truth, to educate herself about the school transportation system and its sprawling infrastructure of laws and policies, and to correct what she increasingly saw as the complacency and mistakes of its publicly appointed leaders.

How she might pursue this mission and what she might do with her newfound knowledge was far from clear in those early days—until Javier's mother, whom she barely knew, decided one day to take up Isabelle's invitation, issued a few weeks earlier at City Hall, to come over for a visit. It was March 1, a Saturday, and once again it was snowing in Bathurst. Ana called Javier's father and asked him to go with her to Lakeside Avenue.

"Let's go to the house of that lady who invited me to go over," she told Francisco. "So I called her and she said, 'Okay, come on over.' We brought a box of donuts and went over for coffee."

...

The Acevedos sat with Isabelle and her sister Linda in the Hains living room—crowded now with photographs and mementos of Daniel and the other dead boys, including Javier—a shrine to the victims of the tragedy.

"We sat there and talked about our boys," says Isabelle. "I felt their pain, because I could see it in their eyes. I could see it in the other parents too, but not so much. Ana and I started to connect. I just couldn't believe that somebody else was feeling the same pain I had, that I could compare it with her and how she felt."

They also talked about the accident and about the possibility of negligence. Isabelle and Francisco discussed the idea of hiring a lawyer, each of them convinced the crash was more than a simple accident, although Ana at this point wasn't so sure. A few days later, Ana and Francisco drove to Moncton with Ana's friend Lydia, to watch Lydia's son play a volleyball game there. As they passed by the crash site just south of Bathurst—with its basketball nets and other impromptu memorials to the boys, standing in the snow—Ana and Francisco broke down in tears.

Bradd Arseneau, one of the survivors of the crash, was also playing volleyball that day in Moncton, and his parents came over to greet Ana and Francisco and offer their sympathies. The conversation was warm and friendly, until Francisco raised the issue of why Wayne Lord had decided to drive their boys home that night in January. At that point, says Ana, the Arseneaus grew defensive, repeating the now familiar view that the tragedy was an accident, and no one deserved to be blamed.

A week later, Ana and Francisco returned for a second visit to Isabelle's house, telling her about their encounter with the Arseneaus in Moncton. Isabelle decided to show them Guidelines 512 and 513 that she had found online, including the long list of recommendations for vehicle safety checks, for snow tires, and particularly the advisory that students not travel on school trips at night or during winter storms. Immediately, Ana understood that, while no firm rules or laws had actually been broken, the school had in fact violated some of the guidelines, which if strictly followed might have saved Javier's life.

"Oh my gosh. It was like somebody slapped me left and right. The guidelines were right there — no night travel, stay in a motel in bad weather, use winter tires, and on and on."

Ana took copies of the guidelines and showed them to friends of hers, a doctor and a lawyer, and they agreed that while the school hadn't broken any laws, it hadn't followed provincial recommendations either. There was a system of safety standards in place for students on sports teams, but it hadn't worked for the Phantoms.

"At that moment I changed," says Ana. "I didn't think like before. I went back to Isabelle and said, 'Okay! We need to do something about this, and you and me, we are going to go to the end.'

"I didn't know what to do or where to go. My life was just going to work, feed my kids, and nothing else. I didn't know anything about lawyers, about guidelines. I was just a simple person, a nobody. But I was angry, and I decided then that I would fight along with Isabelle."

. . .

Unsure where to go or how to proceed, the two mothers got an extraordinary break in March from a neighbour of Ana's who also happened to be a supervisor at the Bathurst branch of the New Brunswick coroner's office. Guilman Roy was a stranger to Ana, but as so often happens in small towns, people with knowledge and influence can also be your neighbours. Ana called the coroner's office one day to get a copy of Javier's official death report. She spoke to Roy, who told her that he also happened to live in Beresford, and he could easily drop by her house to give her a copy in person. He lived only one street away from the Acevedos, and he had often seen Javier waiting at the bus stop on his way into Bathurst. The two had even played a few pickup basketball games together at a neighbourhood court.

"He came to my house to bring me the report, and so I invited him in," says Ana. "We sat together in my kitchen."

Ana says Roy told her that the Bathurst High van "was not in good mechanical shape, and the tires were not good," confirming the rumours that were already swirling around town. "He said we should push for an inquest."

Ana had never heard of a coroner's inquest before, but as Roy explained, the provincial government can order inquests — official, public, court-like inquiries in which lawyers examine experts and witnesses under oath, not to assign blame, liability, or criminal responsibility, but to learn the truth about a death in the community and to seek ways to avoid similar deaths in the future. Inquests, he said, establish the facts in controversial or high-profile deaths, and often change the way society functions by bringing better safety standards to bear.

Ana called Isabelle, told her to come immediately to her house and hear what Guilman Roy had to say. Roy showed the women where they could go online to read the law and the regulations governing coroner's inquests in New Brunswick. He also offered to meet with all the parents and explain the system to them. Isabelle and Ana thanked him and sent invitations to the five other families.

Not long afterwards the parents gathered at Isabelle's house, sitting around her shrine-like living room, surrounded by pictures of the dead boys, as Roy explained what an inquest was. He encouraged the parents to push for one, and explained how an inquest jury could issue a list of recommendations that could lead to changes in the law, and to safer rules for out-of-town school trips. An inquest, he said, could protect other students in the future.

It made sense to Ana and Isabelle. After all, the tragedy had been a huge, high-profile news event. It had killed seven teenagers on a school trip, and questions were now being raised about the safety of the van and its tires. An inquest seemed like an obvious response to the tragedy; yet, two months after the incident, the government had made no suggestion of holding one. Why hadn't an inquest automatically been ordered?

Most of the other parents agreed that an inquest was a good idea if it might produce new laws and safer standards for extracurricular school travel. However, some were also wary that an inquest would force Wayne Lord to take the witness stand and testify, something Krista Quinn said would "torture" the already beleaguered, grief-stricken coach. (Lord had made no public statements, nor had he given any interviews to the media.) There was a lot of sympathy for Lord among many of the grieving families and in the wider community, and a clear fault line had now developed between the views of the Hains and Acevedo families, and all the rest. At the meeting with Guilman Roy, Francisco Acevedo openly blamed Lord for the tragedy, a stance that didn't sit well with others, some of whom were Lord's personal friends and his teaching colleagues at the school. But whether they knew Lord personally or not, the other families simply felt no need to question his actions or assign him blame.

"My family never blamed anybody," says Patrick Branch, who was fifteen when his brother Codey died, and who was interviewed for this book four years later, as a student attending St. Francis Xavier University in Nova Scotia. "We just grieved normally for my brother.

"There were two other families blaming and attacking the system. I wouldn't want to look like that; it wouldn't be healthy for my mind to live in a state of continuous anger. I'm angry that my brother died, of course I am. I wonder to this day what he'd be like now. . . . But two of the families were so angry at the coach. Yes, he was the driver. But he also lost his wife and he almost lost his daughter. My brother loved Wayne Lord. He said he was a hard coach, but he was a good teacher and a good guy. I think in most families, from what I know, people didn't want him held responsible, because he was in the same boat as us. He lost a family member that day. Why should he have to suffer more?"

Isabelle would also tell some of the parents about the guidelines she had discovered on the Department of Education Web site, but there was little interest in discussing them. Isabelle and Ana tried to raise the guidelines during lunch outings or coffee dates with a few of the other moms, but they say the issue was greeted with indifference. Only one parent was clear about offering moral support. Marcella Kelly, Nikki's mother, told Ana that she was "one hundred per cent behind" her and Isabelle's quest for answers and accountability, but she didn't have the emotional strength to get involved in any kind of campaign. "I can't help you, I can't do this," she said.

While the remaining parents were agreeable to an inquest, few of them wanted to fight for one. What they wanted most was to mourn their sons in peace, on their own quiet terms, without the turmoil of a public battle with the government and the school. One way of healing their wounds was to socialize with each other, to share the company of parents also trying to mend broken hearts, and not to talk about investigations or lawyers or issues of liability. An inquest, even if it concluded that the tragedy was a freak accident, would not only put enormous pressure on Wayne Lord, who was dealing with his own emotional scars, it would also dredge up the details of the tragedy in the public eye for weeks to come. Perhaps this was just too painful a scenario for many of the parents to bear.

Isabelle and Ana accepted this reality, even if they didn't share it. But they also believed another dynamic was at work. The two outspoken moms felt there was a reluctance to support their questioning spirit and their demands for accountability out of a desire not to upset the status quo, not to rattle cages too loudly in Bathurst — a quintessentially close-knit town that operated, like any small community, within the comfortable confines of an unspoken hierarchy.

Because the mill and the mine were the only large-scale, private employers in town, and those enterprises were now either closed or on their way out, many of the best jobs in Bathurst were in the health and education systems. The local high schools were, by default, some of the best sources of work. Teachers had some of the better salaries, lived in some of the nicer homes, and, because there was no university in Bathurst, they were at the top of the academic ladder. What's more, teachers at Bathurst High were community leaders; they were role models for students and respected volunteers who brought pride to the town when its school sports teams excelled in province-wide tournaments. Bathurst High was, quite simply, an important and respected local institution. It was part of the social and economic lifeblood of the town.

Some of the grieving parents were themselves either teachers at Bathurst High or good friends with teachers there, including Wayne Lord, Principal Coleen Ramsay (herself a BHS graduate, class of 1974), and John McLaughlin, the school superintendent. Mayor Stephen Brunet himself was a former teacher and coach at BHS, and a friend of Lord's. (And as it happened, one of Brunet's predecessors in the mayor's office during the 1980s, a D-Day veteran named Patrick McLaughlin, was John McLaughlin's father.) Here was a tight-knit town with a close and supportive establishment, led by a network of friends, BHS alumni, and teaching colleagues, most with deep personal connections and loyalties to Bathurst High. Ana and Isabelle, having lost their youngest sons, were now out of the school system for good; they had nothing at stake there anymore. But many of the other grieving parents still had younger, surviving children who were students at Bathurst High, or at other local schools that feed into BHS. As Isabelle and Ana saw it, there was not only enormous sympathy for Wayne Lord, but also a deep reluctance among parents, teachers, municipal officials, and even members of the wider community to put too much pressure on Bathurst High and School District 15, or to ask too many hard questions of a valued institution and its leaders. Hadn't their beloved school, their town, and even their province suffered enough already under the media spotlight in such awful and tragic circumstances? Times were tough enough in Bathurst. What the town needed was to heal, to focus on the positive. Why shake things up any more?

The day after the parents' awkward meeting with Guilman Roy, he called Isabelle to ask whether she could remember him saying anything to the families, on his part, about Wayne Lord. "Did I blame the driver of the van in any way?"

"No," said Isabelle, "Your presentation was very professional."

"Well, someone made a complaint about me to my bosses after the meeting," Roy told her. "One of the families was offended by what I'd said. So I've been ordered not to talk to you, or to any of the parents, any further."

Roy had been reprimanded by his superiors at the provincial coroner's office. Ana and Isabelle were appalled that he was now in trouble at work for trying to help the families, for alerting them to the inquest system. He never talked to them again, and stopped returning their phone calls. But they were undeterred. The idea of an inquest, the chance for a full public investigation into the tragedy, had been planted in the mothers' minds. They seized on it as the best way to find the answers to their questions and perhaps even fix the flaws in the system — the unobserved guidelines — so that other children travelling in winter to future school sporting events might be better protected than their sons had been.

Isabelle had learned enough by this point to become convinced that she wanted some kind of public redress for the boys' deaths. What did this mean? Criminal charges? Perhaps. A civil lawsuit? If that was the only way to hold school officials to account, then yes, although not for the sake of a financial settlement.

"I didn't want to have to sue. I wanted someone held responsible, not for money, but for the accountability."

Money, including the insurance money on its way, was the last thing on hers and Ana's minds. And when the insurance money did finally arrive, neither woman touched it, except to cover their sons' funeral and burial expenses.

"I couldn't touch either the CIBC or the insurance money for myself," says Isabelle, who had to be persuaded by her sister to cash the insurance cheque after it had sat for months, winking at her like an evil talisman on her kitchen counter. "I didn't spend a penny on myself. I always saw it as blood money."

Mostly what Isabelle wanted was some public recognition, some formal acknowledgement, some kind of apology by those in authority, that mistakes had been made, that the tragedy as she viewed it wasn't merely an unavoidable accident.

Other parents, including Krista Quinn, took a very different view. Not only could they not find it in their hearts to point the finger at Wayne Lord, who had been loved and respected by their children, but how could they blame school officials when they themselves, as parents, had allowed their boys to travel to Moncton on the night of the storm? Who among them had called the school to ask why the trip was going ahead in the face of a horrible winter forecast? Who had telephoned the coach after the game to warn about worsening weather conditions back home?

"I don't remember myself calling Wayne that night and saying, 'Don't come back from Moncton, it's snowing here,'" says Quinn. "I could have gotten Wayne's cellphone number. And most of those kids on that van had a cellphone too. I hold myself as responsible as I hold anyone, because I could have called the van and said, 'Hey Nick, let me talk to Wayne, it's terrible here.' But I didn't. I knew it was snowing here, I knew my son was on the road with the coach, and I didn't call. So what makes the principal or the coach or anyone else more responsible than me?"

Isabelle doesn't argue with that. "I blame myself too," she says. "I should not have let Daniel go to that game. Many, many times I've asked myself why I let him go."

But Isabelle also believes that her mistakes as a parent don't somehow cancel out the alleged mistakes of school officials, or remove the accountability of the school system itself, or mitigate the need for a public apology. School authorities were in a position of trust. There were provincial guidelines on extracurricular travel, designed to ensure the maintenance of that trust, but many of those guidelines were ignored.

"I assumed my children were safe at that school, that they had procedures and rules to keep them safe," Isabelle says. "I had trust and faith in the system, and in the school, to make the right decisions."

Although it's unclear what school and provincial officials were thinking, it is possible they had been warned, soon after the crash, not to issue any public apologies or acknowledgement of mistakes, in order to protect themselves and the system from legal action by the parents or the insurance industry. Certainly they tiptoed gently in their dealings with the families. But as far as Isabelle and Ana can recall, no teacher or public official connected with the tragedy has ever formally and publicly apologized for what happened.

...

On Easter weekend, three months after Daniel's death, overwhelmed by grief and a growing sense of disbelief at the silence of school officials, Isabelle picked up the telephone and made a series of calls from her kitchen.

"I called John McLaughlin at home, and I just — I don't know what all I said to him. I just needed to let him know how I felt and what my son meant to me. I told him that what happened was wrong. And he apologized. He said, 'It's my fault. I'm sorry. I'm sorry for what happened.'"

Isabelle then called the Bathurst High vice-principals, and then Coleen Ramsay, the principal.

"I called all of them. Ramsay kept telling me it was an accident. I said, 'Don't you tell me it was an accident.' But she stuck to it. I told each of them that I wished them no happiness in their lives, ever."

Looking back on those calls, Isabelle, the normally polite, soft-spoken Isabelle Hains, says she is ashamed by her rudeness that day.

"Oh my.... Sometimes I really feel like I'm a bad person now," she says. "I feel like I became a bad person. I never would have talked to people like that before."

But she has no regrets about trying to hold school officials to account. Certainly, McLaughlin's private apology on the phone didn't satisfy her.

"What I wanted was a full public apology, and a statement that the school was negligent, that there were guidelines that weren't followed. That would have been enough for me — but they'd never admit to that.

"Look, if children do something wrong, you don't just slap them on the hand. You tell them to apologize for what they did. And these teachers are teaching children that. And here they were, adults running the school system, and they're saying, 'No, I'm not going to openly, publicly apologize for what I did.' And that's not right."

Four

"UNSAFE AT ANY SPEED"

IN THE SPRING of 2008, starting the week of Mother's Day, the grieving families began burying their sons. It was, says Ana, "a hell of a month."

Winter had finally loosened its tenacious grip on the North Shore, and the earth had warmed sufficiently to allow the gravediggers at Bathurst's Holy Rosary Cemetery to excavate seven plots at one end of the graveyard. Holy Rosary is a dry, sandy field of tombstones surrounded by a wall of high trees on a hill overlooking St. Peter Avenue, the city's main commercial strip. The parents had agreed to lay their boys to rest side-by-side in a row, each family ordering a nearly identical black headstone for their son's grave. Only Isabelle couldn't decide what kind of stone, or what inscription, to create for Daniel, so his plot was marked by a large, temporary, white wooden cross, while Isabelle bided her time and considered what to do about the tombstone. Not far from where Daniel would soon be buried lay the tiny grave of his brother, Derek, the premature baby Isabelle and Allan had lost before they married.

Nathan Cleland was the first to be buried. His service was followed by Justin Cormier's and Nick Quinn's later in the week. Each family issued its own invitations to their son's service. Some were small, private affairs, others were opened up to members of the Bathurst High School community, in which case students were allowed out of school early to attend. Ana was invited to Justin Cormier's burial and to Nick Quinn's. The Quinns were friends with many of the teachers at Bathurst High, and Ana stood awkwardly at Nick's gravesite along with Wayne Lord, Coleen Ramsay, and other school officials. She was angry at Lord and Ramsay; she yearned to confront them, to pour out her feelings and her rage, but she was an invited guest, so she kept her behaviour in check and her thoughts to herself.

Nikki Kelly and Daniel Hains were buried in the following weeks. Isabelle had sent an email to Bathurst High ahead of Daniel's service, making it clear that no school staff, aside from a handful of invited teachers who were not involved in the crash, were welcome at his burial. Ana set the same ground rules for Javier's burial on May 31.

The service began at Holy Family Catholic Church. There were prayers and hymns, and a few words about Javier from his soccer coach. During the ceremony Ana's daughter Carla stood between her mother and father, holding their hands. As Javier's coffin was wheeled out of the church at the end of the service, Ana started crying, "Not my baby! Not my baby!" Then to everyone's astonishment, she leaped onto the casket.

"She literally jumped onto it, chest first," says Carla. "And she was crying and screaming. I had to take her off. I grabbed her around her waist, I pulled her off, and I held her two hands. She was saying, 'Not my boy, not my boy,' as they wheeled him out of the church. She had her head on my shoulder as I walked her down the aisle to the door of the church, and all I can remember is seeing all our friends, watching in tears. They were hurting more for my Mom than anything else."

Outside the church, Ana wanted to drive herself to the cemetery. But she was so distraught that Constable Judy Turple, one of the police officers who had dealt with the collision and who was attending the service, begged Carla not to let her mother drive. Carla tried, but Ana wouldn't hear of it.

"I'm going to drive," barked Ana, climbing behind the wheel of her Honda SUV and demanding to have the keys from Carla. "I'm going to make sure my son gets a proper funeral."

Holy Rosary Cemetery in summer. A line of seven graves, each adorned with flowers, starts with Javier Acevedo's grave in the foreground and stretches to the top right of the photograph. (Richard Foot)

"You want to drive?" said Carla. "Okay, drive. Just remember, I have two kids. You do something stupid, they lose their mother."

No one else dared get into the Honda with Carla and Ana, and the procession began making its way, behind the hearse, to Holy Rosary Cemetery. If any of the mourners had expected another hushed and solemn burial service like those held for the other boys in the previous weeks, they were in for a surprise. As she drove to the graveyard, Ana whipped a compact disc out of the Honda's glove compartment, lowered her window, and began blasting Javier's favourite song from the car stereo. The frenetic, angry rap sounds of the hip-hop artist DJ Unk — belting out the words to "Walk it Out," from his hit album *Beat'n Down Yo Block!* — vibrated through the Honda at high volume, attracting the stares of passersby as the procession made its way towards the cemetery. Dozens of mourners had already gathered around Javier's grave. They were standing there, quiet and sombre in their dark suits and dresses, when the vehicle procession arrived. Ana parked the Honda not far from the grave, left her door open, and left the stereo blasting, with the CD on auto-repeat mode, and the rappers shouting, as she climbed out of the car.

Everyone watched — Carla and her sisters, Isabelle, Ana's other friends, invited teachers and Javier's friends from the school, the priest and other clergy, the staff from Elhatton's Funeral Home, the gravediggers — as Ana opened the trunk of her Honda and pulled out three shovels. She marched with the shovels up to the grave, a mother on a mission.

"What is she doing?" people whispered, not sure what might happen next.

"Out of my way!" Ana told the cemetery workers and the people from Elhatton's, who were standing beside the casket, ready to flip the electric switch to lower Javier's remains into the ground. "*I'm* burying my son."

Although few of the mourners knew it at the time, Ana had warned Elhatton's that she planned to bury her son herself. This was an accepted practice in Latin American culture, but not in Canada. Ana had seen some of the other boys' burial services, and no way was she going to simply stand by Javier's grave, sprinkle a symbolic handful of dirt onto the casket, and then walk away, leaving cemetery staff — "Complete strangers!" — to cover up her son's unburied grave.

The funeral home had responded to Ana's unusual request with, "Okay. But we're still going to charge you the full fee."

"Keep the money!" Ana had said.

So Ana stood beside Javier's grave and listened patiently while the priest, Father Greg Culligan, finished reading the burial service, the ancient Roman Catholic prayers competing for everyone's attention with the loud liturgy of DJ Unk, still booming in the background. When the prayers were finished, everyone placed roses on the casket, then Ana waved the gravediggers away and flipped the switch on the hoist herself. As the coffin descended into the ground, Ana picked up one of her shovels and began digging at the pile of earth beside the grave. For a minute everyone watched in stunned silence, unsure what they should do as this small, fearsome lady in her grey suit and tights removed her shoes and stood in the dirt, almost barefoot, tears streaming down her cheeks, shovelling soil onto Javier's casket. Then, Francisco grabbed another shovel and started digging too, as did Carla's husband and then Carla herself, serenaded all the while by the rappers and their staccato chorus.

"My husband, my Mom, and my Dad shovelled the earth until it was done," says Carla. "They went through the whole pile of soil. At the end, my Mom said, 'Not enough!' So she went to a shed in the cemetery and brought more soil from there. It started to rain at some point, so things got a little muddy. But Mom patted the whole thing down, then she sat on the ground and started putting flowers all over the grave, and she made a heart out of rocks. A lot of people had left by this point, but a lot of the school kids stayed, listening to the rap music, amazed at what my Mom was doing. She did it on her terms."

Codey Branch, who'd been cremated, was the last to be buried, his ashes placed in a small hole beside another black granite tombstone alongside his friends. Isabelle and Ana had both been invited to the service, but Codey's mother had informed them that John McLaughlin and Wayne Lord would also be there. Isabelle decided not to attend, but Ana went. She had seen Lord at one of the earlier burials, but she hadn't spoken to him since the wake and the public funeral, five months before. They'd never said a word, in any meaningful way, about the crash.

When Codey's ceremony was finished, Lord briefly visited each of the seven graves. When he reached Javier's, Ana asked him to leave. Lord was surely aware by this point, along with John McLaughlin, Coleen Ramsay, and other school staff, that the Acevedo and Hains parents, unlike the other families, weren't accepting the loss of their sons so quietly or forgivingly. They had been asking difficult questions at the meetings at City Hall and during the private visits from school officials at their homes. McLaughlin and Ramsay had also received those fierce and pointed phone calls from Isabelle. And it's possible that whichever parent had complained to the coroner's office about Guilman Roy had also told Wayne Lord and perhaps others from the school that Ana and Isabelle wanted an inquest into the tragedy. If there was going to be trouble from any of the families, people knew it would almost certainly come from them.

When he was asked not to come near Javier's gravesite, Lord looked Ana in the eye and said, "Mrs. Acevedo, there's nothing I can do to change what happened."

"Oh," said Ana. "You want to talk now? Okay, we are going to talk now. Let's go to the car."

She grabbed Lord by the arm and led him towards her Honda in the cemetery parking lot. Lord protested, as did Alan Doucet, a BHS teacher who had taken over Lord's coaching duties, and who had accompanied Lord to the burial service. Doucet watched as his friend was marched away by Javier's angry, diminutive mother, who directed Lord into the passenger seat of her Honda.

"Don't worry," Ana told him. "I don't have a gun."

Ana then climbed in herself behind the wheel. Doucet parked himself like a guard beside the vehicle, watching through the window as Ana put a CD into the stereo and pressed play. A song, written and recorded by a local musician in the wake of the tragedy, drifted mournfully out of the car speakers.

Ana turned to Lord. "Why did it happen? Why did you drive that night?"

"Well, I thought it was safe," said the coach.

"You thought it was safe? You know what, you can replace your wife, you'll find a new woman. But me, how can I replace my son?"

"I will never replace my wife," he said. "And there's nothing I can do to take your pain away."

Then Lord got out of the car and walked away with Alan Doucet.

What did Ana want from Lord? "I wanted him to say, 'I'm sorry.' He never said that to me. He had no emotion. I would have just loved for him to tell me, 'You know, Ana, I'm very sorry. I thought it was safe. I made a mistake.' But he's never admitted to being wrong."

The cemetery became a second home for Ana and Isabelle that summer. They visited their sons' graves almost every day through June, July, and

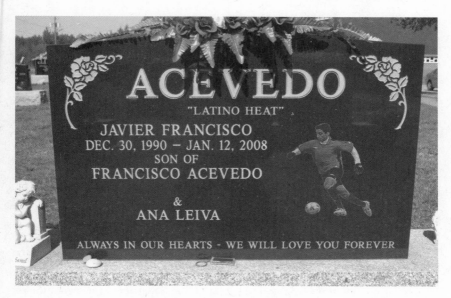

Javier's gravestone. (Richard Foot)

August, bumping into each other so frequently that they just decided to meet at the cemetery and mourn together. One day Isabelle brought Ana a folding lawn chair with a small umbrella shade attached to it. The two moms would sit side-by-side in their chairs, or lay blankets down on the ground and talk quietly, or meditate, while watching the soft, glowing sunlight disappear each evening behind the birch and maple trees that shadowed the cemetery.

Parents of the other boys would often be there too, visiting one of the seven graves. And with every visit, or so it seemed, a group of crows would appear among the tombstones, always seven birds in all, hopping about in the grass or watching the mourning families from the trees.

"They were always there, it seemed to me," says Krista Quinn. "Whenever I was at Nicholas's grave, when I was at my weakest moment, all of a sudden there'd be this, 'Caawk! Caawk!'

"At first I thought I was the only one that noticed them. I didn't talk about the crows to anyone because I thought, 'My God, I'm losing it.' And then, it was Carol Ann Cormier that said it first: 'Hey, did you notice those seven crows?' I think most of us noticed the crows.

"There's one crow that comes right onto the railing now at my home. He visits me still. I'm pretty sure that one is Nicholas."

That summer Krista and some of the other parents also noticed that Ana and Isabelle were always together, even sharing sandwiches at the cemetery. Both Daniel and Javier had loved Subway sandwiches; in fact, sharing a Bacon-Chicken-Ranch sub had been a weekly ritual between Javier and Ana before he died. So Ana and Isabelle sometimes picked up meals from the Subway outlet just around the corner and ate them beside the boys' graves. "We ate with the kids, all summer long," says Ana.

Sometimes the two moms would stay there together late into the night, lying on their blankets in the warm summer air, watching the stars overhead. During those long months of talking and praying and grieving in the moonlit shadows of their boys' graves, the two women forged a heartfelt friendship, and laid plans to honour their sons by seeking accountability for the tragedy by whatever means they could, whether through an inquest, a lawsuit, or even action by the police.

...

"Isabelle and I, at the beginning, were like two fools with so many ideas," says Ana. "We didn't know where to go."

Out of their shared sorrow, the two mothers had cemented not only a partnership, but also a deep conviction that the death of Javier, Daniel, and their friends was not an accident, but a result of what they considered the failures of officials at Bathurst High School, School District 15, and even at the New Brunswick Department of Education. Both women wanted accountability, and changes to the way children would be transported to after-school activities, but neither one had the slightest idea how to achieve these aims. Neither one had ever hired a lawyer for anything more serious than a house purchase. They'd never launched a lawsuit, filed a formal complaint with the police, lobbied a government, written a letter to a newspaper, or launched any kind of public campaign. They were as far from

The makeshift white wooden cross, adorned with a large heart
and other mementos that marked Daniel's grave for years. (Richard Foot)

prototypical activists as any two people could possibly be, and their lives
had been blissfully private until January 2008, when crews of reporters,
photographers, and TV cameramen began knocking on their doors in search
of the human faces of the Boys in Red tragedy. Isabelle had stayed away
from the reporters, but Ana had given a series of tear-filled interviews before
the cameras in her home in the days before the funeral. However, that was
the sum total of her and Isabelle's experience with the news media. Ana
didn't know anything about politics in Canada, or about the way public
responsibilities were divided up between federal and provincial governments,
not to mention municipalities and school districts. She'd never used a computer before Javier died; never in her life had she even sent out an email,
let alone composed a letter to a lawyer, a news editor, a politician, or any
kind of public official.

Yet despite their utter lack of experience in such things, and even their
naiveté, each woman had inner resources to call on. Isabelle had always been
headstrong, especially when her children were involved. Quiet and reserved

in most matters, she could turn herself into a hurricane whenever she perceived that Clark or Daniel had been unfairly treated or misunderstood in the past by teachers, coaches, or anyone else. She'd never been intimidated by authority, or afraid to make herself heard when her children's interests were at stake. As for Ana, here was a woman who had survived the rigours of a desperate childhood and a deadly civil war, who had endured a terrifying journey across the Rio Grande, and had succeeded in building a new life for herself and her children in a foreign country. She had prevailed over the kind of adversity most Canadians would never know. She had reserves of courage and strength within her.

In early April, a month before the burials began at the cemetery, Ana and Isabelle started contacting lawyers in northern New Brunswick, to find out what could be done to take either criminal or civil action against those they blamed for the crash. They hadn't forgotten about the idea of an inquest, they just weren't sure how to go about getting one, and remained hopeful that someone in the New Brunswick government would come to their senses and order an inquest — just because it was the right thing to do. In the meantime they were hopeful that the police, or a sympathetic lawyer somewhere, might hear their concerns and pick up their case.

Some of the lawyers they met with wanted nothing to do with the matter, aware how sensitive a subject it was. Others offered to represent the mothers in a civil lawsuit against Wayne Lord and other school staff, but warned them that they would face years of litigation, perhaps costing hundreds of thousands of dollars, with no guarantee of success. Unable to raise that kind of money, the women then visited the Bathurst RCMP detachment, whose members were still completing a routine, forensic investigation of the collision. The police were friendly and polite when Ana and Isabelle came to call, but informed them that a criminal investigation into the tragedy could not be launched until the Mounties had received a formal complaint.

So Ana and Isabelle began assembling one, although neither had the foggiest notion of how to write or compile a criminal complaint. Ana, however, had friends in the justice system, including a woman named Hilda — Javier's godmother — who was a pathologist living and working in Montreal. In late April, Hilda took the train down to Bathurst and spent a weekend with Ana and Isabelle, working mostly at Isabelle's home. Hilda showed the moms how to put together a "statement of facts" for the police. On the online archives of Environment Canada, they gathered the weather details on the night of the crash and the extensive storm warnings that had been issued for that day. They copied down Bathurst High School's safety mandate, as well as the provincial guidelines on extracurricular travel and other details of the crash.

"Ana and I and the pathologist sat here around my kitchen table for three days," says Isabelle. "We had all these papers, and we wrote a letter to go with the documents, and we made copies for everyone. At the end of the weekend Hilda had to go back to Montreal, but she ended up missing the train that night because she wanted to make sure everything was done right."

The next week Ana and Isabelle gave a copy of their complaint and its "statement of facts" to the crown prosecutor's office in Bathurst and also to the police. "We told them, 'This is what happened, and we feel something should be done,'" says Isabelle. "We just wanted the police to do an investigation and go look at the facts."

Ana says the RCMP accepted the complaint and said they would examine it carefully. "They said they owed it to us and our kids to do the right thing." Ana was relieved. "Okay," she told herself. "Finally, the proper things are going to be done."

What was she hoping for? The two women were mystified as to why, four months after the crash, no one in a position of authority was examining whether negligence had occurred and, if so, whether anyone should be held responsible. "It wasn't about getting any money," says Ana. "It wasn't about sending anyone to jail. Those things wouldn't bring my child back. What I wanted was some accountability, because up to that point, my son had been killed and nothing had been done. It was a big insult."

Most if not all the other families had no similar yearning to cast blame
or seek accountability. Most believed an inquest might prove useful in making
the system safer in the future, but there was little sense, outside the Hains
and Acevedo households, that anyone in the school system had acted ir-
responsibly. Even the crowds of reporters who had covered the tragedy in
January had moved on, figuring there was nothing more to investigate.
Ginette Emond, although shattered by the death of her son Codey, held
views that were typical of many.

"It was an accident," she would firmly say, years after the accident. "That's
how I felt from the very beginning, and it's how I still feel. It could happen
to me, to you, to anybody. The fact that it happened to a coach driving a
team is no different than if I took my three kids and drove to Moncton to
take one of them to a game. It's the same thing, the exact same thing."

Schools transporting students, however, are held to a higher standard
than private individuals. Although we assume parents use care and caution
in driving their own children on highways, society imposes no extra standards
of safety on the private travel choices made by parents, other than those
required of everyone by law. Schools are another matter, which is why New
Brunswick had special guidelines in its Education Act advising principals
and coaches not to transport students in winter, for example, without winter
tires, and not to travel with kids during snowstorms. Were those kinds of
safety standards in place at Bathurst High School?

At the end of July, as the parents were making their summer visits to
the newly consecrated graves of their sons, the RCMP and Transport Canada
summoned the families together to release their dual forensic investigations
into the collision, officially revealing for the first time that the school system,
with its responsibility for the safety of children, had, in fact, ignored rules
and violated the law.

· · ·

The parents gathered on July 28 at the Atlantic Host, a motel and conference
facility on the outskirts of Bathurst. Each family was invited, in turn, into

a private meeting to be briefed on the two investigations — one an exhaustive reconstruction of the collision by RCMP experts, the other a shorter, twenty-three-page report by the Road Safety Branch of Transport Canada, which relied for some of its conclusions on the facts established by the RCMP. As she arrived at the motel, Isabelle noticed that a priest and a handful of grief counsellors were also in attendance at the briefings.

"I thought, 'Why is the priest here? Is the report going to be that bad?' They were obviously worried how the families were going to take this."

In the six months since the tragedy, rumours had swirled through Bathurst about the van being in bad condition prior to the crash. But no one outside the investigation teams knew for sure. To date there had been no official reports, no hard facts, and no witness accounts (except media interviews with one of the survivors, Bradd Arseneau) about exactly what happened the night of the crash, or what might have caused it.

The RCMP report, written by collision investigator Corporal Annie Neilson, came in a heavy, black binder filled with hundreds of pages of forensic data about the state of the highway, the trajectory of the Ford van, and the oncoming Mack truck, plus reams of technical information about the mechanical state of each vehicle. But what surely grabbed each family's attention were a series of grim, colour photographs, taken by the police in the hours after the crash, showing the twisted wreckage of the van, the big Loblaws truck sprawled across the highway, and, between the two vehicles, a debris field of gym bags, athletic shoes, Gatorade bottles, and team jackets, lying across a snowy ditch among the remains of seven lifeless boys, each one covered by a plastic, yellow police tarp and marked by an orange pylon.

Even more startling than the haunting photographs, however, were the official findings inside each report. The RCMP had taken the shattered Ford van to Curtis Bennett of Curt's Auto Repair in Bathurst. His mechanics discovered that even prior to the crash, the van's rear brake hardware was old and worn, and one of the rear self-adjuster brake cables was broken. The body was in poor condition, with rust holes. And most importantly for the investigation, the van was equipped, not with winter tires, but with four worn out, improperly inflated all-season tires, which were scalloped in the front due to the van's steering being out of alignment.

"Mr. Bennett found that the Ford would not have passed a Motor Vehicle Inspection in its pre-collision condition," said the RCMP report. "He concludes that 'this vehicle must have been a handful to drive in this condition, with the front tires worn and scalloped like this, also in winter driving conditions with rear all-season tires worn this bad.'"

The eleven-year-old van, the oldest of the three in the Bathurst High fleet, was due to be replaced by the school in 2008. And somehow, despite its mechanical problems, it had passed a provincial motor vehicle inspection on October 29 the previous year less than three months before the collision.

The RCMP also revealed for the first time exactly how the collision had happened: despite being plowed several times on the night of the crash, Highway 8 was covered by about three centimetres of snow and slush when the van collided with the Mack truck. With the highway markings obscured, Wayne Lord briefly steered the van's right wheels off the edge of the asphalt. When he corrected to get the van back on the road, the van continued sliding leftwards and there was no response to his "steering inputs" as he tried to avoid the truck.

"These events, in addition to the slippery road surface and the Ford's worn and improperly inflated all-season tires, appear to be factors contributing to a loss of vehicle control," the report said.

There was other disheartening news. Of the twelve occupants in the van, only three, including Wayne Lord, were properly wearing seat belts. Lord would later explain that he always ordered students to buckle up on school trips, but on the night of the crash, most of his players were unbuckled. It turned out that wearing seat belts actually made little difference to survivability in this case, because players died when their entire benches, including seat belt assemblies, were thrown from the van. Only in the case of Lord's wife Beth, who was seated in the front passenger seat, was seat belt misuse considered a factor. Beth Lord was using only the torso portion of her strap, with the lap portion tucked behind her. The resulting force of the torso strap on her neck "may have contributed to her fatal injuries," said the RCMP.

The second report, the Transport Canada investigation, said Wayne Lord had done several things right on the night in question. He had a valid Class 4 driver's licence and twenty-eight years of experience on the road behind the wheel of 15-seat vans. He had checked the van's headlights and windshield wipers before leaving Bathurst, and he was credited for driving under the speed limit on the way home during the storm, less than eighty kilometres per hour in a one hundred kilometres per hour zone. "It appears that the [van] was travelling at an average speed that was less than was normally permissible by law, while returning to its destination," the report said. Beyond that, however, the report listed a series of violations of provincial safety laws.

Aside from the Education Act *guidelines* that applied to the school's extra-curricular travel, the BHS van was classified as a "commercial vehicle" under New Brunswick's motor vehicle statutes, and was therefore subject to a stricter set of rules and operating standards than ordinary vehicles. Lord was required to fill out a "driver's daily log" whenever he drove the van more than 160 kilometres from the school. Transport Canada said Lord recorded his name and details of the trip to Moncton in a notebook at the start of the journey, but wrote nothing in an official "daily logbook," which was sitting in the van, but which hadn't been used for nine months before the crash. Lord was also required by law to carry a summary of his daily working hours in the van for the previous fourteen days, but he had no such records. Although the driver of the Mack truck had these documents in order, Lord "was in violation of the logbook requirements."

Despite checking the lights and wipers, Lord also "violated vehicle inspection requirements by failing to perform and record a complete 'pre-trip inspection' of the vehicle prior to the start of the journey," said the report. And he was "in violation of the hours of service limits" for any commercial vehicle driver, having been on duty at the time of the crash for almost sixteen hours, two more than allowed under the law.

As for the causes of the collision, the report was unequivocal, saying three main factors led to the tragedy: "Poor weather and a slippery road surface;" "Driver error," including the possibility of "driver fatigue" with

Lord having been on duty for nearly sixteen straight hours; and the "Poor mechanical condition" of the van. These were hardly the ingredients of a freak, unavoidable accident.

"The most critical maintenance issue with respect to this crash was that the [Ford] E350 was equipped with misaligned, worn and improperly inflated all-season tires," said Transport Canada. "The handling of the E350 on the slush and snow-covered road would have been significantly better had the vehicle been equipped with properly inflated and aligned winter tires that had adequate tread depths."

So who, or what entity, was responsible for the poor condition of the Ford van, for the decision not to equip it with winter tires, and for failing to require Lord and other coaches at Bathurst High to follow the legal requirements for "pre-trip inspections," "hours of service" limits, and "daily logbook" entries? It quickly came to light that the van was owned by a not-for-profit company called Bathurst Van Inc., whose officers were BHS Principal Coleen Ramsay, vice-principals Don McKay and George Willett, and teacher Norman Conde. Because public schools in New Brunswick were forbidden from owning their own vehicles, schools had typically set up arms-length companies like Bathurst Van Inc., headed by school officials, as a way of owning extracurricular vans and buses. The vehicles were paid for by money raised by student councils, but owned and managed by principals and teachers. The whole structure had been put in place years earlier, when the provincial government withdrew funding and active oversight of extracurricular school transport, leaving local school officials holding the bag.

The broken motor vehicle rules and the poor maintenance standards highlighted by the collision reports, plus the news that Ramsay and her deputies, as the van's legal owners, were technically responsible for its maintenance and operation, vaulted the tragedy back into the headlines across New Brunswick.

"Unsafe at any speed," shouted the front-page headline on July 30 in the *Telegraph Journal*, the province's most widely read newspaper. "Probes into Bathurst van crash say vehicle was not fit to be on the road."

Questions now circulated in the news media about why the province's inspection system had given the Ford van a clean bill of health when in fact it wasn't safe. There was also speculation that the collision findings might fuel lawsuits against the province and the school system. Superintendent John McLaughlin, who was handling media calls for the school, reportedly told the *Telegraph Journal* that because Bathurst Van Inc. was a separate entity from the school system, he couldn't answer questions about who was responsible for the van's maintenance.

Many of the parents who'd lost sons were surprised by what they'd learned. While the majority of families still held no ill feelings towards Wayne Lord, they were disappointed to find out that Bathurst High had put a van on the highway in the middle of winter in such poor mechanical condition, and especially without winter tires.

"Everyone should be driving around with snow tires at that time of year," says Krista Quinn. "I don't believe that was one hundred per cent of the problem. But I was kind of surprised to hear the van didn't have snow tires."

For others, the worst part of the collision reports was having to hear them at all, having to relive the pain. "It's just bringing everything back," Dale Branch told the *Telegraph Journal*. "You go through a sort of process to get along for the past six months, trying to do the best you can with your life, and then something like this comes out. It's tough.

"For me it doesn't change the biggest thing—I wish I had Codey back."

Ana and Isabelle, meanwhile, were furious. For them the two investigations read like a catalogue of complacency and carelessness.

"Nobody knew anything about Bathurst Van Inc.," says Ana. "We were all shocked when we found out who the van was owned by, who was directly in charge of that van. You'd think they would have maintained it properly, so when they sent children out, at least it had proper tires and was in proper condition."

Says Isabelle: "The principal of the school is supposed to be in charge. Students look up to them to do the right thing. They expect nothing but good discipline from the students: 'Don't be late. Do your homework. Follow all the rules of the school.' And here they are, and they failed to follow the guidelines and the laws that should have protected our children. That bothered me. The children look up to their teachers, to their principal; they have respect for them. But the teachers and principal didn't have any respect for the children.

"Those reports bothered me so much, I had so much anxiety, I couldn't even talk. I didn't even have a voice to speak."

Mayor Stephen Brunet, who has steadfastly defended his friend Wayne Lord and his former colleagues at Bathurst High in the years since the crash, says it's unfair to conclude from the collision reports that any of the school's staff were reckless or careless with the safety of their students.

"At the end of the day, these coaches, they take care of their kids," he says. "You don't get paid extra for working in the evening, but people like Wayne Lord do it because you see the development of the whole child. For twenty-six years Wayne coached team after team after team. He got many pats on the back from students. He was a respected coach, and a good one."

Brunet says Ramsay and her vice-principals also cared deeply about the boys. They "were hurting too," he says, from the loss of each child. Why then, did these experienced educators not follow all the legal requirements for the safe operation of commercial vehicles or the provincial guidelines for after-school travel? Why did they allow the Ford van to be driven in winter, without winter tires? Brunet dismisses the questions as irrelevant.

"I don't think it was the van's fault," he says.

In Brunet's eyes, the tragedy had nothing to do with driver fatigue, winter tires, or maintenance failures. It was the result of living in an isolated town in a part of the world where winter squalls and bad weather can descend without warning. It was the result of making a choice to travel the province to play sports with other schools, because doing so—despite the risks of winter travel—is a better option, Brunet says, than staying home and not allowing kids to compete in high school athletics.

"When I was a teacher I used to drive for the hockey team or the ski program. We used to run into storms all the way here when we were tripping around with kids. We'd leave Moncton in clear weather, then run into a

School Superintendent John McLaughlin examines the wreckage
of the BHS white van, sitting on a flatbed truck, after the van had been
towed from the highway only hours after the tragedy.
(The Canadian Press/Andrew Vaughan)

squall in Bouctouche and hope it would be over by Rexton. Then you'd
pick another one up in Miramichi, because you were coming north. We
just slowed down to a crawl, and we'd get home. And that's where we lived,
we lived in the snow."

Brunet says the Hains and Acevedo families, because of their sorrow
and anger, "cherry-picked" the mistakes and problems contained in the
reports but ignored one overriding, unmentioned element: the collision,
he insists, was an *accident*.

"They were selecting out negative issues, and forgetting about the whole
situation,"says Brunet. "We have pretty rough conditions here in the winter,
and anything can happen when you're out on the roads. You always hope

nothing happens. I've skidded before and tried to correct, and sometimes it works and sometimes you end up in a snowbank. It just seems to be who we are and where we live."

...

For Ana and Isabelle, such views were no more than excuses. For six months the two moms had been asking questions about the crash, raising the ire of the school establishment and of other parents. But now their suspicions had been confirmed. They had two federal investigations, one finding that the school van was unfit for the road and would have been a "handful to drive," another saying that the school system had violated safety standards under the law. The RCMP made it clear that the reports did not find fault with or assign blame to any individual; the purpose was simply to reveal facts. Yet those reports fuelled Ana and Isabelle's sense of betrayal by officials who had stood in their homes, expressing their condolences, all the while maintaining that the school system had done nothing wrong. As the denials continued, even in the face of the evidence in the collision reports, Ana and Isabelle came to believe that leaders at both the school and the city wanted not to acknowledge or atone for the mistakes of the crash, but to turn the death of their sons into something positive—to whitewash the stain of the tragedy away.

Back in March, before the collision reports were issued, the parents had all been invited to come to Bathurst High for an evening meeting with a visiting celebrity. Jack Lengyel was an American college football coach who was famous for resurrecting the football program at Marshall University in West Virginia, after almost the entire team had been killed in a plane crash in 1970. The story of the disaster and the team's revival had been immortalized in a 2006 Hollywood movie *We Are Marshall*, starring Matthew McConaughey as Jack Lengyel. Lengyel was now in Bathurst to share his own experience in helping a school recover from this kind of tragedy. John McLaughlin and Coleen Ramsay decided to host a gala dinner in honour of Lengyel's visit, a black-tie affair to which they invited members of the

Bathurst establishment: community leaders, as well as federal, provincial, and municipal politicians. The seven grieving families had also been invited, but not for the actual dinner. They were ushered into a room at the back of the school for an hour-long meeting with Lengyel before the festivities started. McLaughlin was there, dressed in a tuxedo, along with Ramsay, hosting the meeting. Things didn't go smoothly.

Lengyel told the parents that in order for Bathurst and its school to heal, the community needed to find positive ways of moving forward from the crash, for example, by celebrating the memory of the dead boys, or by rallying around a basketball revival at BHS. Isabelle, Ana, and Francisco, their emotions raw, were in no mood for cheerleading speeches. They used the occasion to pepper Ramsay with questions: Why didn't she stop the team from driving home from Moncton? What was the mechanical condition of the van, and will the school produce maintenance records for the parents to see? The meeting became heated. In the eyes of just about everyone, the Hains and Acevedo families had now clearly labelled themselves as trouble-makers. In the midst of the angry questions coming at her like torpedoes, Ramsay got up to leave the meeting but Ana shouted at her to stay. Lengyel himself intervened, asking Ramsay not to leave the meeting, but to stay and try to answer the parents' questions. After half an hour of high tempers and raw feelings, the parents went home with their sorrow, and Ramsay, McLaughlin, and Lengyel left the meeting for their gala dinner with the town's elites.

Two months later, school officials called another meeting, this time to inform everyone that the school district was organizing a special event, a posthumous graduation for the seven boys killed in the crash. Five of them would have graduated in June with their classmates, but rather than the awkwardness of remembering them at the school's spring convocation, a large community gala in honour of the Boys in Red would be held in June at the K.C. Irving Centre, the same arena where thousands had gathered for the funeral in January. Called the "Celebration of the Spirit," the centre-piece of the event would be the awarding of posthumous diplomas to the dead boys. But there was much more. The evening would be hosted by a CBC Radio personality and would feature personal reflections delivered by Ken Dryden, the former hockey star and Toronto Member of Parliament; readings by Sheree Fitch and David Adams Richards, two of New Brunswick's leading literary figures; as well as musical performances by students at Bathurst High. Not to be outdone, various politicians including Education Minister Kelly Lamrock and Mayor Brunet would also give speeches.

Many parents were pleased with the idea, but some, including Isabelle and Ana, were upset that they hadn't been consulted first before the celebration had been planned out. Isabelle sent a letter to the editor of the Bathurst *Northern Light*, saying she objected to the event, cementing her reputation in town as one of "those two difficult mothers." Ana, the other difficult parent, confronted John McLaughlin after the meeting where he announced the posthumous graduation.

"Mrs. Acevedo, is there something I can do to help you?"

"Well, what I want, you cannot give me. I want my son back."

"I'm very sorry."

"You killed my son."

"If you want somebody to blame, blame me," said McLaughlin. "I'm the only one to blame."

"What are you going to do, are you going to do your job different?"

"I promise you, things are going to change. Please, Mrs. Acevedo, if there is anything, anything at all that I can do for you and for Mrs. Hains, please let me know. Please tell her, anything at all. I'm very sorry."

Ana's words were harsh, even abusive, some might say. McLaughlin, of course, didn't kill her son or anyone else's. But Ana says she has no regrets about the accusations she flung at him. "They didn't do their jobs, and there were no consequences for anyone," she says. "Is that fair?"

Ana and Isabelle had come to believe that the response to the tragedy by the school and the town was a self-serving one, designed not to meet the needs of the grief-stricken families, or honour the memory of their sons, or even ensure the safety of future students, but to preserve the good reputation of Bathurst High School, the community, and the leaders of each. The large, public wake (which several families now look back on with regret), the massive, televised arena funeral, the visit by Jack Lengyel and the black-tie dinner, and now the Celebration of the Spirit with its parade of dignitaries and celebrities — all were examples, for Ana and Isabelle, of a network of school and municipal officials trying to gloss over the alleged failures of the tragedy, to turn what for the two moms was a story of neglect into a story of community spirit and caring.

Isabelle says the deaths of seven boys and a teacher should have been a wake-up call for student safety. That issue should have been the centre of gravity around which officials responded in the wake of the tragedy. Instead, the focus became the healing of the community and the reputation of BHS, one of the town's most treasured institutions. The fact that two mothers were raising a fuss, asking awkward questions, and standing in the way of the official consensus was merely seen as just another obstacle, she says, for school officials to overcome.

No doubt McLaughlin and Ramsay, confronted with an appalling tragedy, handled it the way they considered best. It's not clear what they make of Ana and Isabelle's "whitewashing" accusations; McLaughlin did not agree to be interviewed for this book, and Ramsay did not respond to a request for an interview. But Stephen Brunet made his views clear. His retelling of the crash is filled with proud memories of the kindness of a community reeling in the wake of tragedy — the outpouring of emails into City Hall; the donations of money, flowers, food, hardware, time, and energy by hundreds of businesses, volunteers, teachers, and city staff who came together to support the families and organize the wake and the mass funeral — all this amounts to an extraordinary example of generosity and deep community spirit. Organizing and pulling off the wake and mass funeral for seven boys in a city of Bathurst's size, with the eyes of the nation upon it, was nothing less, he says, than a logistical triumph. He looks upon that time as proof of his city's strength and character.

"The year of that tragedy, we had a lot of pride, we were a united community, and I feel a lot of pride in the way we responded," he says. "This community hurt during that time. You see the way people pulled together for those families; we just came together like no other."

Brunet calls any talk of whitewashing not only untrue, but deeply unfair. "We're talking about two individuals out of a group who are full of anger and hate. They're handling it in their own way, and the hate is there."

Isabelle says she's never hated anyone. What she hates is an education system whose leaders, she says, were responsible for looking after her son, but who were so convinced of the virtue of their ways, and of their valuable experience as long-time educators and administrators, that they ignored the guidelines and violated many of the rules that might have saved Daniel. Now he was gone, a larger-than-life teenager whom she had dropped off at school one morning, never to see again.

All through that summer Isabelle wrote to Daniel in her journal. "I'm hurting, Dan," she told him one day. "It feels like my heart has been opened and torn apart, and no doctor could sew it back together. I wish I could hold you in my arms again and say that I love you."

...

At the end of August 2008, following a summer of grieving and stargazing at Holy Rosary Cemetery, Ana convinced Isabelle to protest with her in front of Bathurst High School. Ana thought it would be a good idea to remind people, at the start of a new school year, about the documented safety failures that had occurred along with the tragedy in January.

"I heard the teachers were going to be meeting on Monday, before the first day of school. So I said, 'It's time we go picket the school about the importance of keeping kids safe.'"

Along with Isabelle's sister Linda, the three women made sandwich-board-style placards saying: "Safety For Our Children" "Who Can We Trust?" "No More Travelling In Bad Weather Conditions." They paraded for several hours outside Bathurst High, careful to heed a school custodian who'd passed on a message from his higher-ups: "Keep off the lawn." Ana and Isabelle had called a local radio station to explain their plans for picketing the school, so the public was notified about the protest.

"I didn't know how people might react to us," says Isabelle. "And I didn't care. I wasn't really concerned how people felt about me then."

In fact the women, newly transformed from grieving mothers into political activists, were greeted warmly by passersby who honked horns and waved in support as they drove past the school. Some even stopped to offer cups of Tim Hortons coffee. The police dropped by at one point to monitor events, as did a couple of news reporters.

"One taxi driver stopped," says Ana, "and told me that she remembered driving on the night of the crash. She remembered the weather was really terrible. 'I hope you sue the pants off those people, because that's not right, what happened to your sons,'" the cab driver said.

That same week, Ana packed her bags, locked up her house, and moved into an apartment in Moncton. She was going back to school, enrolling herself at the New Brunswick Community College to become a social worker or, as the college described it, a "human services" worker. Among her studies would be specialized training in grief counselling, which Ana hoped might help her find not only a new career, but also some answers to the sorrow that had enveloped her life since Javier's death. Ana's friends had all encouraged her to go, and Isabelle had driven her down to Moncton and helped her get settled there. Ana had decided not to rent out her home in Beresford for a year. She couldn't bear the idea of anyone sleeping in Javier's bedroom, which hadn't been touched since his death in January.

Ana was now a minor celebrity in New Brunswick; her name had been in the news enough that her instructors at the college knew who she was. The first week of classes required her to take a first aid and CPR course. One morning, as the college class was simulating a mass accident scene, with students lying on the floor acting as bleeding victims, Ana was overcome by anxiety and tears. She fled to the bathroom screaming, "He was alive! My boy was alive and they didn't help him!" Ana went home, figuring she'd never succeed at the college, but her professors called and pleaded with her to come back, apologizing for putting her through the CPR course so soon, and saying she could take the course at the end of the year, when she was feeling more comfortable.

"Apart from that first week, it was really positive going back to school," she says. "My professors were really supportive."

One of them, a grief counsellor, heard from Ana that she and Isabelle wanted the government to hold an inquest into the crash and couldn't understand why the province hadn't yet ordered one.

"He agreed with me," she says. "'You need an inquest,' he told me. 'They owe it to you.' But I said, 'I'm only one parent. Most of the other families don't want [to push for] it.' But he said, 'One person is all you need. One person can move mountains.'

"Then Isabelle met him too, and again he said to us, 'Go for the inquest, you have to push for that.'"

Slowly, tentatively, Ana and Isabelle began organizing themselves to lobby the government for a coroner's inquest, Isabelle working from her home office and Ana contributing what she could between classes in Moncton and visits back to Bathurst on the weekend. They wrote letters to the Liberal cabinet: Premier Shawn Graham, Education Minister Kelly Lamrock, and Public Safety Minister John Foran, who oversaw the coroner's office. Ana had a T-shirt made up with pictures of Javier printed on the front, which she wore around town; Isabelle put Daniel's photograph on a Phantoms sports jersey, and she wore that in public too. Later that fall, they would also launch a petition. It read:

On January 12, 2008, the Bathurst High Phantoms, a high school boys basketball team, were returning from a game in Moncton, when the van they were travelling in slammed into a truck shortly after midnight, killing seven players and an adult. Since that time a number of facts have been identified that could have prevented this tragedy ... the public needs to know exactly what happened that night, why it happened and exactly what will be done to ensure it will never happen again.

We are asking for, and need, your support to influence the Government of New Brunswick to listen to our cries and take action by calling for a Coroner's Inquest into the deaths of these eight individuals.

The two mothers circulated the petition around Bathurst and neighbouring towns along the North Shore. They left copies at corner stores and restaurants and gas stations, although some business owners refused to have them in their stores. One Saturday, Ana and Isabelle stood in the parking lot at the Bathurst Walmart, collecting signatures from anyone they could. There was hostility in places, from people who didn't want to hear any more about the tragedy. "Let them rest in peace," said one critical comment written on a petition page they'd left in a convenience store.

"One day in the Walmart parking lot, a teenage boy was with his mom," says Isabelle. "She signed the petition and she wanted her son to as well but he said, 'No Mom, I go to BHS. I don't want to get in trouble.'"

Along with the fear and hostility there was also a heavy dose of encouragement and support.

"Around town, some people would recognize me and give me nasty looks," says Ana. "Some people were saying that Isabelle and I were crazy, that we belonged in a mental hospital. But others came up to me, complete strangers, and told me, 'Don't stop doing what you're doing. Keep pushing.' We had lots of support as well."

More than one thousand people signed the petition as the weeks went by, including, as it turned out, most of the other parents who had lost sons in the crash. Although some parents had become exasperated with Ana and Isabelle's criticism of the school and its staff, they also believed in the need for a public inquest. As petition pages filled with signatures, so the moms would send them off by registered mail to the government ministers they were lobbying.

In November, before the petition was launched, all the parents had been summoned one more time by the RCMP, to be briefed on the results of the criminal investigation that had been triggered by Ana and Isabelle's formal complaint to the Mounties in April. Ana drove back from Moncton and joined the other parents in a meeting room at Danny's Inn, where she had once worked in the kitchen. RCMP investigators said they had read Ana and Isabelle's statement of facts, examined the circumstances of the collision, and discussed the matter with prosecutors. There would be no criminal charges laid in connection with the crash, they said. For one thing, no one had been killed or injured as a result of any criminal "intent," they said. There might be grounds for laying non-criminal charges for multiple violations of motor vehicle laws, but the RCMP inspector overseeing the case said giving someone what amounts to a traffic ticket "would be an insult to the memory of those persons who lost their lives."

Ana couldn't believe her ears. She stood up inside the conference room at Danny's, a tiny figure among the crowd of parents and Mounties, and in her thick Latino accent began yelling at the police. Eventually she grabbed hold of a chair.

"If I took this chair," she shouted, bristling with anger, "and smashed it on this table, or broke the window with it, what would you do? Charge me! But my son is killed, and you do nothing! Your law is only for certain people."

Ana left the briefing in tears. Others walked away in silence and sadness. The RCMP went on to publicly explain their conclusions at a news conference, after which several parents spoke to reporters. Most, like Chris Quinn, agreed with the Mounties' decision not to lay charges of any kind.

"Nobody intentionally killed my son," Quinn told the *Telegraph Journal*, saying he supported the RCMP's decision despite the problems with the van, and its tires, and the motor vehicle violations. "My feelings may be different [from other parents], but I think I can understand where others are coming from. Over the last eight months, I've learned that you don't always know where other people are in this process. We are all different creatures."

Ana and Isabelle were far less sanguine. On television newscasts that night, and in the newspapers the next morning, they expressed their disappointment in the RCMP and the justice system, and said in no uncertain terms that charges should be brought forward.

"I was counting that some kind of charges would be laid, not necessarily to put the people in jail, but some accountability should be laid," Ana told reporters.

"We were robbed by the school," Isabelle said. "Our children were taken from us because we trusted them to make sure those vehicles were safe. We trusted them to make a decision that when the weather conditions are there, they would keep them safe in a motel. I feel that the school, the system, and the government turned their backs on our boys, and I can't let it go."

Later that week, Chris Quinn and a few other parents who had so far been quiet about an inquest, who had let Ana and Isabelle do the heavy lifting in their fledgling campaign, began speaking up. Quinn, Marcella Kelly, and Ginette Emond all told the media that the government must hold an inquest to get at the truth, but most of all to establish safer standards for student travel. What still divided Ana and Isabelle from the others, however, was their continued talk about the failures of Wayne Lord and other school officials. However justified Ana and Isabelle may have felt in continuing their quest for personal accountability against people in the school system, there was too much sympathy for Lord, and little appetite for going after individuals.

Patrick Branch, Codey's brother, sums up the attitude this way: "Did I want people held accountable? Did I even want someone to stand up and make a public apology? That's a tough question. Bathurst is a small community, where coaches, teachers, and principals of schools are well known. Community leaders are well known. To hear someone get in front of a microphone and say, 'I apologize for the wrong that I've done,' that would have been uplifting. It would have helped me. But I look at what's best for everybody.

"To see one person alone saying that, then for the rest of their life people would label that person as the sole person responsible for the accident. They would be walking around town and people would be pointing and saying,

'Look, that's the person who admitted guilt, or was found guilty.' Then rumours would go around, 'That's the person who killed them all.' It would just ruin their lives. That wouldn't be fair to anyone."

It became clear in the fall of 2008 that Ana and Isabelle's drive for legal or disciplinary action against school officials was counterproductive to their cause. It wasn't helping their bid for an inquest, or their wider campaign for changes to the safety of after-school travel. The public didn't share their desire for heads to roll, especially not Wayne Lord's. In Fredericton, a woman named Melynda Jarratt had been quietly watching events unfold, with growing dismay. In November, after reading Ana and Isabelle's comments in the newspaper following the release of the RCMP's decision not to lay criminal charges, she could hold her frustrations inside no longer. She found Isabelle's phone number and gave her a call.

"I can't take this anymore," Jarratt told Isabelle on the phone. "You need to do something different. You need some help."

Five

MELYNDA

FOR TEN MONTHS Melynda Jarratt had watched events unfold in Bathurst with a keen eye, following the news stories and gathering snippets of small town gossip that filtered down from the North Shore to her home base in Fredericton. Her antennae had been up ever since that bitter Saturday morning when she'd been woken by her sister, a schoolteacher, screaming down the line from Bathurst: "They're dead! People we know! Their children are all dead!"

Bathurst High was Melynda's old school. She'd helped organize the BHS reunion in 2004. She'd been good friends with Allan Hains, a happy-go-lucky guy she had hung around and partied with during those carefree teenage years of the late 1970s. Melynda and Allan had once hitchhiked together from Bathurst to Moncton, to hear Supertramp play a rock concert. To learn now that Allan had lost his youngest son Daniel, and to hear that her hometown had been struck by such awful tragedy, sent Melynda bee-lining it back to Bathurst — like many other BHS alumni who had moved away — so that she could attend the public funeral, grieve with her old hometown friends, and comfort those who had lost children.

In any case, Melynda was never one to sit on the sidelines. She was a force of nature, constantly on the move, talking at top speed, her brain firing on all cylinders, always passionate about something, always overflowing with ideas and opinions and calls to action. She had a look of permanent youthfulness and a blazing big smile. Being in her presence was like standing next to a brightly buzzing neon sign; Melynda hummed with an energy that seemed to radiate, inexhaustibly, from some internal nuclear reactor that couldn't be turned off.

At the time of the crash Melynda was a well-connected Fredericton writer, historian, and Internet business consultant. She owned her own company, New Maven Media, where she and a small staff developed Web sites and online content, and provided graphic design services for a host of clients including Fredericton's Beaverbrook Art Gallery and the New Brunswick Liquor Corporation. The provincial government and its agencies were an important source of contracts and business income. Melynda was also the country's leading historical authority on Canadian war brides, that generation of young European women who married Canadian servicemen during the Second World War and followed them across the Atlantic at war's end. War brides had been the focus of her Masters history thesis at the University of New Brunswick, and she had parlayed her passion for these women's stories into several books and film collaborations. War brides had also led her to the cause of the Lost Canadians, another generation (that included the children of some war brides) who, due to accidents of birth, had been denied Canadian citizenship for decades and were now fighting a long legal and public relations battle with the federal government. In 2008 Melynda was advocating for the rights of the Lost Canadians, giving testimony to Parliamentary committees, and would end up playing a vital role in the passage of new legislation that year, granting citizenship to thousands of people and correcting a long-standing historical wrong.

Injustice of any kind was like catnip to Melynda. She couldn't resist wanting to stand up for people whenever her sense of fairness was offended. She came from a large, working-class family in Bathurst, and as a young adult had become active in the social justice causes of the political left. She never saw herself as a victim, she had far too much chutzpah and confidence for that. Instead, she played the role of social justice superhero, always quick to denounce laws or government actions that in her view victimized others.

Melynda had left New Brunswick after high school to travel and study in Europe and in western Canada in the 1980s, before moving to Fredericton and becoming a history student at the University of New Brunswick. She soon found her way to the forefront of the big human rights issues of the day, rising through the ranks of the anti-apartheid forces in Canada, and working as a volunteer coordinator for Henry Morgentaler's highly controversial abortion clinic, which opened in Fredericton in defiance of the New Brunswick government's wishes. By 2008, Melynda was busy running her own business, and travelling across Canada promoting the history of the war brides and advocating on behalf of the Lost Canadians.

She was due to travel to British Columbia to attend a Lost Canadians event the same weekend that tragedy descended on Bathurst. But she was back in New Brunswick by Monday and travelled immediately to Bathurst, arriving there in a snowstorm, just in time for the boys' big public wake. Although Melynda had known Allan Hains for years, she met Isabelle for the first time inside the Bathurst arena, standing beside Daniel's open casket.

"What do you say?" she remembers thinking as she stood among the seven ashen-faced families at the public wake. "It's so tragic! The words—you can't say anything. Me, who writes and speaks for a living, I couldn't think of a thing to say. It was just so horrific. There's no well of words you could find that are suitable to that occasion. It was surreal."

Melynda knew that Daniel had been popular in high school, and that there would be a large crowd at the Hains house that night, a real Irish wake. She showed up with a case of beer, ate a piece of the birthday cake that said "Happy Birthday Daniel" on it, and stayed until three a.m. She returned the next night, after the mass funeral service, trying once more to comfort Allan and his family. By midnight Isabelle had gone to bed and Melynda was one of a handful of guests still hanging around. Allan didn't know anything about Facebook, so Melynda took him onto the computer and showed him the page set up for the Boys in Red.

"I said, 'Allan, there's a whole world out there mourning with you on Facebook. You should see what they're saying.' So we got on the Internet and we were probably there until six the next morning. There were something like forty-five thousand 'friends' on the site at that point. And he started answering some people — 'Hi, I'm Dan's father, thank you for your thoughts.'"

A few days later, Melynda went back to Fredericton, picked up her life again, and had little to do with the tragedy and its grieving families for months. She became aware, as anyone would by following the news, that Isabelle Hains and Ana Acevedo had turned into outspoken critics of the school and of Wayne Lord, and were now demanding a coroner's inquest from the provincial government. Melynda sympathized immediately with their plight. She sensed that the full story behind the crash wasn't yet known, and would only be uncovered by an inquest. She also feared that Ana and Isabelle — "two naive, innocent women," she called them — would get "squished by the state" if they fought the government on their own. Her social justice superhero instincts were tingling away and telling her to help the mothers out. But she had mixed feelings.

"I didn't want to get involved," she says. "I knew there were things I could do to help things along, but I didn't want to. I thought, 'Oh my gosh, this is way too big, it's over my head! I'm not getting involved in this one.' I had too many other things to do."

It wasn't just that Melynda was busy with her own work. She knew that if she took up the mothers' cause, she would alienate many of her professional contacts in Fredericton, including those in the provincial government who sent work her way, putting her own business at risk. Even her husband counselled caution, telling Melynda that if she stepped into the fray she wouldn't just be offering advice from the sidelines. "You're going to be right in the middle of this storm," he said.

On November 13, Melynda arrived home from a war brides' speaking engagement in Saskatchewan to find Ana and Isabelle on the front pages of the New Brunswick papers, attacking the RCMP's decision not to lay criminal charges and not to prosecute Wayne Lord. She knew then she had to do something.

"These ladies were calling for Mr. Lord's head. And at the same time they wanted an inquest. It looked bad, it looked yucky. The story was too negative. I thought, 'My gosh, it's not going to happen. If they continue to be interviewed without some professional help, by journalists who are going to quote them — because they're going to say whatever comes off the top of their heads, because they're so angry . . .'

"I just saw them drowning. They had no media savvy at all. They were complete neophytes! Innocents! They were little, innocent women caught up in a world of vultures."

Melynda believed Ana and Isabelle had the power to force the province to launch an inquest if they applied the right kind of pressure. But first they needed public opinion on their side, and there was no way they would win the sympathies of New Brunswickers if they continued to argue for the prosecution of individuals at the school, especially Wayne Lord, a man who had lost his own wife in the tragedy and who had an injured and traumatized daughter at home who was struggling, understandably, to heal from her emotional wounds. Melynda looked up Isabelle's phone number and called her in Bathurst. They spoke for half an hour. Isabelle told Melynda that things weren't working out, despite her and Ana's efforts. The police weren't going to lay charges, and it didn't look like the province would ever announce an inquest. Melynda explained her feelings, gently criticizing Isabelle's approach so far and telling her, "I can help you get an inquest." Two weeks later, Isabelle picked Ana up at her apartment in Moncton, and together they drove to Fredericton to meet Melynda and begin plotting a new strategy.

• • •

In Melynda's eyes, Ana and Isabelle appeared much the same as when she'd first seen them back in January, standing beside their sons' caskets — two wounded figures, haunted by sorrow and trauma. Yet there was also something new about them, a spark of fire, a sense of purpose and drive. Having learned the facts about the poor mechanical state of the van, about the violations of the Motor Vehicle Act and of the provincial student travel guidelines, and having been denied any chance at a police prosecution, the two moms were now fixed on a concrete goal, more determined than ever to have an inquest into the tragedy.

Melynda didn't mince words. If she was going to help them, she said, there would be no more talk (especially in front of reporters) of blaming Wayne Lord or holding him personally to account. Targeting Lord, she said, wouldn't bring back their children or win them an inquest. The focus from now on would be the system itself, finding out why it failed their children, and how it could be changed to keep kids safe in the future.

"I have changed laws. I know how to get things done," Melynda told them. "If you are dedicated, if you are willing to go to the end of the road, if you want something bad enough, you can get it.

"Politicians have to be forced to do the right things. How do you do that? You've got to hit them right in the jugular, press a nerve, resonate with people. But you just can't go off half-cocked. You can't just say whatever you think. It's got to be planned. You've got to think before you speak. And in our case you can never say Mr. Lord's name. Ever again. Because Mr. Lord is not the issue."

Putting aside their hard feelings towards Lord and other school staff was a bitter pill for Ana and Isabelle to swallow. They sat inside the offices of New Maven Media and listened in silence as Melynda outlined her plans. They would hold a news conference in a few weeks in Fredericton, formally placing their demands for an inquest before the media. At the same time they would launch an online blog through which to explain their purpose and champion their cause. She said they should all meet again in Bathurst the next weekend to brainstorm ideas and make videos for the blog.

Ana remembers Melynda, fully in command, dictating strategy like "an army colonel" explaining the plan of attack for an impending battle. But she knew that she and Isabelle needed help, and she was grateful for it.

Isabelle was similarly taken aback. "I didn't even know what a blog was. It sounded horrible to me. And then she said we were going to make videos. 'Videos?' I said. 'Oh my gosh. Videos of what?'"

The next weekend they gathered again at Isabelle's house in Bathurst. Melynda had asked the mothers to buy flip charts, masking tape, markers, and other supplies from Staples. They turned one of Isabelle's basement bedrooms into a "war room"—the nerve centre of their campaign—and in there they sat together through the weekend and brainstormed, making to-do lists, dividing up responsibilities, setting out media talking points and plans of action.

Melynda brought with her an acquaintance from Fredericton, Charles LeBlanc, an eccentric media gadfly who was New Brunswick's best-known online blogger. LeBlanc was an unemployed, unsophisticated but highly successful pioneer in the world of blogging, using the Internet as a tool to self-publish his random thoughts, observations, and opinions. He had started his own blog as a platform to raise awareness of attention deficit hyperactivity disorder (ADHD) from which he suffered, but that soon morphed into something bigger. LeBlanc had become well known in the small pond that is Fredericton's political scene, by turning up at the provincial legislature, or at any public place where the city's social or political elite were gathering, wearing his trademark blue jeans and baseball cap, with his camera in hand, and posting pictures and rough commentary of any public figure, reporter, or government official who fell before his lens. Politicians in nice suits and silk ties learned to suck it up and smile for his camera, rather than be ridiculed on his increasingly popular site. Although he was often the butt of jokes, and a major irritant to Fredericton police and security staff at the legislature, LeBlanc earned a grudging respect among the media and the public for his tenacity, his plain-spoken ways, and his ability to poke fun at the self-importance of the establishment. He was a living symbol of the power of individual free speech.

Melynda knew LeBlanc could be hard to handle, but she needed his expertise to help her and the two moms set up a blog of their own, and show them how to post YouTube videos on the site. LeBlanc was only too willing to assist. He and Melynda spent the weekend in Bathurst, using Isabelle's computer to build a blog, which they called VanAngels.ca. The name was inspired by the title of at least one American Web site whose owners, like Ana and Isabelle, had lost loved ones in a 15-seater van crash, and who were campaigning to have the vans outlawed by governments across North America.

"This Web site is dedicated to Javier Acevedo and Daniel Hains, two high school basketball players from Bathurst, New Brunswick, Canada, who were killed along with five others in a tragic 15-passenger van collision on January 12, 2008," said the greeting at the top of the new blog, next to high school photos of the two boys, and a picture of their mothers standing side-by-side: Isabelle in Daniel's Phantoms shirt, Ana wearing a T-shirt imprinted with Javier's photograph.

The blog became Ana and Isabelle's campaign calling card. Every letter they would write to politicians, every response they received back, every story about their cause that appeared in the print or broadcast media, as well as a continuous stream of public statements, videos, and links to relevant government legislation all would be posted onto VanAngels.ca for anyone with an Internet hookup to see. LeBlanc installed a live-action traffic monitor on the site, allowing the moms to know how many people were reading it and what city their audience was reading it from.

Their very first post, on December 2, 2008, was a link to the New Brunswick Department of Education guidelines for student extracurricular travel safety, which school officials in Bathurst had ignored for years. Their second post, on December 10, was an amateur video, made on the weekend of their gathering with Melynda and Charles LeBlanc. Titled "In Quest of the Truth. Bathurst Mothers Demand Coroner's Inquest," it shows images of Highway 8 outside the city, the crash site itself with its memorial of basketball nets and flowers still sitting in the ditch beside the road, followed by on-site interviews with Isabelle and Ana describing their campaign: "There ees many unanswered questions," says Ana on the video, speaking in her thick accent. "There ees not even an answer, why they were out that night in that kind of weather."

At the end of the video is a written plea: "You can help us. By emailing, phoning or writing the Acting Chief Coroner and the Minister of Public Safety and tell them you want a Coroner's Inquest into the Bathurst Tragedy of January 12, 2008."

Neither Melynda's name and picture nor Charles LeBlanc's appeared anywhere on the blog. Anyone reading it and watching its videos would likely imagine that Ana and Isabelle had created everything themselves, an impressive achievement for two middle-aged mothers without any media training and limited computer skills. The heartfelt, though haphazard, efforts they had made so far to push their cause in public—the protest at the school, the letters to cabinet ministers, the petition, the off-the-cuff comments to reporters—would soon take on a more sophisticated and carefully crafted tone. Melynda was more than happy for people to think Ana and Isabelle had upped their game all on their own. Still wary of getting too involved, she had even asked two friends in Fredericton, professional communications consultants, if they'd be interested in helping Ana and Isabelle organize a formal news conference. She said Isabelle was willing to pay fifteen hundred dollars for their services, but both men turned the offer down. One of them, Duncan Matheson, who ran his own public relations firm and had lost his own daughter in a highway crash, wanted nothing to do with them. "They're out to get Wayne Lord," he said. "It doesn't look good."

So Melynda resigned herself to guiding and advising the two moms on her own, albeit from the shadows. Together they plowed ahead and organized a formal news conference in Fredericton, booking a meeting room at the Crowne Plaza Hotel, the historic, once-grand lodgings beside the Saint John River formerly known as the Beaverbrook Hotel, named after the legendary Canadian press baron, Lord Beaverbrook. Melynda had joked about holding the news conference on December 10, to coincide with the annual Christmas dinner taking place at the Crowne Plaza that night for Liberal Premier Shawn Graham and his cabinet. The women mused fancifully about crashing the cabinet festivities and putting their demands directly before the celebrating ministers and their wives. But it was too far-fetched, and everyone knew it. Several times in the coming years, as Melynda would organize campaign events or ghostwrite press releases, her toughness and take-no-prisoners enthusiasm had to be reined in by one of the moms.

"A lot of times in the coming months I had to say to Melynda, 'That's not me, we can't do that,'" says Isabelle. "Sometimes she would write something in a press release, or for the blog, and I'd say, 'Change that word, that's not polite.' I felt you just can't take someone and make fun of them in different ways. You have to be respectful, that's how I felt."

"My activist side of me would often overwhelm them," Melynda says, laughing at the memory. "Isabelle was focused on our goals, but she and Ana always wanted to be kind, or at least be respectful."

The trio decided to hold the news conference on December 11. They sent out press notices and invitations to the media, and alerted the government about the event too. While Melynda couldn't persuade any public relations experts to work with Ana and Isabelle, she did manage to create the illusion that the moms had a communications professional representing them. In fact Melynda had simply hired a film industry insider named Jim Lavoie for a one-time job — to "act" as the mothers' official "spokesman." Lavoie had worked for years as an actor, crew member, and facilitator on local film projects, but was not widely known in public. He agreed to host the news conference and introduce the moms to the media, creating the impression for anyone watching that this was no fly-by-night campaign, but a serious effort with professional expertise on board. It was a clever piece of theatre. And in the coming months Lavoie actually became the moms' *real* spokesman, supporting their campaign and their media relations efforts for months to come.

Ana and Isabelle spent the night before their big news conference in a room at the Crowne Plaza, rehearsing their speeches and getting last-minute coaching from Melynda. She had prepared them well. "I told them, 'You guys are never, ever going to say Wayne Lord's name again. If you're asked about him, if his name ever comes up, you're going to say that punishing Wayne Lord is not going to bring our children back. Your message is that we need a coroner's inquest.'"

Both moms were anxious. Although they had talked to reporters over the past year about their grief and their anger, neither one had ever addressed a formal press gathering before, under the glare of the television lights. They knew the provincial media would all be in the hotel tomorrow, including some of those hard-nosed political types from the legislature press gallery across the street.

"I was so nervous," says Isabelle. "I'm sure I only went to bed at four a.m., and I was up again at six, reading through my notes. I was thinking, 'Oh my, I don't know if I can do this.'"

The next morning more than a dozen people arrived to hear what the mothers had to say, mostly reporters and television cameramen. Charles LeBlanc was there too, videotaping the event for his blog and for VanAngels. ca, which debuted formally for the first time that day. Melynda was hovering in the background. Also watching and taking notes at the back of the room was Valerie Kilfoil, director of communications for the Department of Education, who approached Ana when it was all over and handed her a business card. "Anything I can do," she told Ana cryptically, "give me a call. Keep in touch."

Ana, Isabelle, and Jim Lavoie sat at a table covered with a white cloth and adorned with not only reporters' microphones, but also pictures of the mothers' sons, Javier's soccer and basketball medals, Daniel's favourite rugby ball, and other mementoes. A short distance from the table was an intimidating wall of television tripods, with their fancy cameras and bright spotlights glaring down at the moms.

"I was scared to death," says Ana. "I had never been in anything like this before in my life, live on TV."

After introductions by Lavoie, Isabelle read carefully and nervously from her prepared statement.

"We are just ordinary people," she said, her voice soft, her eyes darting anxiously from the page in her hands to the journalists in the room, scribbling away in their notepads. "We lived a simple life before our sons were killed eleven months ago. Like Ana, my life has changed forever since this terrible tragedy. We want to put a face to our voice, as we call for a coroner's inquest. All we want is some answers. . . . We would like some consolation, knowing that what happened to them will never happen to another student travelling to a school-related event again."

When it was Ana's turn, she spoke from the heart, without looking at her notes.

"Who would have thought that I would be sitting here today demanding a coroner's inquest?" she said. "Last year at this time I was planning for Christmas, planning for my son's birthday, and what we were going to do for his graduation. He was going to attend university; he wanted to be a doctor, that was his dream."

Ana then stood up. She held Javier's picture to her chest and with her voice breaking, pleaded with Greg Forestell, the province's acting chief coroner, for an inquest.

"After this tragedy, there is a big lesson for everybody to learn. . . . I don't want to see sports taken away from children, it's really important to them. What I'd like to see is more safety rules, to bring them back and forth from activities. A coroner's inquest is the only thing that can bring us those changes. It's not going to bring my son back, I know that. But it's going to save lives," she told the reporters, "even those of your own children."

There was a long, emotional silence after Ana sat down, and finally reporters started asking questions, one of which was, "Why do you think the government hasn't called an inquest yet?"

"I would like to know that too," said Isabelle, "why they didn't call a coroner's inquest yet, after forty-seven weeks?"

When it was over and the reporters had packed up their gear and gone back to their offices, Melynda congratulated the two women on a job well done. Both moms were wearing identical pairs of shoes — black Clarks with medium heels, which Isabelle had bought for herself and Ana on a recent trip they'd made together to Ottawa to visit Ana's oldest daughter. Before leaving the room at the Crowne Plaza, Ana hugged Isabelle and made her friend a solemn promise:

"I will go with you on this, to the end," she vowed.

Isabelle smiled. "We'll walk together in the same shoes."

•••

Later that afternoon the two moms were taken to the CTV studio for an interview with supper-hour news anchor Steve Murphy, the most famous journalist in the Maritimes. The interview was broadcast across Nova Scotia, New Brunswick, and Prince Edward Island to tens of thousands of viewers. Then they bid farewell to Melynda and drove back to Moncton, where Ana had community college classes the next day. They drove through the evening, listening in tears to the news on the radio, amazed to hear their words being broadcast right across the radio dial.

"Wow," said Isabelle. "All over New Brunswick people are driving home from work and they're listening to our cries for a coroner's inquest."

Earlier that day, one of Ana's community college instructors had projected live television coverage of the news conference onto a big screen in front of Ana's class in Moncton. When she arrived back at the college the next day, she was showered with hugs and handshakes and congratulations from her teachers and fellow students. In fact, Ana and Isabelle's story had been picked up by the national news wires. It was broadcast right across Canada, and published in newspapers from coast to coast, even in the big national dailies in Toronto.

At that moment, Isabelle felt certain they would get an inquest. But there were still powerful forces opposing them, including school officials in Bathurst, and the school system's friend and ally, Mayor Stephen Brunet, who made it clear that he and many other local residents were opposed to an inquest. Why dredge up the details of this painful tragedy from the past, he told CBC Television. Why force people like Wayne Lord to testify? Brunet said people were pulling him aside at places like Tim Hortons, grumbling about the persistent media spotlight, and the never-ending attention surrounding the crash.

While most of the other parents were now publicly in favour of an inquest, some were still wary, and many were emotionally exhausted by having to see and hear the tragedy mentioned, over and over again, in the news media. "We stopped getting the paper at our house, because we just couldn't take it any more," says Krista Quinn.

The families were also keenly aware that the debate over an inquest had divided their town; they were caught in the middle, which only added to their emotional burdens. Ana and Isabelle's campaign was drawing comments on the CBC Web site and elsewhere online, including the new VanAngels. ca blog. Many people were supportive and encouraging: "Keep it up," they said. "I admire what you're doing." But others were critical, even hateful, calling the moms "gold diggers," or telling them to "Let those boys rest in peace."

Amid the tension, Ana was worried for her safety. She warned Isabelle, who had a habit, even in winter, of staying beside Daniel's grave late into the night: "We better not go to the cemetery after dark any more."

Melynda understood the negativity in her hometown. "Bathurst is an inherently small-c conservative place," she says. "People just wanted the episode to be over — 'We gave you your big hurrah, we came out to the big funeral, we made our donations and bought the Boys in Red T-shirts. Aren't you satisfied, isn't that enough?'

"I also believe that people in authority and power in Bathurst, who like to present the idea that this is a lovely little town, they would really prefer if it was just swept under the carpet and forgotten, and everybody moved on."

But Melynda wasn't prepared to let up the pressure. She contacted the moms the day after their news conference to remind them to make a series of targeted phone calls, as part of their plan.

"Don't just settle for your fifteen minutes of fame," she told them. "Keep up the pressure, keep it going."

Isabelle called John Foran, the minister of Public Safety, who oversaw the coroner's office. She left messages and he called her back, politely thanking her for the calls and agreeing to look into her demands, but making it clear that he couldn't promise anything. She also left messages at the offices of the ministers of Education, Justice, and Transport, but none of them called back. When Ana phoned the office of premier Shawn Graham, his secretary told her that "the premier doesn't speak to just anybody."

They blogged about the premier that day on their Web site:

We remember [Graham] and his wife at our sons' funeral at the
arena in Bathurst. He flew in from Fredericton and we met him
downstairs. He spoke to each one of us and gave us his condolences. I remember seeing him on television. He said this was a
sad day for New Brunswick and that his heart went out to the
parents. Now he cannot even pick up a phone and talk to us for
two minutes to assure us that Greg Forestell, the Acting Chief
Coroner is doing his best and will come to a decision soon.

A few days later, however, the moms did get a call from Forestell, asking
them to meet with him at Danny's Inn on December 18. All the families
who lost loved ones in the crash were invited to the meeting, after which
there would be a news conference. On the morning of the meeting the
Telegraph Journal, the provincial newspaper owned by the influential Irving
family, ran a strongly worded editorial saying an inquest should not only
be held, but that the law should be changed to make inquests automatic for
any student deaths in the school system.

"Grieving parents should not be forced to fight for a thorough review,"
the paper said. "The Coroner's Act must require mandatory inquests for
deaths of students on school property, engaged in school activities, or otherwise under the guardianship of the education system."

Despite that moral support, said Isabelle, "We had no idea which way
the government would go."

Forestell, however, brought with him exactly the Christmas gift Isabelle
and Ana wanted. As he told the parents at Danny's Inn—and would soon
announce publicly at a news conference that day—the government would
hold an inquest in the new year to fully investigate the tragedy, and produce
recommendations for student safety.

"Yeahhhhhhhhhhhh!" yelled Melynda when she heard the news.

"Parents prevail," shouted the front-page headline the next morning in
the *Telegraph Journal*.

Ana and Isabelle had prevailed indeed. They had started, eleven months ago, asking hard, uncomfortable questions about why the crash had happened. They had summoned the energy, in the midst of their grief and of all the critics and doubters, to demand answers from a school system that had circled its wagons, and from an apathetic government that had to be poked and prodded into doing the right thing. They had made some enemies to get to this point, but were also winning admiring fans among ordinary New Brunswickers who couldn't help but respect these two courageous Bathurst moms. After Forestell's announcement some of Ana and Isabelle's detractors claimed that the province would have called an inquest eventually, even without the mothers' campaign, once bureaucrats had reviewed the accident reconstruction reports and the RCMP criminal investigation. That's pure speculation, but even if it were true, why was the government still undecided on an inquest, still noncommittal, a month after the police report had come out, and eleven months after the deaths of seven teenagers in the care of a school?

"That inquest should have been called minutes after the accident occurred back in January," scoffs Melynda. "Why did these mothers have to go through all that? Why did they have to ask any questions whatsoever? When you force people into a position where they don't know what's going to happen, what do you think they're going to do? They're going to fight for it. And if we hadn't fought, they wouldn't have held the inquest.

"The nerve and arrogance of those people who put them in that position!"

Ana and Isabelle, despite a considerable victory, shared none of Melynda's euphoria toward the outcome.

"Ana and I were both relieved," says Isabelle. "I felt, 'Oh, thank goodness we don't have to push any more, after what they'd already put us through.' I felt this inquest could change the face of student safety for after-school travel. But did I feel victorious? No. Melynda felt that way, but not me. I didn't feel empowerment. That's not how I deal with life. My goal was just to get that inquest."

...

The inquest would begin on May 4 and run for two weeks. Rather than rest easy and savour the result of her successful campaign — or take time alone to quietly mourn Daniel through the dark days surrounding the first anniversary of the crash — Isabelle immersed herself once again into the details of the tragedy, to prepare for the coming inquiry. She spent her days and many of her nights, soldiering on in the "war room" basement office of her home, surrounded by computers and printers and fax machines. There was also a steadily rising forest of filing boxes stuffed with information on motor vehicle laws, accident reports, government safety guidelines and advisories, school board documents, and other bits and pieces of data collected over the past year, including printed copies of hundreds of emails between herself and various officials, all carefully organized into file folders. Added to this mountain of reading material, now, was information about how coroner's inquests worked, and Isabelle was not happy with what she was learning.

In the weeks before Forestell's announcement, as the mothers were tightening the screws on the government in their public campaign for the inquest, there had been a series of stories in the *Telegraph Journal* about the shortcomings of the province's coroner inquest system. It turned out that two experienced Saint John lawyers, David O'Brien and John Barry, had for years been asking the government to reform the Coroner's Act, saying New Brunswick was one of only two provinces, along with Newfoundland and Labrador, whose inquest systems had not been properly updated since the nineteenth century. Coroner's inquests are all about getting at the truth of unexpected deaths, and making sure similar deaths are never repeated. This was harder to do in New Brunswick, the lawyers said, because the recommendations of inquest juries are not binding on the government. The families of dead victims who are the subject of an inquiry also have no legal standing at the hearings. They cannot call their own witnesses, present evidence, or cross-examine government witnesses — rights afforded to families in the more up-to-date systems in British Columbia, Alberta, Ontario, and other provinces. In New Brunswick the whole process is a one-sided affair, presided over by a government coroner and a Crown lawyer, and that's it.

David O'Brien, a civil litigator and a heavy hitter with the New Brunswick Branch of the Canadian Bar Association, wrote a report for the group in 2003 titled "Bringing Death Investigations in New Brunswick into the 21st Century." It said the Coroner's Act "lacks the ability to respond to the modern day requirements of death investigation, to provide answers and to provide recommendations that will be respected and implemented in order to protect the safety of its citizens." The province had ignored the report, however, and the issue had languished until the Bathurst tragedy placed the inquest system under the public spotlight. Suddenly, Ana and Isabelle realized that their hard-won inquest might in fact turn into a superficial affair, organized by the government merely for the sake of public optics, without any real hope of bringing changes to the education system. Melynda put the two moms in touch with O'Brien and Barry, and together they agreed to pool their efforts and fight for changes.

The lawyers recognized immediately something that wasn't yet fully appreciated by woolly headed senior bureaucrats in the government, or by the province's political leadership: Ana and Isabelle, as unlikely as it seemed, had real political power. Whatever their perceived faults — anger, naiveté, a misplaced desire to penalize Wayne Lord — here was a pair of grieving, small-town mothers who had lost their sons and who had nothing personal to gain from their activism, except the discovery of the truth and a safer future for other children. These qualities resonated with the public and the media, and gave their crusade a David-and-Goliath-like quality in the face of government arrogance and intransigence.

As John Barry told the women in an email: "If out of an unbelievable tragedy you could achieve substantial law reform in death causation investigation, that would be an accomplishment in the public interest and the memory of those young men.

"You are both politically a formidable duo formed out of tragedy. I admire your determination and forbearance . . . Call on the Premier to do the right thing."

Ana and Isabelle did call on Premier Shawn Graham, once again. They sent letters to him and to other members of the Liberal cabinet. And they were joined this time by Debbie Harquail, an aboriginal woman in the town of Dalhousie, just up the coast from Bathurst, whose family had gone through the unhappy experience of a New Brunswick inquest the year before. Debbie's sister Leona was found dead of a drug overdose in 2005 after signing herself out from a provincially operated addiction centre. For two years the Harquail family had begged the government for an inquest, finally getting one in 2008. But at the end of it, Debbie Harquail said her family's needs had been ignored during the inquiry, and months after it was over, none of the nine recommendations put forward by the jury—aimed at improving the health and safety of mentally ill aboriginal women—were enacted by the province.

"The Coroner's Act must be amended to allow [families] to get all their answers met," Harquail wrote in a letter to Ana and Isabelle, after hearing about their coming inquest. "My heart is with you, and so is my spirit of Motherhood. A Mother will go through fire for her children. I support you to help you save the lives of all our children and grandchildren."

In mid-April, after weeks of letters and emails and continued public pressure, Harquail joined Ana, Isabelle, Melynda, and their new "spokesman," Jim Lavoie, in a meeting in Fredericton with Public Safety Minister John Foran and his officials. After introductions by Lavoie, Ana and Isabelle made it clear they wanted the best inquest possible for their sons, and they didn't believe they would get one under the current system. They knew the government couldn't fully change the Coroner's Act, and pass new legislation, in time for the start of their inquest in early May. So they asked instead for an amendment to the existing law, giving them, and future families, full legal standing and the ability to call and cross-examine witnesses.

Foran was friendly and polite, and listened patiently to the women. However, his most senior official, the department's deputy minister, a young, brash, thirty-something civil servant, tried to hurry the women along as they put forward their demands. He was particularly disrespectful, says Ana, rolling his eyes while Melynda was making her own arguments. At the end of the meeting, as Foran got up to leave, Ana could contain her frustration no more. She wasn't as fond of Melynda as Isabelle had become — Ana was often irritated at Melynda's take-charge, overbearing manner — but she was appalled by the behaviour of this young, self-important bureaucrat.

"Hey, I might have my issues with Melynda, but whoa, she's one of us," says Ana. "Oh my gosh, I was boiling, watching him at that meeting, trying to stay in control of my emotions. As we were about to leave, I said to this man, 'Excuse me, I don't mean to be disrespectful, but are you like this in every meeting? Are you always rolling your eyes at people?' I embarrassed him [the official apologized for upsetting Ana] but I just couldn't hold it in."

Despite their efforts, the government would not bend, refusing to make any changes to the Coroner's Act or give the families legal standing at the inquest. Perhaps it would have been logistically impossible to amend the legislation in a matter of weeks. Perhaps officials felt they had done enough for the two mothers already and simply decided it was time to stand up to their demands. If the moms got what they wanted on the Coroner's Act, who knows what they might ask for next?

What the government did do, however, was go out of its way to make sure the upcoming Bathurst inquest was a carefully planned, fully explored, and comprehensive review that met all the needs of Ana, Isabelle, and the other families. It's hard to know whether the government did this out of a genuine desire to find the truth or whether it simply wanted to prove its critics wrong, by showing that New Brunswick's inquest system wasn't a "relic of the nineteenth century" but was in fact perfectly capable of examining the Boys in Red tragedy.

Ana and Isabelle had their own clear view. "They gave us a good inquest because we made such a fuss about it," says Ana. "They had to prove to us that there was nothing wrong with the Act, so we got the best."

Six

TESTIMONY

WHILE ANA AND Isabelle wouldn't have legal standing or representation at the upcoming coroner's inquest, they were invited to help shape its tone and direction. Greg Forestell, the province's acting chief coroner who would preside over the inquest, and George Chiasson, the Bathurst lawyer appointed by Forestell to ask questions on behalf of the Crown, each consulted with the moms in advance, both in person and by email, asking them to submit the names of potential witnesses and suggest areas that the inquiry should explore.

Ana was busy attending her college classes in Moncton, but Isabelle took up the coroner's challenge with gusto. For six weeks she toiled in her basement office, pouring over the RCMP and Transport Canada accident reports, studying the motor vehicle laws, the Education Act, the van maintenance records, and even the weather reports from January 12, 2008. Almost every night, she and Melynda would talk for hours via Skype, Isabelle explaining what she'd learned through her research that day, and Melynda turning Isabelle's new knowledge and her queries into formal, coherent questions for Chiasson to ask at the inquest. For Isabelle the task became on obsession.

"Some days I was up at six or seven in the morning, working in my downstairs computer room," she says, "and I often didn't leave that room until two or three the next morning. I just slept down there. I'd work all day and late into the night, then crawl into Daniel's bed in the room next door, and go back into the computer room the next day. My sister Linda would come down and feed me.

"I just wanted the best for the boys. I didn't want to leave any stone unturned."

In the end Isabelle submitted a list of more than a dozen people she wanted called to the witness stand, along with as many as two thousand detailed questions for Chiasson to ask. Not twenty questions, or even two hundred, but *two thousand*, a sign of Isabelle's relentless, single-minded, uncompromising handling of all matters relating to Daniel's death. Some of the witnesses she requested were never called to testify, but many were, and many of the questions so doggedly researched and crafted by Isabelle and Melynda would end up shaping the very heart of the various lines of inquiry pursued by Chiasson at the hearings.

During Isabelle's research she stumbled across an extraordinary, long-forgotten document on the New Brunswick government Web site — a 2001 safety review of the school transportation system by the provincial auditor general. The audit was mainly focused on the use of yellow school buses to transport eighty-nine thousand New Brunswick students each day between home and school. But the audit also included a review of extracurricular travel — the safety of the "vans or cars that student councils own and operate for the purpose of transporting students to and from various school related activities" — precisely the system that was in place at Bathurst High School at the time of the crash.

The audit was highly critical of the Department of Education's safety measures for school transportation in general. "Parents have entrusted the Province to implement a safe and reliable pupil transportation system. [Yet] the Department lacks an overall monitoring function," the audit said. "There is little or no monitoring of superintendents, principals or bus drivers to ensure they are fulfilling responsibilities assigned to them in the regulations."

Most importantly for the Bathurst case, the audit said although there were guidelines in the Education Act for the safe maintenance and operation of extracurricular vehicles — the same guidelines unearthed by Isabelle in the months following the tragedy — there was in fact no enforcement of those guidelines, and little monitoring of motor vehicle inspection standards, driver training and licensing, vehicle maintenance, or winter tire use.

The auditor general cautioned: "We discovered some confusion over responsibility for these vehicles. Officials we interviewed admitted to us concern over this area. In some respects, no one is sure who would be held accountable if anything were to go wrong."

There it was. In 2001, seven years before the Bathurst tragedy, the government was formally warned — ominously warned, as it turned out — that students in its public schools were being transported to after-school activities in cars and vans whose ownership, maintenance, and operation existed in a regulatory vacuum. Some schools told the auditor general they had lists of teachers, coaches, and parents who were authorized to drive students to off-site events, but others had no idea who was properly trained and licensed to drive their kids. Some schools were aware of the safety guidelines in the law, others were not. And no one, according to the report, knew who was ultimately responsible for the vehicles and the enforcement of the rules. Was it the provincial government? The school boards? The schools themselves? Or even their student councils?

Certainly the province abdicated its responsibility: by 2008, nothing had been done about these gaping holes in the system. So when Ana and Isabelle began asking questions about why their sons were travelling, under school supervision, on a snowy highway late at night, in a van without winter tires, driven by a coach who had been on duty for more than fourteen hours — all contrary to the unenforced, unmonitored guidelines — it was only natural that they couldn't get any satisfactory answers from the coach, the school principal, the superintendent, or the minister of education. Because no one knew, as the auditor general had predicted, *who would be held accountable if anything were to go wrong.*

Clockwise from top left: Justin Cormier, Daniel Hains, Javier Acevedo, Nathan Cleland, Codey Branch, Nick Quinn, and Nikki Kelly. (The Canadian Press/Andrew Vaughan)

...

On the morning of May 4, Greg Forestell convened the "Inquest of the Bathurst High School Van Collision" with the following words: "A coroner's inquest in New Brunswick," he said, serves as a "means for satisfying the community that the circumstances surrounding the death of one of its members will not be overlooked, concealed or ignored."

For more than a year Ana and Isabelle had fought to make sure the circumstances of their sons' deaths, and those of the other victims, would not be overlooked or ignored, despite deep opposition from inside their own community. Whatever the outcome of the inquest, whatever the jury's recommendations, or whether any change at all would come from it, Ana and Isabelle could hold their heads high; they had succeeded where many doubted them, they had carried the day in their campaign for truth and accountability, simply by the fact that the inquest had now come to life.

Ana took two weeks off from her college classes in Moncton and temporarily moved back to the North Shore for the duration of the hearings. On the first day, she, Isabelle, and Melynda gathered at the Bathurst courthouse, a sprawling stone-and-concrete complex only a few blocks from Bathurst High, and walked inside through a waiting crowd of reporters and photographers. Ana remembers feeling something akin to a harassed and hounded "movie star," overwhelmed on all sides by news crews and paparazzi, "with all the cameras on us." For the next two weeks the hearings would dominate the newspaper headlines and television broadcasts across New Brunswick. The three women would attend every moment, sitting in the front row of the court's public gallery, listening intently to the testimony, scribbling notes, and passing requests to lawyer George Chiasson, who would question the witnesses.

Melynda's decision to take time away from her work and sit openly with the moms through the hearings was a bold one. She had grown up in Bathurst and knew many people there. Once she was recognized as Ana and Isabelle's associate and ally, there would be no doubt about who was giving them strategic advice, who was helping to craft their public statements and manage the often provocative content on VanAngels.ca. Among the first to recognize Melynda at the courthouse was school Superintendent John McLaughlin, who in the 1970s had been a fellow student with Melynda at Bathurst High. Although he was a year older than her, they had always been friends. McLaughlin was also in the courtroom every day of the inquest, and he had spotted Melynda on day one, sitting beside Ana and Isabelle.

"John came up to me and said, 'How are you?'" recalls Melynda. "He realized that I was with the parents who were causing all the fuss. What can you say under those circumstances? I put my arm around him and gave him a hug, and of course Isabelle didn't like that — 'Oooh, the enemy!' — but I said to Isabelle, 'John is my friend, I've known him all my life. I'm not going to ignore him.'"

In the weeks and months to come, as word spread in Bathurst and Fredericton about Melynda Jarratt's collaboration with Ana and Isabelle, some old friendships became harder to maintain. Even her professional life suffered, she says, as government contracts that might once have been awarded to her company went elsewhere instead.

"I've encountered people who are very, very angry with me," Melynda says. "And I still get nasty looks. I have old friends in Bathurst who I grew up with, they won't look me in the eye. It's all different now. It would be very hard to have a happy conversation about old times."

Only one other grieving family was represented through the entire inquest. Alan Cormier, Justin's dad, sat through every single hearing. Codey Branch's father Dale and Nick Kelly's dad Bruno Blanchard showed up later in the proceedings, as did Francisco Acevedo. Aside from Ana, Isabelle, and Alan Cormier, however, the other parents avoided the opening days, which was when many expected Wayne Lord to be called to the witness stand. Some parents believed Lord shouldn't be put through the "torture," as Krista Quinn called it, of having to testify about the tragedy in public.

Lord was actually the second person called to the witness chair, following a quick, emotionally charged appearance by Austin Ward, the Loblaws truck driver, whose memories of that awful night had never been publicly documented before, and still haunted him more than a year later. After stoically recounting his brief role in the tragedy, Ward left the courtroom. He was replaced by Lord, who sat nervously in front of the court for more than an hour, his hands folded in his lap, looking directly at Chiasson, answering the lawyer's questions, and never averting his eyes to anyone else. Lord spoke quietly and matter-of-factly — he had always been a man of few words — and on this occasion his soft voice was made even harder to hear due to a noisy air conditioning system that forced Chiasson to plead repeatedly with Lord, and with all subsequent witnesses, to speak loudly so they could be heard above the mechanical din of the courthouse ventilation.

By this time, Lord had withdrawn from teaching and coaching. His teenage daughter Katie, who had also survived the crash, had withdrawn from school and was being treated for post-traumatic stress disorder. Ana and Isabelle, the crowd of reporters, and everyone else in the room were on the edge of their seats as Lord talked publicly for the first time about the horrifying events of January 12, 2008. Although the weather looked good in Moncton before their trip home, he said, conditions worsened in Miramichi and "got progressively worse as I approached Bathurst... the wheel tracks were no longer visible. The road was completely covered with slush and I had no idea where the centreline was.

"I was meeting the transport as it was coming over the crest of the hill," he told the inquest. "I wanted to make sure I gave it as wide a berth as I could, so I turned, moved to the right slightly, and when I — all of a sudden, I hit either what I thought was a rut or the edge of the shoulder. I found out later it was the edge of the shoulder. When I felt the vehicle pulling towards the ditch, I corrected, put it back onto the pavement, but it continued in the same path and I could not get it straightened out again. It turned into the southbound lane and was struck by the transport."

Lord said he was vaguely aware of various provincial safety guidelines concerning after-school travel but couldn't pinpoint them exactly. He was also aware of pre-trip vehicle checklists that had to be filled out. The checklists were once filled out routinely and regularly at BHS, but those checks and forms, he said, "had not been used for the past few years."

Isabelle had only set eyes on Lord a handful of times since the crash. "His appearance at the inquest was hard for everyone," she says. And for the first time, her attitude towards him softened. "I felt kind of sad for him. He didn't know where to put his eyes, or how to sit. He looked very alone. I felt bad for him. But at the same time, I was still angry."

In the days following Lord's testimony, the inquest heard separately from Bradd Arseneau and Tim Daley, the two Phantoms players who had survived the crash. Arseneau, by this time in grade twelve, had little to contribute, saying he couldn't remember many details of the event, not even the colour of the van they were travelling in. Daley, who had graduated from Bathurst High and wanted to become a police officer, but who was still recovering from a broken pelvis, was more helpful. He talked in detail about his memories of the trip, including a rush for a coveted spot in the van's back bench seat for the journey home from Moncton. It was a scramble he would lose, thereby saving his life.

"On your way back from Moncton, where did you sit, getting in?" asked Chiasson.

"I was too slow to get the back seat, so I had to sit up front," said Daley. "We always sit in the same spot [but] always between me and Codey, we always try to fight for the back seat. He won that time."

Codey Branch and the other six players seated in the van's two rear benches all died in the collision. Daley, Arseneau, and Katie Lord, who were sitting together towards the front, survived.

The public also heard for the first time from Sebastien Morrison and Julie Chiasson, the young couple that stopped to help the victims moments after the collision, and from RCMP Corporal Mario Dupuis, the first police officer on the scene. Dupuis was overcome by emotion, breaking down in the witness chair as he recalled his tormented memories. Later in the inquest other police and emergency witnesses would also break down, sometimes outside the courtroom, sometimes in Ana or Isabelle's arms.

Both mothers were themselves emotionally drained by the end of the first week of hearings, but they were comforted at the same time by the reassurance of strangers. A few days earlier Ana had been approached in a

Bathurst store by a woman she'd never met, who told her she'd been watching news of the inquest every night on television and that Ana and Isabelle were constantly in her thoughts. She handed Ana a bouquet of flowers and said, "People like you guys are what it takes to make changes." Another stranger sent flowers by courier to Isabelle's front door, with a note bearing a similar message of support.

The two moms were also pleased that by the end of the first week, the parents of many of the other boys began appearing in the public gallery at the inquest. News reporters also noticed the new arrivals, and asked Isabelle how she felt about the growing number of grieving family members in the courtroom.

"I'm happy they're there," Isabelle said. "It brought tears to my eyes to see them today. It shows that they are behind us."

•••

While the first half of the inquest was gut-wrenching, the second week made Ana's and Isabelle's blood boil. Having finished with eyewitness accounts of the crash and its aftermath, the inquest now adopted a wider focus. There was testimony from mechanics and motor vehicle inspectors about the condition of the van, from a yellow school bus driver about the higher training standards of Class 2 professional bus drivers, and from officials at the departments of education and transportation. But what most raised the ire of the two mothers was testimony from teachers and school officials, including BHS Principal Coleen Ramsay and Vice-Principal Don McKay.

Ramsay, a long-time educator who herself had grown up in Bathurst and graduated from BHS in 1974, said the school would have happily reimbursed the hotel expenses of any coach who chose to keep their team in another city overnight because of weather concerns. She said she knew of the existence of provincial guidelines for after-school travel. Yet she didn't know that the van's pre-trip checklists were not being filled out, or that the school's vans were supposed to have mechanical safety inspections every six months, or that the van driven by Lord didn't have winter tires. Ramsay and other school staff said they believed the tires on the van — labelled "M and S" for mud and snow—were winter tires, when in fact they were only all-season tires, not winter ones.

As for why the Phantoms had travelled that day in bad winter weather, Ramsay said she always "erred on the side of caution" when it came to after-school trips; however, on the day of the crash, she didn't feel caution was necessary, despite the storm warnings.

"If a coach asks me [whether or not to travel on the day of a forecasted winter storm], I have no problem in saying, 'Don't go,'" Ramsay told the inquest.

"OK," said Chiasson. "On the date in question of this accident, do you recall if you had received such a request?"

"I did not."

"Any discussions on it?"

"No."

"During the day, during bad weather, do you go check the weather for yourself?"

"If I'm aware of it. In my office, I'm in the centre of the building. There are no windows. And if it's a busy day, I may go through the whole day and not know whether it's daylight or dark."

"Do you recall if on that day, you had any notification of an impending storm coming that evening?"

"There were reports. There was a weather warning."

"Do you recall discussing that with the coach, or any coaches?"

"No," said Ramsay. "It was one of those days like it seemed like it never transpired. We do have those days where they predict weather and then it doesn't happen. And it didn't seem to happen that day, it seemed like it was one of those days where, while we were in school, the weather was still holding."

"So you're saying that you yourself had no concerns on that day?"

"No."

Earlier at the inquest, a climate technician from the Meteorological Service of Canada testified that the snow started falling in Bathurst at about two p.m., became mixed with ice pellets at eight p.m., and changed to freezing rain after midnight. Twelve centimetres of snow, ice, and freezing rain fell from two p.m. on Friday to two a.m. the next morning.

Don McKay had retired from teaching by the time of the inquest, but during the tragedy was the vice-principal who supervised student travel and after-school sports. He, too, said he knew about the existence of the provincial travel guidelines. Yet, like Ramsay, he didn't realize that the BHS van did not have winter tires; he didn't know a mechanical safety inspection was required every six months; and he didn't know about the guideline recommendation for defensive driving courses for anyone who drives students. As for the weather on the night of the crash, he said he'd discussed the storm warnings with Wayne Lord that morning. They had even talked about the possibility of the Phantoms staying in Moncton overnight if the weather was bad. But McKay also said the school had no formal process in place for himself or other school leaders to monitor the progress of winter storms once students were already out on road trips. There was no mandatory system to call coaches on the road, and get updates about the state of their weather, and advise them about conditions at home.

"Is there a protocol for you to check with the coach, how does that work?" asked Chiasson.

"A call could've been made from here to Mr. Lord, indicating what it was like, yes," said McKay.

"Is there someone in place to monitor that?"

"Not at this particular point in time, other than, you know, knowing where each of us are kind of all responsible."

"That night, did anything come to your attention? Did you want to make that call?"

"No," said McKay. "It never crossed my mind."

The jury was particularly interested in this issue, and asked its own questions of McKay, once Chiasson had finished.

"Sometimes schools are cancelled on the pretense of a snowstorm; this is assumed because of the safety of the students," said one of the jurors. "Do you know why a trip would not be cancelled on the pretense of a snowstorm? What would make, who would make the decision to cancel the trip because of an impending storm?"

"Often the coaches would," said McKay. "They would bring their concerns to us and we would follow through on it and see, based on checking with the other school and those types of things. So on some occasions, the decision was made that the team wasn't gonna go, and then we would follow through by contacting the other school."

Admissions like that left Ana and Isabelle shaking their heads. At times, however, the women were more upset by the conduct of observers in the courtroom than by what the witnesses were saying. As the inquest wore on, Ana grew increasingly irritated that some witnesses, mostly the school and government employees, came to the hearings with a lawyer or even a team of lawyers at their side. Some witnesses, the moms noticed, were being quietly coached by their lawyers from the sidelines.

"All these people have high-priced lawyers sitting there in suits," says Ana. "These lawyers would nod their heads up and down, or shake their heads side-to-side, telling their clients, 'Don't answer,' 'Good job,' and so on. Well, it came to the point that I'd had enough. I said to George Chiasson, 'George, you tell those lawyers to stop telling the witnesses how to answer your questions, because I'm going to get up and I'm going to tell them to 'BE QUIET! STOP THAT!' He said, 'OK,' and he went to talk to them, and those lawyers gave me some nasty looks back.

"I was not content," says Ana. "It took a lot of effort for me to keep my butt on that seat!"

Then it was school Superintendent John McLaughlin's turn in the witness chair. McLaughlin is a large, looming man with an accommodating, down-to-earth style whose presence fills a room. His family had lived in Bathurst for generations—his dad was once mayor—and as school superintendent, the old mayor's son now occupied his own high-profile position in town. As befits such a leadership figure, McLaughlin was also a polished professional; he knew when to be tough and when to be gentle, and he now tried hard to be helpful and conciliatory as he answered Chiasson's questions.

McLaughlin, who also had a lawyer with him in the courtroom, said that
the team of principals he supervised on the North Shore had known for
years about the province's student travel guidelines. He admitted what many
others were afraid to: that there was no auditing or monitoring of whether
the travel guidelines, or the rules of the Motor Vehicle Act, or any safety
protocols at all, were ever followed by staff in the various schools. And that
was about to change, he said, explaining that most of those guidelines had
been turned into provincial policies in the wake of the Bathurst crash. They
were no longer just suggested best practices; they were mandated.

"There are no more 'shoulds,'" he said. "They have been replaced with
'musts.'"

Yet McLaughlin still hedged, pointing out that enforcing such government
policies in a myriad of schools across a wide geographic area is always easier
said than done.

"The devil is in the details?" said Chiasson.

"It certainly is."

On the day of McLaughlin's testimony, Ana and Isabelle sat in their
usual spot in the front row of the public gallery, wearing T-shirts with their
sons' faces emblazoned across the front. The moms weren't satisfied with
the testimony of any of the school officials. On every day of the inquest,
they had retreated with Melynda to Isabelle's home office to post their
observations of the day's proceedings on their VanAngels blog. On the very
last day, following McLaughlin's testimony, they posted a list of "Frequently
heard phrases during the coroner's inquest into the death of our sons." Their
list included:

"I forget"..."I cannot recall"..."I'm not trying to pass the buck"..."It's
not my job"..."It's not my department"..."I just trust that it's inspected"..."I
never read the Guidelines"..."I didn't know about the weather"..."the
roads weren't bad."

"These people should be ashamed of themselves," the moms wrote. "To
think that we entrusted our children to their responsibility."

Despite their disappointment in some of the witnesses, Isabelle and Ana were, on the whole, feeling satisfied with the inquest by the end of the hearings. It had been a gruelling and heart-wrenching two weeks. They had been in the public spotlight—on television and in the province's newspapers—every day, yet the mothers believed the coroner had delivered a comprehensive inquiry that had looked carefully at not all, but many of the areas they wanted examined. The process had been empowering for the two women and for some of the other parents who had also attended. Most importantly, Ana and Isabelle felt that the five people on the jury had taken their role seriously, had listened carefully, and had asked some good questions of their own. The moms had high hopes that some good might come of the whole affair.

• • •

Before the final day of testimony, Ana, Isabelle, and Melynda submitted, at the coroner's request, their own recommendations for the jury to consider before the panel delivered its own official list. Of the twenty recommendations the mothers submitted, the most important from their point of view was that students should be driven to after-school events, not by teachers or volunteers, but by paid, professional bus drivers (with Class 2 bus licences), driving either standard yellow school buses or mini school buses known as Multi-Function Activity Buses (MFABs). They also wanted the Department of Education to take over responsibility for student travel from the local schools, by properly funding extracurricular transport and monitoring all such travel around the province from a central office in Fredericton. And they wanted a new "weather law" requiring the cancellation of all games and off-site activities in the event of serious winter storms. The women shared their proposed recommendations with the other families, who added a few suggestions of their own. Nick Kelly's mother, Marcella, who began coming to the inquest towards the end of the hearings, wanted a requirement for schools that host visiting teams to have supplies of pillows and blankets on hand so that outside students can stay overnight instead of driving home in bad weather. Alan Cormier, who had faithfully attended the entire inquest, also wanted the government to widen Highway 8, so his recommendation was submitted too.

By now most of the parents had started coming to the courthouse to attend the hearings, even those who had remained quiet or hadn't publicly advocated for an inquest, and many told reporters that they were feeling optimistic and had high expectations of the jury.

"I am confident the jury will come back with good recommendations," said Ginette Emond, Codey Branch's mom. "I knew this process was going to be hard, but I knew we had to get through it for changes to be put in place."

No one knew how long the jury would take. The news media hounded Isabelle and Melynda to contact them as soon as they'd heard when the jury would be ready. In the end, the jury deliberated for only two days, and then everyone was summoned back to the courthouse to hear jury foreman Jeff Causey read the official recommendations to the government.

There had been a violent windstorm in Bathurst the previous day, so severe that it tore the roofs off homes in the trailer park opposite Isabelle's house. The next day, as the moms were driving back to the courthouse with Melynda to hear the jury's findings, each woman filled with anticipation and anxiety, the tail end of the windstorm was still whipping around the city, flinging up the remains of the sand that snowplow drivers had spread on icy streets all through the winter. As the women drove over the causeway that leads across Bathurst Harbour into the city's downtown, a terrific gust of wind swept in front of them, rattling their car and driving a huge funnel of sand up into the air like a prairie tornado.

"We'd never seen anything like that," says Melynda. "The sand was turning and turning in the air. We were like, 'Holy cow, what's going on?' It was like a message to us. We interpreted it as, 'The boys are speaking to us, that something big is going to happen.'"

All the parents, including some who hadn't attended many of the hearings, gathered inside the courtroom, along with their surviving children. Ana and Isabelle described the moment on their blog:

"The courtroom was tense as families, friends, the public, and the media gathered to hear the Jury's recommendations. The first two rows were filled once again with parents and relatives and everyone was quiet. You could hear a pin drop in the courtroom. We didn't know what to expect: were they going to listen to the parents' recommendations that we delivered as a group on Wednesday?"

Then, as the jury foreman read through the list, "One by one we breathed a sigh of relief, as we realized they actually listened to what we had to say, and acted upon the witness testimony."

There were twenty-one formal, jury recommendations; some, but not all, mirrored those submitted by the parents. Greg Forestell added three of his own to the list, for a total of twenty-four recommended changes. Among the most significant:

- Both 15-seat and 7-seat vans should be banned, across Canada, for student travel.
- The Department of Education should assume legal and financial responsibility for extracurricular student travel.
- Only trained school bus drivers with Class 2 licences should transport students to off-site school events.
- There should be a weather law prohibiting school travel in bad winter weather. Games should be cancelled, or teams should be prepared to stay where they are overnight, rather than travel home in storms.
- Only principals and vice-principals — not coaches or drivers — should decide if students travel for school events during inclement weather. And there should be provincial training programs to help school leaders make informed decisions about travel.
- Schools that host visiting teams should have contingency kits with bedding and other supplies, and be prepared to house or provide billets to visiting students in the event of bad weather.

- All vehicles used to transport students should have winter tires
  in the winter, and vehicle maintenance should be paid for by
  the government, not by student councils.
- No driver should be on duty, or driving, more than fourteen
  hours.
- There should be external audits to monitor compliance with
  student travel policies.
- Education staff who do not fulfill student travel safety
  standards should be reprimanded or dismissed.
- Highway "drop edges" should be seamless; in other words,
  there should be little or no drop-off between the edge of the
  asphalt and the gravel shoulder.

This drop-off recommendation was the result of a startling piece of testimony, delivered on the first week of the inquest by RCMP Corporal Annie
Neilson, the collision specialist who reconstructed the details of the crash
for police. She revealed that a second serious crash had occurred, almost a
year after the Boys in Red tragedy, on the same stretch of highway. A driver
had steered onto the shoulder of Highway 8, just south of Bathurst, to give
a wide berth to an oncoming tractor-trailer, and had then lost control when
trying to straighten out the vehicle. People were injured in that incident,
but no one was killed. As with the BHS crash, slippery road conditions and
a drop in elevation from the highway to the shoulder were considered factors
in the second crash. This evidence suggested that perhaps Ana and Isabelle
weren't entirely right to lay blame for the BHS tragedy on the failures of
school officials who didn't follow rules and guidelines, and on provincial
bureaucrats who didn't enforce them. Perhaps the crash was the result of a
dangerous highway drop-edge? Perhaps the Phantoms were doomed the
moment Wayne Lord steered the white van toward the far edge of the road,
at which point, perhaps no vehicle, no driver, and no kind of winter tire
could have safely handled that hazardous section of asphalt? This is what
coroner's inquests do, when they're effective — they ferret out facts and

evidence, and connect once unseen dots, painting a fuller, clearer picture of deadly events for all to see.

Certainly the jurors recognized this, and recommended a fix for the severe drop-edge on Highway 8. But they also recognized that this wasn't the whole story, that the tragedy was also—as the official accident reports had shown, and as the inquest had made clear—the result of a deadly concoction: a series of decisions, or non-decisions, to travel in the face of a winter storm forecast, plus a slippery slush-covered road, a faulty vehicle, lousy tires, and a coach on duty for too many hours. The jury's other recommendations reflected these facts too, loudly reinforcing what Ana and Isabelle had been arguing alone, from the wilderness, for more than a year.

"We were right," they proclaimed on their blog that same day. "It was an almost surreal experience to be sitting there, almost sixteen months to the day that our boys were killed, and to hear a Coroner's Jury affirm what we had been saying all along."

When the proceedings were finally over and the media interviews were finished, Melynda, Ana, and Isabelle left the courthouse parking lot and drove through the small, dusty downtown to the outskirts of Bathurst, finally reaching Highway 8 and driving south for a few kilometres before pulling over onto the shoulder of the road at the crash site. The memorial basketball net was still there, adorned with flowers and notes of grief and love, standing in the grassy ditch in front of a wall of green forest.

"They wanted to talk to their sons," says Melynda. "It was very sad; it was hard."

Ana stood silently, gazing at the net. Isabelle walked down into the ditch and whispered through her tears, "Daniel, it's over now."

Many of the families, even those who hadn't supported Ana and Isabelle in their campaign, believed they'd won a collective victory, that changes would now come to make travel safer for students, meaning that their sons did not die in vain.

"It was a hard process, but now that it is over, what I really feel is that

Codey didn't die for nothing," Dale Branch had told reporters back at the courthouse.

Melynda knew better.

"How little did they realize that they'd done nothing, that true success was going to be measured in the enforcement of these recommendations; and within a very short time we found this out. They thought it was over," she says. "But geez, it was just the beginning."

. . .

It was the end of the line, however, for Ana. By the close of the inquest she and Isabelle were physically and emotionally exhausted. For more than a year they had been fighting the school system and the province: they had organized the petition and the protests; they had taught themselves how to write emails and research public documents; they'd held a press conference and given countless interviews to the news media, seen their names and faces splashed across television screens at home and on newspapers around the country; they had written letters and emails to politicians and bureaucrats, and participated in dozens of official meetings; they had absorbed both the bouquets and brickbats of public opinion, all the while coping with their own personal grief. After the inquest, Melynda went back to Fredericton to pick up her work and her life there. Isabelle retreated into her home to await the government's response to the inquest recommendations; after taking some time to rest, she was prepared to keep fighting if necessary. But Ana had no more of herself to give. She was distracted by her college studies in Moncton. She was tired of all the campaigning and lobbying. And she was increasingly frustrated with Melynda, who in the weeks before and during the inquest, had taken over all public messaging in the mothers' campaign, including the press releases and the scripting of most of what appeared on the VanAngels.ca blog. Melynda worked hard for the two mothers, but she could be brash and pushy. As her role in the campaign and her influence with Isabelle grew, so did Ana's resentment. By the spring of 2009 all three women desperately needed a break, and as Ana returned to

Moncton, she also retreated from active participation in the moms' campaign. She still supported Isabelle, and her name and image would remain on the blog and on all future public statements issued by Isabelle and Melynda. But Ana could no longer keep the solemn pact she'd made with Isabelle the previous year — to walk together "in the same shoes" to the end.

Ana's adult daughters were also telling her that she'd done enough, that it was time to stop fighting the school and the government. Carla, especially, was worried about Ana's close relationship with Isabelle. In the months after the crash the two women had become almost inseparable.

"I was proud of my Mom and everything she fought for," says Carla. "It's what she wanted. My only concern is that with Isabelle, Mom wasn't taking care of herself. She wasn't sleeping, and she wasn't eating. They were together all the time; they'd share half a coffee, half a salad, half a bagel.

"And when I saw her picture in the paper, my friends would say, 'Look, look, your mom's in the newspaper,' but I didn't want to know. I didn't want to get involved in all that stuff. I just wanted to keep my mother-daughter bond with her."

Ana needed to grieve quietly for Javier, and to try pulling her life together. But her retreat from Isabelle's side, from the kindred spirit who had supported her through so much pain and sorrow and with whom she'd won such important victories, was itself a painful reality for Ana. Even though Isabelle herself remained a steadfast friend, the guilt of Ana's withdrawal would haunt her for years.

* * *

One of Ana's last public acts as a member of what lawyer John Barry had called that "formidable duo" came in mid-summer, when she joined Isabelle and all the other parents in Bathurst to hear the New Brunswick government's response to the inquest findings. The families assembled on July 28 in a small conference room at the Atlantic Host motel, where Roland Haché, the province's new education minister, would reply to the twenty-four recommendations put forward by the jury in May.

Haché was a sixty-two-year-old former schoolteacher from the North Shore, who represented Beresford and other communities to the west of Bathurst in the provincial legislature. He was a jovial man with a large smile, a long-time municipal and provincial politician, and a loyal Liberal foot soldier. Haché had replaced the much younger, more fiery, Kelly Lamrock as education minister during a cabinet shuffle only weeks earlier in June. His first difficult job when he took over the portfolio would be to stickhandle the government's response to the inquest, or at least be the public face of the provincial government in what Haché and his officials must have hoped would be their final dealings with the grieving parents and with this politically awkward, highly-publicized file.

In the months since the inquest, the government had held roundtable meetings with various players in the education system, including sports associations and local school officials. Based on these consultations and on the government's own decision making, Haché announced to the families that the province and its schools simply couldn't afford to transport students to extracurricular activities in yellow school buses, or even in smaller-version multi-function activity buses, driven by paid, professional drivers with Class 2 licences. School buses would be used where possible, but mostly the existing ad hoc system of school-funded vehicles, and private vehicles driven by parent volunteers, would remain in place. Haché tried to soften the blow of this disappointing news by announcing that teachers, parents, and other volunteer drivers would now be required to take a short, mandatory driver training course before taking students on the road.

The government would also not be implementing a weather law prohibiting school road trips in bad winter weather. It would, however, adopt almost all the other jury recommendations. New Brunswick had already banned 15-seat vans for student travel in the wake of the Bathurst crash. It would now go ahead and fix the drop-edge on Highway 8 and require host schools to have contingency kits with bedding, or billeting plans, to be able to host visiting teams overnight in the event of bad weather. And, Haché said, the government would begin to enforce mandatory safety policies for all extracurricular travel, including hours-on-duty limits for drivers, mandatory vehicle checklists, more rigorous monitoring of mechanical conditions and inspections, and mandatory winter tires on school vehicles during winter months. Although the province wouldn't pay for the vehicles, it would take over responsibility for their regular maintenance and for equipping them with winter tires.

While Ana, Isabelle, and other parents were pleased by these positive changes, they were surprised, and deeply disheartened, by the decision not to bring in a weather law and not to require school buses and professional (Class 2) drivers for after-school travel. These two recommendations were dear to Ana's and Isabelle's hearts, and popular among most of the other parents too; they were central to what the inquest had been all about.

"We really thought they were going to implement ALL the recommendations," says Ana.

Haché tried hard to be sympathetic and conciliatory with the families. He said there just wasn't the money to pay for school buses and professional, Class 2 drivers. Valerie Kilfoil, his communications director who had quietly attended the mothers' press conference in Fredericton the previous year, made an emotional plea to the parents not to assume that Department of Education bureaucrats didn't take their concerns seriously, didn't also grieve for their lost sons and share their desire for improved safety.

"I have children too," said Kilfoil.

Still, many of the parents were unconsoled. They had expected more.

"I wish they had implemented Class 2 drivers," Dale Branch told reporters as he emerged from the private meeting with Haché. "There are a lot of things good in what they're doing. But as parents we'd all prefer yellow school buses, and bus drivers, driving our kids."

Ana, as usual, put the issue more starkly: "They didn't learn anything," she said. "How many more children must die?"

After the meeting Haché held a brief news conference with reporters in the parking lot outside Bathurst High, with a supportive John McLaughlin at his side. One of two, shiny new red minibuses, or multi-function activity buses (MFAB) that had replaced the high school's remaining 15-seat vans, was positioned in the parking lot as a backdrop for the two men, who pointed to it as proof that standards had indeed improved for student safety. But the truth is, many New Brunswick schools didn't have high quality buses like this for their extracurricular needs, and they wouldn't be getting them now from the province. In fact, the government had nothing to do with the arrival of the new buses at BHS, because both had been donated by private sources in the aftermath of the tragedy. Following the loss of eight lives, Bathurst High now had the best extracurricular vehicles. But dozens of other schools did not.

Ana and Isabelle had followed Haché to the school and stood in the background, watching and listening as the minister spoke to the media. Afterwards, Isabelle told the reporters that she wasn't satisfied with the government's response. She'd come too far, and fought too hard, to get to this point and not to have school buses and Class 2 drivers required for all student travel. She vowed to continue her campaign, and never stop, until the government implemented this recommendation.

Her campaign would indeed continue, more vigorously than ever before. But what Isabelle didn't yet know is that the battle lines would take an unexpected turn. Any politician or bureaucrat who believed the public struggle against the Bathurst mothers had come to a blessed conclusion was in for a rude awakening.

Seven

THE TEST

JOHN MAHLER DIDN'T know who Isabelle Hains was when she called him up out of the blue, one October morning in 2009. Mahler was an automotive columnist at the *Toronto Star*, Canada's largest newspaper. A long-time journalist and former news photographer, he'd joined the paper's "Wheels" section later in his career and had made a name for himself as an expert on tires. In his spare time he also raced cars as a hobby. Mahler still sported the hard-nosed, tell-it-like-it-is demeanour of a newspaperman, but behind his no-nonsense exterior and his moustache was a big smile and a passion for anything automotive. As Isabelle talked, her story jogged Mahler's memory. He vaguely recalled hearing something in the news a year ago about a highway collision in New Brunswick that had killed a bunch of kids. At first it seemed odd that one of the mothers of those dead boys would now be telephoning him in Toronto, but as she talked and explained her problem, he thought he could be of some help.

Mahler listened carefully as Isabelle told him, in her sweet and cautious voice, about the highway crash and the inquest, and about the new minibus—or Multi-Function Activity Bus (MFAB)—that had replaced the 15-passenger vans at Bathurst High School. Isabelle then said she had just discovered, quite by accident, that officials were installing winter tires on only the rear wheels of all school MFABs in New Brunswick, while putting "all-season" tires, designed for summer use, on the front. Did Mahler have an opinion on that? Was it safe? Was it the correct policy to mix tires like this, or should there be winter tires on both the front and rear wheels?

For Mahler this was a no-brainer. Everyone in the business, from professional drivers to mechanics to tire makers, knew very well that you never mix tire types on a vehicle. If you're going to use winter tires, you need to put them on both the front and the back. "The school board and the province are wrong," he told Isabelle without hesitation. "It's so basic. One of the basic knowledge building blocks about tires is that you never mismatch them. It's a guarantee of trouble if you have two different handling feedbacks on different ends of the wheel, even on a bus."

Mahler said he'd be happy to relay his thoughts to officials in New Brunswick and give advice to them if they wished. He also said he would do a small write-up on the issue in one of his upcoming columns. What Mahler didn't know at the time is that he was about to insert himself into the middle of a brewing public storm that would make headlines in New Brunswick for the next several months. Isabelle wasn't merely asking Mahler's opinion; she was quietly amassing an arsenal of information, data, and expert opinion for another all-out campaign that she and Melynda were preparing to wage against the government.

It had been five months since the end of the coroner's inquest, and more than two months since the provincial government had announced its response to the jury's recommendations. Since that time the public and the media hadn't heard any more from Isabelle and Ana. Through the dog days of August and on into September and October, as the summer warmth faded into the cool of autumn, so the heat and hard feelings had finally seemed to dissipate from the Bathurst tragedy. There had been no more press releases, no more petitions, no more angry letters to the editor penned by the grieving mothers. Even their online blog had fallen silent. To many, the long, painful aftermath of the tragedy appeared to have wound its way to an end. Certainly, officials at School District 15 and the provincial government hoped it had. They'd all had quite enough of their dealings with Isabelle Hains and Ana Acevedo.

"The New Brunswick government wanted these women gone—gone from its affairs and gone from the headlines, there's no question about that," says John Mahler, looking back on the moment.

Indeed, Ana and Isabelle wanted and needed a rest. Among other pressures, Isabelle was also now coping with her failing relationship with her husband Allan, who was still working in Alberta. Their marriage was giving way, not only to the stresses of long distance, but to Isabelle's all-consuming campaign efforts. In mid-October, just as all the women were looking forward to a badly needed break from campaigning, the winter tires conundrum popped suddenly and unexpectedly into their lives. What appeared at first to be a minor technical disagreement with the authorities would spiral into an extraordinary dispute, a public tempest that would ensnare officials in two levels of government, and even cross international borders, before it was ultimately settled. Once again, the Bathurst moms decided to take on the political and bureaucratic powers that be in the name of their sons. During their previous winning campaign for the coroner's inquest, they had fought anyone who stood in their way with icy determination and nerves of cold steel. This time, stoked by anger, they would take on their foes with fire. And they would be joined in their quest by an important new ally—a third Bathurst mother who, until now, had sat mostly on the sidelines, but who would turn out to be the angriest and the most fiery of the bunch.

• • •

In the wake of the Bathurst High collision, New Brunswick had banned 15-passenger vans from its schools. At the same time, an anonymous donor had given Bathurst High two new, safer vehicles for driving its students to sporting events: a 26-passenger school bus and a 21-passenger MFAB, which resembled a school bus but was smaller and shorter. Each vehicle was painted red and had "Bathurst High School Phantoms" stencilled in white lettering on the back and sides. Both buses went into service for the first time at the beginning of the new school year in September 2009.

On October 19, about five weeks after classes had started, Melynda was visiting Bathurst when she heard from her brother David that he'd seen the 21-passenger MFAB sitting at the Goodyear Tires shop in town. She got hold of Isabelle that afternoon and the two women drove to Goodyear to take a look at the new minibus. They were curious about what it was doing at the shop, and they were especially interested, after all their work on the coroner's inquest, in knowing if the province was honouring its commitment to have winter tires installed on school vehicles through the winter.

Isabelle was well known in Bathurst by this point in time, and she was instantly recognized by the young mechanic at Goodyear when she and Melynda drove onto the lot. He was friendly and helpful, and told the women the minibus had been brought in to have its winter tires put on. The work was now finished.

MFABs have six wheels, four on the back and two in the front, and sure enough, there were four winter tires on the rear of the minibus, but for some reason, there were only all-season tires on the front. Isabelle had learned during the inquest that proper winter tires have a small, three-peaked mountain symbol, with a snowflake in the middle, etched onto the tire wall. The four rear tires all sported the mountain-snowflake symbol, but not those on the front. The mechanic confirmed her suspicions that the front tires were all-seasons. "That's what the school wanted," he said, shrugging his shoulders and getting back to work.

One of the teachers from Bathurst High, who had been loading the old tires into the back of the MFAB while eyeing Isabelle and Melynda suspiciously, was suddenly joined at Goodyear by Shaun MacDonald, the school's new vice-principal, who had arrived at the shop in his car. MacDonald approached the two women.

"What are you doing here?" he asked.

"Well, we heard the vehicle was here and we wanted to see what kind of tires it has," Isabelle said. "It has mixed tires, but you're supposed to have winter tires on these vehicles. The coroner's inquest said you have to have winter tires."

"We've got the right tires," MacDonald informed them before turning to Melynda, who had taken out her video camera and was filming the encounter.

"Turn that camera off, please." MacDonald looked again at Isabelle. "We're following our policy."

Then MacDonald and the other teacher drove away without further explanation.

Isabelle and Melynda were stunned. "We were like, 'Holy cow, what just happened here, man?'" says Melynda. "'What's going on with these tires?'"

Tires were at the very heart of the Bathurst High tragedy. The school's old white van had worn, all-season tires on its wheels at the time of the collision. Transport Canada's report into the crash said the school's failure to equip the van with winter tires was one of three main contributing factors in the disaster. As a result, tires had been a central issue at the inquest, and the coroner's jury had recommended that all vehicles used for student transport be equipped with winter tires between November and April. It was less than three months after the government had agreed to implement that recommendation on extracurricular school vehicles across the province. And now, the very school that had lost eight lives on a snowy highway, in a van without winter tires, was installing only all-season tires on the front wheels of its new vehicles.

Isabelle and Melynda were furious, but also confused. They knew that after the tragedy, the government had taken over the responsibility for maintaining extracurricular vehicles from schools. So, although Bathurst High teachers had driven their MFAB to Goodyear, they were likely following provincial rules in terms of what tires should be installed. Either the school was wrongly interpreting the province's policy on winter tires or the policy itself had not been properly written in the wake of the inquest recommendations. It's also possible, they imagined, that the province or the school were deliberately cutting corners on the new winter tire standard in some way, perhaps to save money. Whatever the case, Isabelle and Melynda were determined to get to the bottom of the matter. But first they needed to confirm for themselves what the correct tire configuration should be. What did the experts think?

The women went immediately from Goodyear to the provincial Department of Transportation depot in Bathurst. Staff there were courteous but wouldn't discuss the matter. So Isabelle and Melynda drove to Curt's Auto Repair, the shop owned by mechanic Curtis Bennett, who had been hired by the RCMP to inspect the white van after the crash and who had testified at the inquest. The women told Bennett what they'd discovered at Goodyear, and his response was immediate: the MFAB should have winter tires all around. The school was wrong to be putting winter tires only on the rear wheels. The women got the very same reaction that afternoon from another mechanic in town who also warned them: "It's going to be hard for you to get this changed, you know. It's hard to fight the government."

By now, of course, Isabelle had some experience in that area. So she drove home with Melynda, sat down at her computer, and wrote a letter to John McLaughlin, the superintendent at School District 15:

"We have just found out today that the new, smaller, Multi-Function vehicle currently being used by the High School does not have winter tires in the front," the letter said. "If, at this point, the Department [of Education and the school district] has not learned its lesson when it comes to winter tires on vehicles transporting students, how can one blame us for a complete loss of faith in your Department?"

They also issued a press release to the media, their first in months, explaining their discovery and accusing the government of "violating its own policy" on winter tires. "They haven't learned a thing," the women wrote.

And with that, the whole BHS tragedy that had traumatized a province and troubled its government for more than a year was suddenly thrown back into the public spotlight. The story was picked up by news media around the province, and within days a reporter from the *Telegraph Journal* had even travelled from Saint John to Bathurst to interview Isabelle on the matter.

"Bathurst school accused of not following standards," said the headline in the paper the next day. "Proper tires not installed on school vehicle, say mothers who lost sons in crash."

The "mothers" in the headline referred in this case not to Isabelle and Ana, but to Isabelle and another mom, Marcella Kelly, whose fifteen-year-old son, Nikki, had died in the collision. Ana, worn out by the inquest, at loggerheads with Melynda, and trying to start a new life as a human resources counsellor, was still publicly a member of the "Van Angels" group but behind the scenes she was no longer actively participating. As Melynda would later explain, "Ana was taking a break, she needed one, and she was licking her wounds," which were still raw, more than a year after losing Javier.

Isabelle telephoned all the parents of the boys to tell them about the tire problem she and Melynda had stumbled upon. Even though she often received only lukewarm support from the other families, Isabelle felt duty-bound to keep them informed of every new development. When she called Marcella's house, her husband Bruno Blanchard picked up the phone, and he was shocked by what Isabelle told him. Blanchard was a machinist and millwright with Barrick Gold Corporation, whose work frequently took him away from home to Barrick's mines in Africa. But he happened to be home the week the tire issue reared its head, and he went straight to the high school parking lot to see the MFAB for himself. He confirmed with his own eyes Isabelle's claim that there were all-season tires on the front. The news troubled Blanchard, but it fairly ignited his wife's anger. Like all the parents, Marcella had welcomed the government's decision back in July to endorse the inquest jury's call for winter tires on school vehicles. Now, on the cusp of winter, with student athletes set to head out again onto the highways, to learn that the school's new minibus wasn't properly equipped with winter tires felt to Marcella like a slap in the face, a betrayal by those in authority who had promised, in the wake of the boys' deaths, to fix this problem and never again put students on snowy roads without the correct tires. Marcella, who still had two other sons at home, called Isabelle to say she was ready to fight.

"Thank God for Marcella," says Melynda. "We welcomed her getting involved in the tire campaign. She helped Isabelle, and Isabelle needed the help because Ana was now no longer around."

Marcella — younger, more charismatic and articulate than the other moms — brought valuable skills and a new dynamic to the group. Isabelle and Ana had both proven themselves to be tough and determined activists, and no one disputed their courage, but neither was terribly polished, or savvy in the ways of government or the media. Isabelle and Ana's lack of sophistication sometimes played well in the media — they were authentic — but this also had its disadvantages in terms of getting their message across. Marcella, on the other hand, was a persuasive advocate and a fearless public critic.

"Marcella was not afraid of anyone," says Melynda. "She'd pick up the phone without hesitation. She'd tell people off; she'd wag her finger right in their face, and they were afraid of her. Whereas Isabelle was very quiet and demure, Marcella on the other hand, Marcella had no problem telling people off, and for darn good reason. Marcella knew this issue, she could speak, and she carried herself well."

"I was grateful," adds Isabelle, "that she was coming on board to help me."

Marcella started working the phones. She called Yvon Godin, the New Democrat Member of Parliament for Bathurst, and told him about the problem. She called Bernard Richard, a former Liberal New Brunswick cabinet minister who was now the provincial ombudsman. At first Richard wouldn't even take her call, but Marcella refused to simply file a written complaint with his office and then go away. She persisted until he agreed to come to the telephone. He told her, however, there was nothing he could do to help. Marcella then called the Quebec government, which ran a fleet of school MFABs of its own. She learned that Quebec used winter tires on both the front and back wheels of its school minibuses.

Marcella also helped Isabelle during this time to keep in touch with the other families that had lost boys in the crash. Some, like Codey Branch's father Dale, were upset and angry about the matter. Others were disappointed but weren't interested in joining the campaign or creating a fuss. As one of them told Marcella, "We all have to handle this situation in our own way. You do what you feel you have to do."

...

The first public official to come under fire over tires was John McLaughlin, who was being criticized by Isabelle and Marcella, both in the media and directly in private letters and emails. He responded by saying that his school district was under orders from its provincial masters to put winter tires on only the back wheels of the MFAB.

Although the Bathurst High minibus and others like it nominally belonged to the schools that used them, they were now legally owned and maintained by the provincial government. McLaughlin revealed that while the government had publicly accepted the inquest recommendation for winter tires, it had in fact adopted a rather different policy put forward by a private engineering consultant in Fredericton, who was advising the bureaucrats to put all-season tires on the front wheels of MFABs, even in the winter. The consultant, David Hoar, believed that winter tires all around was indeed the best option for MFABs travelling at low speeds, for example, on city streets. But at high speeds on highways, he said, the minibuses were safer, and less prone to loss of steering control, with ribbed, all-season tires on the front steering-axle wheels, and winter tires only on the rear drive-axle wheels. That was a technical point Hoar would stick to, and argue in the media, for weeks to come, in contrast to the views of the majority of experts on the subject. And yet it was Hoar's advice that the government followed.

Even before the Bathurst tragedy, the high school in nearby Miramichi had owned an MFAB, not a 15-passenger van, for driving its students to sporting events around the province. Miramichi had always put winter tires all around on its minibus. Marcella called the school and learned that now, with its MFAB under the maintenance direction of the provincial government, the school had been ordered to put all-seasons on the front and winter tires on only the back. Those, said John McLaughlin, were his precise orders too.

"All decisions about vehicle maintenance are being made by the Department of Transportation as the vehicles themselves are owned by the Province of New Brunswick," wrote McLaughlin in a letter to Isabelle and Marcella. He made the same argument to inquiring reporters, pushing responsibility for the issue onto provincial bureaucrats.

Privately, however, McLaughlin must have been feeling the pressure. For the past two years he had weathered not only the ordeal of the crash itself, but also the mothers' campaign for accountability, and then the inquest. Whatever his shortcomings in the eyes of Ana and Isabelle, McLaughlin no doubt believed he had done his best in the toughest of circumstances, and had come through the long crisis with his professional reputation intact. It would have been fair for him to assume at the start of the 2009 school year, before the tires controversy erupted, that the whole unhappy tragedy had now been put to rest.

When it exploded again in October, McLaughlin would have been as surprised as anyone. He called all the parents of the dead boys to explain that the tire issue was out of his hands, that he hadn't dropped the ball on safety, but was in fact strictly adhering to the new provincial policy. Marcella had no time for his excuses when McLaughlin called her. She felt bitterly betrayed and she let him know it. "You have the recommendations on winter tires from the inquest," she scolded him. "I trusted you to do the right thing."

"Marcella was really upset with John," says Isabelle. "He didn't expect that reaction from her. But by then, she had lost all respect for him."

Isabelle also didn't accept McLaughlin's claim that he was an innocent bystander in the tire furor. "Rather than simply following the new provincial policy, why didn't he do something about it?" she says. "Why didn't he try to change it? He could have done some research, just like us, to find out what the experts believed. And once we had informed him of the problem, he didn't pressure the government enough either. I mean, this was his school. After all they'd been through with the deaths of our sons, why wouldn't he be more on top of this, more concerned about this?"

Provincial officials and politicians had mostly stayed quiet during the early days of the tires dispute, but became agitated when a federal bureaucrat entered the fray. In her search for expert opinion, Isabelle had contacted Transport Canada's offices in Ottawa to see if they had any recommendations about winter tire use on multi-function activity buses. Nigel Mortimer, a senior official in their Road Safety Department and the Government of Canada's top expert on winter tires, told her that winter tires should be installed on every wheel of the minibus. Mortimer then sent an email to McLaughlin, saying he'd been contacted by Isabelle Hains and this was his advice:

"Transport Canada highly recommends the use of winter tires, designated with the mountain snowflake symbol, on all wheel positions," Mortimer wrote. "Since [New Brunswick's school] MFABs currently have all-season tires on the front and winter tires on the rear, we highly recommend that the same Nokian tires be installed on the front as well as the rear."

The email was one of several pieces of government correspondence Isabelle would later obtain through the access to information law. In another email, McLaughlin thanked Mortimer for his information: "This issue is of great concern to all of us as student safety is of the highest importance," McLaughlin wrote. Then he forwarded Mortimer's advice to the New Brunswick Department of Education in Fredericton.

Education officials, worried about the escalating media controversy, asked the provincial transportation department to check in with their engineering consultant in light of Nigel Mortimer's unequivocal statements. So began a not-so-friendly, back-and-forth email conversation between Mortimer and Hoar, in which Hoar outlined his technical reasons for favouring all-season tires on the front wheels. Mortimer disagreed, saying that decades of testing and road-accident data, plus recommendations from the rubber industry, made it clear that winter tires should be used all around. Hoar didn't back down. He needled Mortimer to produce the specific tests supposedly proving that winter tires were superior on the front wheels of MFABs. The trouble is, there weren't any.

The MFAB was a relatively new vehicle. No one had ever formally tested winter tires on that type of minibus. Transport Canada assumed that years of testing done on cars, trucks, and sport utility vehicles, all of which favoured winter tires all around, would yield the same results for MFABs. Transport Canada owned a large, test track facility north of Montreal, but the cost of running a new vehicle tire test specifically for MFABs could run between fifty and eighty thousand dollars. And in any case, the New Brunswick tire dispute was not Ottawa's problem. Transport Canada had given its opinion, both to the private citizen, Isabelle Hains, and to the New Brunswick government.

That opinion, however, sparked a minor constitutional kerfuffle between Ottawa and Fredericton. Nigel Mortimer's advice to outfit MFABs with winter tires, issued first to Isabelle and promptly made public by her, not only cast doubt on the province's tire policy; it was seen in Fredericton as interference by another government into a sensitive topic that was none of its business. After complaints were made, an assistant deputy minister at Transport Canada, one of the department's most senior officials, felt obliged to write to his counterpart in Fredericton with the assurance that Transport Canada will "continue to recognize and respect the provinces' jurisdiction in all matters involving driver and vehicle licensing as well as vehicle usage laws and their enforcement." The official added that Nigel Mortimer hadn't been aware of the context of the Bathurst tire dispute, nor did he know who Isabelle Hains was, when she contacted him for an opinion on the matter. The advice Mortimer gave to Isabelle was no different, he said, than the consumer responses Transport Canada issues to "enquiries from thousands of callers and writers each year."

As bureaucrats hashed out their jurisdictional sensitivities, and New Brunswick officials scrambled to figure out whether their tire policy was right or wrong, Isabelle and Marcella were busy recruiting a growing army of experts who claimed the New Brunswick position was faulty. Along with the two Bathurst mechanics and Transport Canada, they now added John Mahler at the *Toronto Star*. After assuring Isabelle that the policy was wrong, Mahler called David Hoar to discuss it. "He was just apoplectic that I wouldn't go along with his plan," says Mahler. He also called the New Brunswick government, but no one there was interested in getting advice from a tire journalist in Toronto. So Mahler wrote a column in the *Star*, taking New Brunswick to task.

He quoted Hoar telling him, "'If you put snow tires on [all around], you improve your traction, you improve your braking. At low speed, yes. But there are no studies we can obtain that prove this is true at highway speeds.'

"'If I am incorrect,' Hoar told Mahler, 'prove me wrong with data.'"

Mahler reviewed Hoar's position with the experts at four major North American tire makers — Michelin, Toyo Tire, Bridgestone, and Continental Tires — all of whom were puzzled by the New Brunswick policy and all of whom advised that all around winter tires were the safest option, even on MFABs.

Guy Walenga, Bridgestone's director of North American engineering and commercial product technology, put it simply: "A front [all-season] tire setup may be okay for a pro driver," he said. "On the minibus, is this the best setup? No. In braking on snow, when weight transfers forward, winters on the front will stop better than all-seasons." Walenga and others also said winters on front would give minibus drivers better control on icy and slippery corners.

"New Brunswick's policy," concluded Mahler in his column, "is just plain wrong."

To all this was added the voice of the Rubber Association of Canada, whose members included the tire manufacturers. The group agreed with Transport Canada that winter tires all around were the safest option. The women also posted on the VanAngels Web site a YouTube video by Canada's Automobile Protection Association, a consumer advocacy group, showing footage of vehicle tests in snowy conditions that proved the benefits of winter tires all around.

"We can't understand," they wrote on VanAngels.ca, "why the New Brunswick Department of Education chooses to ignore the advice of experts who know winter tires better than anybody else in Canada."

Isabelle and Marcella presented all their expert information to the province. They wrote letters and emails to Premier Shawn Graham, to Transport Minister Denis Landry, and to Education Minister Roland Haché. They said if the province wouldn't change its policy, then it should conduct new tire testing on an MFAB to settle the matter once and for all. Instead, Landry publicly refused any testing, and the government simply dug in its heels.

"I think the province just thought, 'Two moms, what do they know about tires?'" says Isabelle, who also saw a darker side to the government's response.

"You think they would have been happy to help us resolve this," she says. "Instead, they saw us as the enemy. They tried to destroy our credibility, and the credibility of the little guys who we had been speaking to, the experts who owned tire shops and car shops. The politicians fell back on the advice of their communications people and their senior bureaucrats who refused us. Their strategy was the same one as before the inquest: deny, deflect, delay."

Valerie Kilfoil, the Education Department's spokeswoman, responded to John Mahler's column in the *Toronto Star* by repeating David Hoar's views and by criticizing Mahler's article as inaccurate. "The Government of New Brunswick is following the advice of experts. Experts agree in most instances four winter tires [as opposed to six] are safest," she wrote.

In fact the only person advocating this view up to this point was Hoar. Later, however, the government produced letters from two tire makers, Goodyear and Michelin, each saying, in response to a query from the province, that they agreed with the consultant's recommendation to put all-season tires on the front of MFABs. Michelin's letter was in flat contradiction of the company's earlier statements to John Mahler.

This not only confused the issue; it was a clear setback for Isabelle and Marcella. David Hoar was no longer a lone wolf with an unusual opinion, but could now claim two major tire companies on his side. Michelin, however,

quickly backed down — sort of. The company issued a new letter clarifying
its position, saying winter tires all around offered the "optimum balance of
performance and overall vehicle stability." Putting all-seasons on the front,
the company said, while not preferable, was in fact "permissible."

Despite the Goodyear and Michelin letters, the majority of expert opinion, both from government and private sources, still claimed that New
Brunswick's tire policy was wrong. Yet the province wasn't budging. And
it was still refusing to set up an MFAB tire test. It became obvious to Mahler
that bureaucrats and politicians in Fredericton were less interested in knowing
the truth about tires than in thumbing their noses at the Bathurst moms.
"I think New Brunswick's policy was driven totally by hubris," he says. "It
wasn't a question of money. There were about fourteen of these buses in
New Brunswick. For a few thousand bucks they could all have been outfitted
with full sets of winter tires, and the problem would have gone away. But
no, the government couldn't suck it up and admit they were wrong. They
didn't want to be told what to do by a bunch of women — by these women.
It really came down to that."

An apparent breakthrough came following a lengthy, face-to-face meeting between Isabelle, Marcella, and Education Minister Roland Haché, in
which Haché agreed to follow Transport Canada's recommendations. Nigel
Mortimer had already made Transport Canada's views clear, but that wasn't
good enough for Haché. He and his advisers now wanted the federal government to conduct new research into the best tire options for MFABs.
Whatever the result of those tests, New Brunswick would follow. The
mothers were pleased, but cautious, and they told Haché they would hold
his feet to the fire.

"We would like to know what are the next steps in the process with
Transport Canada, and the timeline for implementation of policy changes
should Transport Canada's findings point in that direction," they told the
minister in a public letter, which also contained a warning: "We parents
struggle every day with the reality that we will never be able to see our sons
grow into adults. It is not easy for us to put ourselves in the public eye, to
lobby politicians . . . but we do it because we know our children would want

us to raise awareness of these issues in the hope of preventing similar tragedies from occurring again.

"It is for that reason that we will never give up."

The problem with Haché's strategy was that Transport Canada hadn't agreed to carry out any tests. "Transport Canada hadn't promised to do anything," says Mahler, who was in touch with Nigel Mortimer throughout the whole affair. "New Brunswick was saying they'd do whatever Transport Canada told them to do, but Transport Canada totally did not want to get involved."

Frustrated by the impasse, and worried that winter was passing by and, along with it, the window of opportunity to conduct new tire testing in freezing conditions, Mahler pitched a new solution. "Let's do our own test," he suggested to Isabelle and Marcella. Sure, neither woman knew the first thing about organizing research at a professional test track. Nor did they have the tens of thousands of dollars required to pay for such a test. But Mahler knew the engineers at the companies that owned those tracks. Perhaps they could be persuaded to do a favour for the Bathurst moms?

• • •

One of the companies Mahler called was Continental Tires, a huge auto supplies multinational headquartered in Germany, with a state-of-the-art outdoor test track known as the Brimley Proving Grounds, located in northern Michigan. Mahler explained the New Brunswick issue to a testing engineer with Continental named Jay Spears, who then discussed the matter with his boss, Joerg Burfien, the company's director of research and development for the Americas. Burfien, appalled by New Brunswick's policy, was eager to help.

"Continental took offence to what was going on in New Brunswick," says Mahler, who says running tests to compare the performance of winter tires to all-seasons was, in the eyes of the company's engineers, like trying to find out if water is wet. "They couldn't believe a professional engineer would make a recommendation like the one being followed by the province. They thought this should not go unchallenged."

Continental agreed to do the test at no charge, as long as Mahler, or the Bathurst mothers, could come up with a multi-function activity bus and get the vehicle to Michigan. "Their facility is very busy," says Mahler. "So they gave me a specific time frame when they could have the test site available. I thought this was wonderful. I was ecstatic. I couldn't believe it. Finally, we were going to show the government of New Brunswick how silly they were."

Mahler didn't believe he'd have much trouble finding an MFAB to borrow, but after a week scouring the Internet and writing letters and emails to bus companies, he came up empty. Either a company didn't have the right model, or it was located too far away from Michigan, or the rental fees were too high.

In Bathurst, Isabelle and Marcella weren't having any luck either. They asked the provincial government to send one of its MFABs to Michigan for the test, but the province just stonewalled. Valerie Kilfoil, at the Education Department, said it would take several weeks for their request to work its way through the government. She said the mothers should consider renting their own vehicle for their test.

Isabelle then pinned her hopes on Ron Campbell, a salesman with Girardin Minibus, a Quebec company that builds MFABs just like the one they needed. For several years Campbell had been working with the Canadian Standards Association to promote the virtues of MFABs as a safe alternative to 15-passenger vans. Campbell had closely followed news of the Bathurst tragedy and had come to know Isabelle in the wake of the crash. She had hoped he might be able to lend the mothers an MFAB to drive to Michigan, but Campbell couldn't pull it off with his company. Girardin was willing to loan a new minibus for the test, but it didn't want the vehicle driven all the way to Michigan, accumulating mileage. It would only provide a minibus if Mahler or the mothers could find a way to transport it there on a truck or train, a costly proposition.

By now it was January, the winter was ticking by, and Mahler, Isabelle, and Marcella were getting desperate. So Isabelle and Marcella launched a public appeal. They wrote letters to the editors of newspapers across the country, explaining their situation, and asking for some company or agency to lend them a minibus of the model they needed, and let them drive it to Michigan. Many of the letters were published, including in the New Brunswick newspapers, but still no MFAB could be found. Mahler then wrote an open letter to Premier Shawn Graham, published in the *Toronto Star*.

Dear Premier Graham,

I am writing to ask you to lend one of your province's school vehicles for winter tire testing. It is approaching the second anniversary of the tragic collision that claimed the lives of seven New Brunswick high school students. Since then, a group of mothers who lost their sons has been advocating for school vehicle safety.

...Your Minister of Transport, Denis Landry, recently said, "The Department of Transportation will not be undertaking its own study of tires on 21-passenger multi-function activity vehicles. However, officials and technical experts along with Transport Canada are in discussions to resolve this issue, with the safety of students foremost in their minds." But nobody I know has heard who these people are, or when a resolution is expected.

...Continental Tires, one of the largest tire companies in the world, is offering to perform the instrumented scientific testing for your province at no cost.... New Brunswick has an opportunity to set a gold safety standard for the rest of the country. Let the memory of the lost "Boys in Red" from Bathurst High school motivate you to promote the highest level of school vehicle safety possible.... Instead of seeing these saddened families as a problem, why not see them as presenting an opportunity for your government to show it does what's right? Loan them the MFAB minibus for a test.

Mahler's letter, and the mother's appeals, failed to move the government, which continued to insist it was negotiating with Transport Canada for its own vehicle test. But there were no details on when or where that might happen. Marcella was fed up and she said so on VanAngels.ca:

> The time has long since passed for "discussions." We arrange for an offer of free testing at one of the world's top research and development facilities and this is the answer we get from our government.
> We know better than anyone what happens when you leave the safety of your children in the hands of the government. We aren't going to stand around and wait for another tragedy to occur while they sit around and "discuss."

On January 11, on the eve of the second anniversary of the crash, Isabelle was at Marcella's house when the telephone rang. It was Jay Spears at Continental Tires, who revealed that he'd been contacted by a senior official at Transport Canada, asking Spears and his company not to proceed with their tire test for the Bathurst moms. Continental had also invited Transport Canada to attend its test in Michigan, but the government declined.

"Spears was really angry; he couldn't believe it," says Isabelle, who suspects Transport Canada's call to Spears was made at the request of the New Brunswick government. "Jay Spears said, 'There's no way we're not doing this test.'

"It proved to us," adds Isabelle, "that the province was hiding something."

•••

New Brunswick's hard line against the women, and its refusal to loan them a minibus for the tires test in Michigan, was striking a chord with the public and winning the moms a measure of sympathy. In January Isabelle received a phone call from a New Brunswick woman whom she'd never met before. "She was a stranger to me," says Isabelle. The woman told Isabelle she was appalled by what the government was doing to the Bathurst moms, and by its failure to co-operate on the test. "She said, 'How much do you think this is going to cost, renting a minibus and getting it to Michigan?'" Isabelle was touched by the caller's offer of support, but she said she didn't know exactly what the costs would be. Two days later, an envelope arrived via courier at Isabelle's house. It was from the lady on the phone — a cheque for eight thousand dollars.

"I just couldn't believe it," says Isabelle. "I called her up and said, 'That's a thousand dollars for each person who died that night in the crash.' She said she'd never thought of it that way." The benefactor said Isabelle was free to use the money in any way she felt necessary. The only condition was that the donor wished to remain anonymous. Isabelle was never to reveal her name. And she never has.

"She's never told me who it is," says Melynda. "One thing about Isabelle, she is true to her word," says Melynda. "There's nobody quite as honest as Isabelle."

Before Isabelle even had a chance to spend her benefactor's money, a news story broke that would have a profound impact on the tire campaign. A staff lawyer for Loblaw Companies, the grocery chain whose truck had collided with the BHS van, had filed a lawsuit in the New Brunswick courts in December against Wayne Lord and Bathurst Van Inc., the school organization that had owned the white van. The Loblaws lawyer, knowing the law but lacking in common sense, was suing Lord and the school to recoup the forty-one thousand dollars his company had spent towing their tractor-trailer from the crash site and emptying its fuel tanks. On the one hand the lawsuit was just a corporate formality, a routine application by the company's legal department seeking to dot all its i's and cross all its t's. On the other hand, it was a public relations debacle. Lord had lost his own wife in the crash, he and his daughter were still suffering the emotional aftershocks of the event, and now a national grocery giant, for whom forty-one thousand dollars was mere chump change, was going after Lord and other teachers for the money. The news sparked outrage, especially in Bathurst, where many residents vowed to boycott the company's stores. Two Facebook protest sites were also created, quickly attracting hundreds of followers, all condemning the company's decision.

Once news of the lawsuit reached Loblaws's executive suite, the claim was immediately withdrawn and the company's president, Allan Leighton, issued a statement of contrition:

> We thoroughly apologize for the alarm and concern caused by the statement of claim against Wayne Lord and Bathurst Van Inc., and we will not seek further action. While it is normal legal practice to look for reimbursement, this decision was clearly made without consideration of the specifics of this accident. We would like to thank all our customers that voiced their concern regarding our decision, allowing us to reconsider our actions.

Eager now to repair its reputation in New Brunswick, Loblaws asked the City of Bathurst if the company could help the community honour the Boys in Red, perhaps by donating money for a new monument in their memory. News of the offer was broadcast that morning on CBC Radio, and one of the first people to hear it was Peter Jarratt, one of Melynda's brothers, who worked an early morning shift as a security guard at the Bathurst lumber mill. At daybreak, Peter called Melynda with an interesting proposal: "Melynda, you want to get your minibus? This is how you're going to do it!"

Melynda thought Peter's idea might just work. That same morning she contacted Loblaws's head office at 1 President's Choice Circle in Brampton, Ontario, and asked for Inge van den Berg, the vice-president of corporate affairs, who had been handling the lawsuit controversy in the media. "I told her who I was, and said we needed an MFAB to complete the studies that were being offered by Continental Tires. I said the testing was not going to happen if we could not get a bus." It was probably a long shot, but Melynda figured there was a chance Loblaws might be willing to pay the costs of renting a minibus and transporting it to Michigan. She was wrong.

"How much does a bus cost?" asked van den Berg.

Melynda paused. A new minibus? "About eighty thousand dollars," she said.

"Then we'll just buy one," said van den Berg, without hesitation. "We'll buy a bus, and sell it again after the test."

Melynda couldn't believe what she was hearing. She quickly informed Isabelle and Marcella of the good news, and told them to expect a phone call from Loblaws. Within hours Allan Leighton, the president and deputy chairman of Canada's largest grocery store chain, was phoning Isabelle in her kitchen in Bathurst to express his condolences and to place his company's resources at her disposal. Like most Canadians, Isabelle had never spoken to the chief executive officer of a large corporation. She then talked to van den Berg, and passed on the names and numbers of John Mahler and of Ron Campbell, the auto executive and MFAB salesman, thinking the vehicle could be purchased from Campbell's employer, Girardin Minibus.

It was all settled by the end of the day. After hearing that Loblaws was on board, Ron Campbell said there was no need for the company to actually buy an MFAB. Girardin would loan the mothers a minibus as long as Loblaws could transport it to and from Michigan on one of its tractor-trailers. He called Isabelle that afternoon to explain what had been decided. That conversation was quickly followed by a phone call from a Loblaws truck driver, who told Isabelle he'd received clear instructions to get the Girardin minibus to Michigan. Isabelle and the minibus, he said, were his top priority for the next few weeks.

Suddenly, Isabelle was awash in emotions she hadn't experienced in years. She had been battling the government and butting heads with the establishment in her city and province for so long, it was hard to get used to the rather exhilarating notion that people with money and influence were now actively supporting *her*. No longer were she and her small band of women standing alone against the world of power. They had found potent allies who wanted them to succeed: Loblaws, the people at Continental Tires, John Mahler at the *Toronto Star*, and all the other experts. Together their support began to buoy Isabelle's exhausted spirit. "I felt really encouraged," she says. "People were coming into our lives at this point, and all they wanted to do was help. It was like an army of angels."

One of those angels was her new anonymous benefactor. Isabelle called the lady back to say she wanted to return the eight thousand dollar cheque, now that Loblaws and Girardin had stepped in. "I felt bad taking the money," says Isabelle. "But the lady said, 'No. I don't want it back. You're still going to have expenses. You're going to need a hotel.'"

Isabelle, Marcella, and Ana would all be going to Michigan for the tire test, now scheduled for late February. Isabelle and Marcella were determined to witness the test first-hand, and they had persuaded Ana, despite her recent hiatus from the campaign, to join them. Isabelle purchased three airline tickets from Bathurst to Sault Ste. Marie, Ontario, where they would rent a car and drive the short distance across the U.S. border to the Continental test track.

The women's tire showdown with the government was now major news in New Brunswick. Every major newspaper and broadcaster in the province had carried stories of their recent battle, and was now awaiting the results of their impending test at Continental. "Bathurst crash moms on way to Michigan," said the headline on the CBC's provincial Web site on February 22. The public had watched Loblaws and Girardin Minibus throw their weight behind the Bathurst moms, and many people waited eagerly to learn the results of the test. The New Brunswick government was still promising to carry out its own test with Transport Canada, but the timing, details, and whereabouts of that study were unknown. Isabelle and Marcella, meanwhile, laid out their own test plans for everyone to see. They also sent an eighteen-page package to the New Brunswick cabinet explaining, once again, why they wanted a test, why they wanted winter tires, and what the experts were telling them, as well as a summary of what they'd been through for the past several months.

As the countdown to the test approached, the board of directors of the Bathurst airport decided to pitch in and give Isabelle, Marcella, and Ana three free airline tickets to Sault Ste. Marie. Isabelle wasn't sure she could use the freebies because she had already purchased three tickets with Air Canada. She called the airline and spoke to a ticket agent in Saint John. Refunding the tickets was officially against Air Canada's rules, but the agent relented. "I've been following what you've been doing, and I think it's really great," she told Isabelle, whose fame was growing by the day. "I'm going to cancel your tickets, give you back your money, and use your free tickets to reserve the seats you already have. Good luck in Michigan."

...

The three moms gathered at the Bathurst airport on February 23, each wearing their black fleece Van Angels jackets, on top of white T-shirts imprinted with large photographs of their sons. There had been a few moments of drama that morning when Ana had second thoughts about joining the trip. Isabelle had tried to reach her throughout the previous day, but Ana wasn't returning her calls.

Ana felt guilty that she hadn't helped Isabelle with the tire campaign. She was also worried about working again with Melynda, who was flying out from Fredericton that day and planned to meet the other women at Pearson Airport in Toronto. Isabelle woke up on the morning of departure, her stomach in knots over the big trip and sick with worry about Ana. Finally, only moments before they had to go to the airport, Marcella drove out to Ana's house in Beresford, convinced her to pack her suitcase, and the two of them met Isabelle at the airport. The three moms all shared a hug inside the small terminal, spoke to news reporters waiting for them there, and received the handshakes and well wishes of airport workers, from the airline check-in crews to the security staff, all of whom knew where the mothers were headed.

It was dark by the time they arrived in Toronto, where they would catch their connecting flight to Sault Ste. Marie. Inside the terminal at Pearson Airport, they met Melynda, and all the tension between her and Ana melted away and was forgotten as the four women embarked on their adventure.

They were surprised, however, to learn that Pearson was being shut down due to a local snowstorm. "It was nothing compared to the kind of stuff we see in Bathurst," says Isabelle. "We couldn't believe the airport was closed." With their connecting flight delayed until the next morning, the airline was giving out hotel room vouchers to its stranded passengers. But that meant waiting in a long line with hundreds of other cranky travellers. It was already late, so the foursome opted instead for a night in the empty departure lounge, curling up on the hard airport seats or trying to sleep stretched out on the floor.

Early the next morning, the exhausted women flew to Sault Ste. Marie, where they rented a car, drove across the border to Michigan, and checked into their motel near the Continental Tires facility. John Mahler, driving down from Toronto, was due to meet them at the motel later that day, along with a professional videographer Isabelle had hired to document the test, which was scheduled for the next morning.

The women were just settling into their rooms and getting showered when Melynda's cellphone rang. It was Benjamin Shingler, a reporter with the *Telegraph Journal*. The New Brunswick government, he told Melynda, had announced that morning that Transport Canada had quietly conducted a minibus test for the province, and the results proved what the women had been saying for months: winter tires on all wheels gave better performance than a mix of winters and all-seasons. The province was now promising to equip its fleet of MFABs with full sets of winter tires. As Shingler read Melynda the headline on the province's news release over the phone, she repeated it for the moms in the motel room:

"Released . . . today . . . on the government wire . . . 'Winter tires . . . to be mandatory . . . on Multi-Function Activity Buses.'"

"What," Shingler wanted to know, "did the moms have to say to that?"

Melynda didn't know what to say. She was flabbergasted. The three mothers were stunned. Within minutes the four women were inundated with similar calls and emails — from the CBC, the *Northern Light* in Bathurst, from every local radio station in New Brunswick that had followed the tire saga, even from reporters with the *National Post* and the *Globe and Mail*—all wanting to hear the mothers' reaction to the province's surprise announcement, on the very cusp of the Michigan test. Would the women, in fact, go ahead with their test?

As their cellphones were buzzing, Melynda told her friends to sit tight and not say anything for the moment. "Shit, hold on," she ordered. "We don't know what we're doing. Before we say anything to the media, let's call John."

It appeared the women had won a momentous victory. It was an infuriating victory—with the government declaring, the day before their long-awaited Michigan test, that it now agreed with their position on tires —but it was a victory nonetheless.

"They caved under public opinion," the moms said, talking among themselves as Melynda tried to contact Mahler.

"Those sneaky, conniving —"

"It's sleazy as hell."

"That's the kind of government we're dealing with. But it won't look good on them."

The women had won their showdown with the government and achieved their policy goal. But what now? Should they now go ahead with the Continental Tires test? What if that test produced an unfavourable result?

"I was certainly afraid," says Melynda. "And I was having second thoughts: 'Maybe we should cancel our test?'"

Melynda reached Mahler on his cellphone, while he was on the highway en route to Michigan, and filled him in on the startling news. He was taken aback but adamant that the Continental Tires test should proceed. "Of course you're going to do the test," he said. "We know the test is going to prove that winter tires are the best. We're not stopping, the show must go on."

Melynda also spoke to Jay Spears, the Continental Tires engineer, who also agreed the test should proceed as planned the next morning.

"We were very upset," says Isabelle. "We'd come all this way, gone to all this trouble, we'd even slept in an airport. But we regrouped, we called back all the reporters who had been leaving messages with us, and we told them our plans."

Said the headline on the Canadian Press story written that day out of Fredericton: "N.B. changes tire policy after repeated calls from crash victim parents." The story quoted a statement issued by Education Minister Roland Haché and Transport Minister Denis Landry.

"Now that a clear federal recommendation — one that takes into account the specific vehicle, its use, our climate, travel routes and speed limits — is in place, we will take immediate action to ensure our MFABs are equipped with six winter tires," the statement said. "Ensuring student safety is our No. 1 priority."

Once the media calls were out of the way, Marcella phoned Haché to let him have a piece of her mind. His office said he was unavailable, so she asked for him to call her back on her cellphone in Michigan. Haché did call, but instead he called Ana's cellphone. Ana had kept a low profile during the tire campaign. The moms say that Haché couldn't have known Ana was in Michigan with the others, and that he called her as a way of avoiding Isabelle and Marcella's wrath.

"So he calls my cell," says Ana. "'Hello, this is Roland Haché. I've been looking for Marcella, but she's not at her house.'

"So I said, 'Just a minute, Mr. Haché, she's right here!'"

Marcella took Ana's phone, and for the next half hour unleashed two years of pent-up pain, frustration, and fury on the cabinet minister on the other end of the phone.

"I wouldn't have wanted to be Roland Haché at that moment," says Melynda. "And I've got to hand it to him, he didn't hang up. And he couldn't hang up. If he had, imagine what the mothers would have said about him in the media."

At one point during the tongue-lashing, Ana ran into the room next door to fetch Melynda and Isabelle. "Come!" she begged. "You guys have to get Marcella off the phone. She's going nuts!"

After pouring out her anger, Marcella passed the phone to Isabelle. If there was any life left in Haché by this point, Isabelle finished him off, not with yelling and cursing, but with a stark reminder to the politician about the unrelenting sorrow of the Bathurst families. It was a knife to the heart, delivered calmly but forcefully in Isabelle's low-key signature style. Melynda captured the whole moment on video:

"Roland, you know what? This is a victory for us, the parents. . . . Could I speak please?. . . Our children were killed in a vehicle with all-season tires. And now the children that are travelling to after-school activities are going to be in vehicles with all winter tires, like our children should have been that night. Now all children are going to be safe. There'll be no more second-guessing. . . just a minute Roland. . . there's not going to be any more opinions or second opinions. Now we have scientific data. Isn't that great? I speak the truth. I go only by facts, what I read and what I see. I will not repeat something if it's not true. And I know what happened to my son that night. And we all know it was neglect. It's been going on for years and years. And now we all know, you don't put all-season tires or combination tires on those vehicles."

Isabelle was crying now. She sat on the carpet of the motel room, her back against the foot of a bed, wearing a sweatsuit and a black scarf, holding the phone against her ear as the tears fell down her face.

"We thought the schools put the priority of our boys first, but you didn't. So we had to take things in our own hands. We spoke with you, we wrote you emails. But it took four months for any test to get done.

"I'm ashamed to say that our government doesn't listen to its citizens. You defend, you deny, you delay. And it's disgraceful, it really is. And we lost our children because of it, because your government didn't put children's safety first. And you continued to do it after their deaths. And it's a shame. So who's going to get reprimanded for this? Nobody. Just like when our children died. Nobody. Everybody just walked away. So how are people going to learn? No one will learn. All these recommendations for our boys have to go into the Education Act. Otherwise, four or five years from now, people will forget, and they'll go out in storms, and people will forget there are supposed to be winter tires on that vehicle, because it never became a law in the Education Act. Am I right? I am, because that's what will happen. And if we don't push for this, it will happen again.

"Well Roland, thank you for listening. I know you hear me, but you know what? It's only a job for you, it's only a job. After a while, you get comfortable in your job as a politician, and you kind of forget what people really want, and really need, and what we really value in life. And that's what happens with government after a while. You get greedy and selfish after a while, and you don't realize what citizens need. You don't even consider the citizens.... Now seven families are trying to live a life, but we know the government is not doing everything in its power to keep children safe, because it took four months to even get a tires test done, when you knew, everybody knew, the tires were not safe. It's not fair that you didn't jump at the chance to do something and do it right away. You should have demanded it. How far do people have to go with the government? We worried everyday about the children that travelled in those vehicles for four months this winter, we did, mothers did, but the government didn't, not once. Because if you did, you would have done that test a long time ago. OK Roland, I'm going to say goodbye now. Thank you for listening."

...

The following morning was bright, cold, and crisp, a perfect winter day. The four women arrived at the headquarters of Continental's Brimley Proving Grounds, along with John Mahler, whom they had met in person for the first time at the motel the night before, plus the videographer and another tire expert who had come down from Toronto. They were all warmly greeted by Jay Spears and other Continental Tires staff, including the professional drivers who would put the MFAB, freshly delivered by Loblaws, through its paces.

The Brimley facility is a sprawling, nine-thousand-acre complex of office buildings, parking lots, and carefully manicured test tracks, set among the flat tablelands of northern Michigan, not far from the St. Mary's River that forms the Canada-U.S. border. In some parts of the complex, the ground is prepared by snow grooming machines so the snow and ice conditions are exactly as researchers want them for particular tests. On the day of the MFAB test, new-model cars still in the design phase were being tested at adjoining tracks for winter handling abilities.

Mahler had found videos, recently posted on Transport Canada's Web site, of the MFAB test conducted by the department for the New Brunswick government. To his eyes and to the experts at Continental, it bore no resemblance to the professional vehicle tests normally performed by Transport Canada or the auto industry. In the short, shaky videos, a white MFAB is driven across what looks like the bumpy, uneven surface of a frozen lake or a snow-covered field somewhere in the countryside. Transport Canada says the videos were made at its modern, motor vehicle testing facility at Blainville, Quebec. The to Mahler and other experts. the whole thing looked like an amateur job, put together on a shoestring budget.

"We showed the video to Jay Spears, and he just shook his head and rolled his eyes," says Mahler. "It wasn't even a low-quality test. If I said, 'Here, go do a tire test, go drive up and down on a frozen lake somewhere a couple of times so we can get some video'—that's essentially what [it appears] they did.

"Why did they do it? My opinion is that the New Brunswick government needed an out. They had said they'd do whatever Transport Canada wanted. So they hastily arranged a test and paid for it. They deliberately wanted to undercut these women and make them look foolish, before we could do our test in Michigan. It was just mind boggling."

It was a brief, five-minute drive from the headquarters building at the Brimley facility to the actual test area where the minibus was waiting. Continental had arranged for a vehicle to transport everyone out to the test site—a white, 15-passenger Ford van, exactly like the one in the Bathurst collision. Isabelle, Marcella, and Ana stood outside the headquarters, gaping in horror at the van, seemingly paralyzed and unable to climb inside. Finally, Isabelle spoke: "That's like the van that killed our boys." Realizing his mistake, Jay Spears and his embarrassed staff apologized

Melynda Jarratt and John Mahler. (VanAngels.ca)

and offered to find cars to take everyone to the test area, but the mothers said no. They climbed inside the van, each one drawn instinctively to the seats where their sons — Daniel, Javier, and Nikki — were sitting on the night of the crash. There was nothing but silence inside the van on the short journey out to the track.

At the test area, the moms pulled out peel-and-stick banners they'd brought with them, saying "The Boys in Red," which they stuck on the sides of the yellow MFAB loaned by Girardin. They then stood on the snowy, sun-speckled tarmac, bundled up against the cold, and watched as Continental drivers put the minibus through a sequence of tests: cornering ability, braking ability, and stability control. Each was run at low and high speeds, on three tire configurations: all-seasons all around, all-seasons on the front with winter tires on the back, and winter tires all around. In every test, the full-winter tires configuration easily outperformed all the others. The minibus, when fitted with all-season tires on the front, went skidding into the mock barriers,

The Multi-Function Activity Bus (MFAB) that was used as the test
vehicle by Continental Tires. Although this model is painted in typical
school bus colours and has flashing lights, many MFABs do not have
school bus colours. (VanAngels.ca)

sending pieces of Styrofoam flying through the air. There was no question
which tire policy was the right one.

That night, everyone gathered for dinner at the hotel restaurant. The
mood was celebratory: the Canadians thanked Spears and his team for their
help, and the Americans congratulated the moms on their achievement in
getting the policy changed in New Brunswick. There was no doubt in anyone's
mind that if Continental Tires hadn't stepped into the dispute, promising
to test the MFAB for free, nothing would have changed in New Brunswick.

"The people at Continental treated us like queens," says Ana. "And our
own government treated us like we were nothing."

Back in New Brunswick, Roland Haché had been pressed by reporters
to answer whether his government had deliberately chosen to announce

the changes to its tire policy on the eve of the Michigan test to take the wind out of the mothers' sails. Haché said it was pure coincidence. But not everyone believed him, including the editors at the *Northern Light* in Bathurst.

"If that's your story, stick to it," they wrote in an editorial the following week. "We doubt the [timing of the announcement] was a coincidence. The government did not keep the mothers advised of what was happening behind the scenes, and didn't make a phone call to formally advise them of the change in policy."

The whole winter tires affair, said the paper, "was a black eye for the government."

Shouted the headline on another editorial, this one in the *Miramichi Leader*: "Van fiasco shows real lack of class." The editorial said:

> Could the provincial government have handled the issue any worse? It's difficult to imagine how. [On] Tuesday, the government announced, via news release, it will ensure all tires on the buses used to move student athletes around the province will be winter tires. Total cost five thousand dollars. Total cost in terms of terrible publicity for the government—priceless.
>
> The education minister should have been ashamed to put his name to that release. Instead, he should have sent heads rolling down the steps of his department for such a mess.

At Bathurst High, Principal Coleen Ramsay wrote a letter to Ana, Isabelle, and Marcella, congratulating them on their tire campaign and their "perseverance and hard work on behalf of the safe transportation of students to extracurricular activities. I personally am very glad to have a definitive answer to your question regarding 'winter tires.'"

Isabelle was astounded by the letter. During Ramsay's time as principal, the lives of seven children and a teacher had been lost in a school van, driving in a winter storm without winter tires. The official crash reports had said the lack of winter tires were an important factor in the tragedy. The inquest had explored the issue at length and its jury found that winter tires should be mandatory on school vehicles. A multitude of experts had since made it clear that winter tires should be installed on all wheels. In the face of this evidence — not to mention common sense — why didn't someone, anyone, in the education system ever speak up publicly against the province's stubborn, oddball tires policy when it was first handed down to the schools? Why didn't education officials take more of an interest in the tires being installed on the BHS MFAB? Why didn't they ask their own questions about it, as Isabelle and Marcella had, from the very beginning? Ramsay had written to express her gratitude for what the mothers had accomplished. Yet why did it fall to parents to confront the government and investigate the matter?

In her letter, Ramsay also made no mention of the professional testing done at Continental Tires. Instead, she credited the haphazard Transport Canada test for bringing the matter to a close.

"Rest assured," wrote Ramsay, "that the findings of Transport Canada were acted upon immediately by Bathurst High School. Six new snow tires were installed on the [minibus] as soon as the results of Transport Canada's testing were made known to us. There is no doubt that it was your determined efforts that brought this decision about. And never doubt that I appreciate everything you have done."

The handling of the tires issue by the provincial government, including its reluctance to treat the mothers' complaints seriously from the earliest days of the dispute, raised questions about how much public officials genuinely cared for the safety of children in the school system. If the death of seven boys and the subsequent inquest hadn't shaken up New Brunswickers' trust in the system, the behaviour of authorities during the winter tires campaign finally had.

When the tires controversy first erupted, many New Brunswickers had been skeptical of the small group of activist moms. Although Isabelle, Ana, and Marcella certainly had their share of public support, there was also a good deal of exasperation. Many people were simply tired of seeing them constantly in the media and hearing their seemingly incessant complaints.

"It's time to move on," said one comment on the CBC New Brunswick Web site in November, beneath a story announcing the moms' call for winter tires all around on school MFABs.

"Seems these moms just can't leave the spotlight," said another.

"What has happened, has happened, and there is nothing that can change that," said yet another reader. "It is over and it is time to move on."

Three months later, however, the winter tires campaign had not only proven the province's policy wrong; it had revealed, for everyone to see, the arrogance and carelessness of the government on the question of children's safety.

Paul Chapman, a freelance columnist at the *Northern Light*, summed up the matter on March 2:

> I do know that there are people who feel squirmy, or very uncomfortable and even annoyed with the whole issue. Many feel these mothers have pushed this issue too far. I have had the feeling myself on occasion, after hearing yet another news report about the winter tires. But have they? Doesn't look like it now, does it?
>
> The way I see it, by announcing the [tires policy] change while the mothers were away, and without telling them the change was coming, is an insult. It makes the government look petty and self-interested.
>
> This whole sorry issue falls at the feet of the provincial government, for deciding to dig in its heels, and in the end, having to change its policy. It did so without acknowledging the efforts of these mothers, but rather taking the credit itself for changing the policy. It would do this government and the bureaucracy some good to be a bit more humble. They were just shown up.

Marcella, Isabelle, and Ana, at the snow-covered Continental Tires test
track with company engineer Jay Spears. (VanAngels.ca)

Isabelle rarely touched alcohol, but she accepted a glass of wine at the
dinner that night in Michigan. She needed to be able to raise a glass, to join
in the toasts being made around the table. She was certainly pleased by the
outcome. Once again she had stood up to the government, and against
enormous odds forced change upon her province. Yet, as before, Isabelle
felt no real sense of victory or triumph. Daniel and the other boys, after
all, were still gone.

"I was relieved that we didn't have to do it anymore," she says. "It was
a long, four-month campaign. Every day we had to write letters and push,
push, push. We knew schools were putting children in these vehicles with
the wrong tires."

In his many weeks of working with them via telephone and email, followed by two days alongside them in Michigan, John Mahler had developed
enormous respect for the Bathurst mothers.

"I liked them a lot," he says. "They were energetic and they were tough."

But there was something else about Isabelle, Ana, and Marcella that disturbed Mahler, and it was evident that evening over dinner. While others were happily celebrating the tire tests, the mothers remained more subdued.

"They were still deeply, deeply troubled, and you could see it," he says. "There was a very heavy sense of sadness there."

Eight

OTTAWA

DESPITE ITS UNEQUIVOCAL success, the winter tires campaign had been an enormous, energy-sucking distraction for Isabelle, an unwelcome detour from her real mission since the spring of 2009: the pursuit of two unrealized jury recommendations from the coroner's inquest. She returned to Bathurst from Michigan determined to carry on where she had left off, fighting to have professional drivers and yellow school buses used for all extracurricular travel in New Brunswick and for a national prohibition on 15-seat vans in Canadian schools.

The battle over winter tires had exhausted her. Certainly Ana and Marcella were emotionally spent, and neither one would find the will or the energy to join Isabelle on the front lines of her ban-the-vans campaign. Yet the tires fight had also strengthened Isabelle's confidence and fuelled her resolve, convincing her that she could take on a government and win. She would need all of that resolve and more, as she now looked beyond New Brunswick and trained her sights on that omnipotent creature called the federal government, a more imposing, powerful, and complicated target than she had ever tackled before.

Isabelle believed that Ottawa was the most sensible place to seek a Canada-wide ban on 15-seat vans in schools. New Brunswick had outlawed the vehicles from its schools in the wake of the BHS crash, as had Quebec. They became the second and third provinces to do so, after Nova Scotia banned the vans for student travel in 1994, following a highway tragedy there that killed three young hockey players and a parent. In May 2009 the Bathurst inquest had recommended a national prohibition on student travel in 15-seat vans, but most other provinces weren't listening. Alberta had a fuzzy, informal ban; after the Bathurst tragedy, insurance companies there were reluctant to insure Alberta schools that used 15-seat vans to transport kids, creating a de facto, if not a statutory, prohibition. And in Prince Edward Island and Newfoundland and Labrador, there were province-wide school board policies against 15-seat van use. But so far, no other provinces aside from Quebec, New Brunswick, and Nova Scotia had formal, legislated bans.

Rather than spread herself thin lobbying the provinces and territories where vans were still legally permitted in the school system, Isabelle turned her attention to Ottawa, and to her Member of Parliament, Yvon Godin, who represented Bathurst in the House of Commons for the opposition New Democratic Party. The federal government couldn't order the provinces to outlaw 15-seat vans in their schools, because Ottawa has no jurisdiction over education. And even if it did, Godin himself was only a member of the parliamentary opposition; he had little real influence with the government. But Isabelle wanted him, as her local MP, to try anyway. In the fall of 2009, just as the tire issue was rearing its head, she and Marcella paid a visit to Godin's constituency office in Bathurst.

"I didn't know where we could go with this," Isabelle says, "so I went to talk to him to see what he could do."

Godin had been the MP for Bathurst for more than a decade. In 2008, on the weekend of the BHS tragedy, he'd happened to be in town and had gone immediately to the high school, where he'd wandered the hallways, greeting and sharing his sympathies with the red-eyed, shell-shocked kids and teachers, huddled in groups throughout the building. When he'd first heard the names of the dead, his mind didn't properly register who the Boys in Red and their families were. Hains...Kelly...Branch...Cormier...and the rest.... Aside from Javier Acevedo, they were all fairly common names on the North Shore. Godin didn't think he knew any of them personally. It wasn't until four days later, when he walked into the big hockey arena for the public wake and saw the seven boys lying in their open caskets, that he realized he *did* know some of the victims, and many of their parents.

"I'd heard the names of the families, but I had not put faces to them until I went to the arena," he says. "When they'd said Daniel Hains was one of the boys that died, I didn't put a face to him, it didn't come to me at all. So when I got to the wake and saw Allan Hains and Isabelle standing beside one of the caskets, I was in shock."

Godin, a former mineworker and long-time labour organizer before he got into politics, knew Allan Hains from the pulp mill, where Allan had served on the executive of the mill's union. A few months before the crash, Godin had given a speech at a union banquet, where he and Allan had shaken hands and shared a few laughs. Now the two men were sharing a hug beside the body of Allan's dead son. Suddenly, Godin also noticed other families he knew:

"I recognized the Kellys. Nick's grandfather had once worked with me at the mine. The Branch family — Codey's dad was the guy who brings the mail to my constituency office. I couldn't believe it when I walked into that arena and realized I knew so many of these families."

Godin first rose to prominence in his community as local president of the United Steelworkers union at the Bathurst zinc mine. A North Shore Acadian, he jumped into national politics in 1997 and made headlines by winning the riding of Acadie-Bathurst for the NDP for the first time, and by doing so in grand style, knocking Liberal heavyweight Doug Young, a member of Prime Minister Jean Chrétien's cabinet, from power. Godin held onto the riding through five subsequent elections. In 2011 he swept all his challengers with an astonishing seventy per cent of the local vote. The NDP is a party with a split personality, and Godin belongs firmly to the organized labour wing, the blue-collar crowd from which the organization once drew most of its strength, as opposed to the newer, more intellectual, and ideological social-justice wing.

After attending the Phantoms' wake and funeral in 2008, Godin returned to his work in Parliament, and had nothing more to do with the aftermath of the tragedy. Ana's and Isabelle's struggles were with the school and the province; the federal government had no formal role in the running of either the education system or regulating traffic safety on provincial highways, so the moms had no need for political help in Ottawa. Like everyone else, however, Godin had followed the news, watching with growing fascination the way the mothers had demanded and won changes to student travel policies, had successfully campaigned for an inquest, and then had their pleas and warnings validated by the inquest jury.

He also had special sympathy for their cause. Not only had he known Allan through their union connections—every Labour Day, he had socialized with both Allan and Isabelle at the Bathurst labour hall—Godin also knew something about the profound pain of losing a child. Several years before the BHS crash, Godin's brother Alfred had lost his twenty-three-year-old son in a motorcycle accident. Four years later, Alfred's other son, a twenty-seven-year-old man with four young children of his own, was killed by a falling tree while cutting timber in the woods. Although the deaths had been hard on Godin, they had devastated his brother, whose pain overwhelmed him for many years. After the death of his first son, Alfred had buried himself in sorrow, refusing to allow his boy's photograph to be seen anywhere in his house until, after a long, extended period of profound grieving, he finally came to terms with his losses by choosing to live his own life again, re-engaging with the world and making the best of every day.

So, although he hadn't lost his own children, Godin understood some of the grief Isabelle and Marcella were suffering when they came to see him in 2009.

"I had known Isabelle before the crash. Afterwards, she wasn't the same person," he says. "She took it hard, and I felt so sad about it, to see her in that condition. I saw that she wanted to change things, and I wanted to help."

...

Isabelle was well informed about the long, ugly history of 15-seat vans. She had read the many stories in the American media about van tragedies there, digested the stream of U.S. government safety advisories on the vehicles, and poured over the Web sites of American families who were campaigning to outlaw the passenger vans across the U.S. Her own blog was a reflection of many of those sites.

Until the BHS tragedy, concerns surrounding 15-seat vans had not penetrated the public consciousness in Canada. However, it was a big issue in the U.S., where more than one thousand people died in the vans in the decade between 1997 and 2006. Since the turn of the millennium, the U.S. government's National Highway Traffic Safety Administration (NHTSA) has issued an unprecedented four safety advisories on the vans, more than for any other type of vehicle. A series of public and legal campaigns by the families of children killed in van crashes has led to tough restrictions on their use. In the year 2000, South Carolina was the first state to ban student travel in 15-seat vans, and since then similar prohibitions have taken effect in at least forty states. Although not always well enforced, there is also a nationwide ban by the U.S. government (which regulates the sale of new vehicles) on the sale or lease of 15-seat vans to schools and daycare centres.

Critics in that country consider both 12- and 15-seat vans dangerous because they were originally designed by the American automakers to function as cargo vehicles. In 1971 they were extended in length and equipped with bench seats to meet a growing market demand for a simple, versatile vehicle — as opposed to an actual bus — that could carry more than ten passengers. Even though such vans are now used for group-passenger travel, they lack some of the features common to other passenger vehicles, such as airbags, protective seats, and steel-reinforced sides and roofs in case of rollovers or collisions. Some vehicle safety experts compare them to pickup trucks with bench seats in the back, enclosed by little more than a thin, metal skin. Like pickups, 15-seat vans are strong vehicles front and back, but on the sides they are tin cans, with almost no protection for passengers.

Unlike cars or minivans, 15-seat vans also have a higher centre of gravity, which becomes especially dangerous when the vans are fully loaded. Because so much weight is concentrated in the back of the vans when full, they also have a propensity to fishtail and lose steering control during driving emergencies at high speeds. The Safety Forum, a private U.S. consumer watchdog, once called them "death traps," a sensational label that became widely repeated in the media and was reinforced by a continuous stream of fatal van crashes.

Starting in the 1980s, 15-seat van disasters began claiming lives in Canada: three schoolchildren and a parent in Nova Scotia in 1984, seven college tree planters in Alberta in 1990, a farmworker in British Columbia in 2003, two high school basketball players in Alberta in 2004, and three more farmworkers in B.C. in 2007. But it wasn't until the widely reported Bathurst High crash the following year that 15-seat vans, and questions about their suitability for children, finally came under serious national scrutiny.

Although the annual number of U.S. deaths in 15-seat vans actually began to decline after 2001, they continued to be a safety concern for the NHTSA. In October 2010, more than a year after Isabelle first went to see Yvon Godin, the NHTSA warned that 15-seat vans are particularly dangerous when equipped with the wrong tires or with worn or under-inflated tires, just as the BHS van had been. That year the agency also warned:

"Pre-primary, primary and secondary schools should not use 15-passenger vans for transporting school children, as they do not provide the same level of safety as school buses."

Traditional yellow school buses are considered by most experts the safest vehicles in which to transport groups of children. They aren't immune from crashes, of course, but they are designed, partly through the use of side steel barriers and reinforced roof frames, as well as their general sturdiness, to minimize death and injury to their passengers in case of a collision or rollover. Most importantly, in most North American jurisdictions yellow school buses are also governed by strict legal regimes with an elaborate safety infrastructure—special mechanical and maintenance standards, daily inspection checklists, highly trained professional drivers, government-enforced hours-of-duty limits—all of which reduces the likelihood of fatal incidents.

Isabelle gave all this information to Yvon Godin. She also brought copies of recent articles by Canwest News Service, a national newspaper chain that had just published a series of investigative stories at the beginning of the 2009 school year about the safety of extracurricular school travel in Canada. In a series titled "Precious Cargo," Canwest wanted to know whether any of the recommendations of the Bathurst inquest in May had brought about change, not only in New Brunswick, but in school boards and provinces across the country. Canwest, which owned newspapers from British Columbia to Quebec, surveyed every provincial government as well as thirty-seven rural and urban school boards from coast to coast. It discovered that the inquest's findings were being ignored outside New Brunswick, including the recommendation for a national ban on 15-seat vans. In most provinces, strict safety and regulatory regimes were in place governing the daily transport of millions of Canadian children between home and school; however, no similar regimes governed the transport of those very same children, by the same schools, to extracurricular events. Instead, Canwest identified what it called "a regulatory vacuum," and a "hodge-podge of practices in place across the country, and large differences in safety standards from one [school] district to another."

Some districts surveyed had high standards. The English Montreal School Board, for example, used only yellow school buses and professional drivers to take kids to after-school sports and other events. Other districts had little or no safety policies at all, operating the way many schools in New Brunswick had before the Bathurst crash, using an assortment of vehicles from 15-seat vans, to teachers' cars, to taxi cabs—even a pickup truck at one school board on Vancouver Island—to transport students to events after school.

In Bathurst, Codey's father, Dale Branch, was interviewed by Canwest. He had a message for parents of Canadian school kids everywhere:

"I had assumed those vans were being properly maintained by the education system," he said. "I had assumed if there was a winter storm warning, the team would not be travelling. It's kind of late for me now, but as parents, we have to educate ourselves. Don't assume that everything is just so."

The Canwest investigation also showed how the Canadian Standards Association, the not-for-profit group that develops safety standards for governments to enforce on every kind of consumer good from light bulbs to lawn mowers, had been working for years on a standard for an extracurricular school vehicle to replace 15-seat vans. The CSA was only months away from announcing it when the Bathurst tragedy happened, shocking the members of the CSA technical committee who were working on the matter.

The "D-270" standard, as it was called, established formal design and manufacturing criteria for Multi-Function Activity Buses (MFABs), specifically for school use. MFABs were relatively new on the market and no safety standard had ever been established for them in Canada. Adopting one now would create a new category of minibus in federal law, a vehicle built to the same, exacting standards as yellow school buses, only half the size and without the flashing stop signs and other traffic-control features of school buses. By formally endorsing the new standard, the federal government could not only standardize MFAB design, it could raise awareness about MFABs and encourage provinces and school boards to use them — rather than 15-seat vans — as the vehicle of choice for extracurricular transport.

"The [D-270] standard needs to be adopted or it won't be used," CSA vice-president John Walter told Canwest. "The CSA wouldn't have gone into this if we felt [15-seat] vans were providing the safety that was needed. We obviously felt there was a need to fix what was there."

Transport Canada had worked with the CSA in the development of the standard since 2000. The government's engineers had sat in on many of the CSA technical committee meetings, and were well aware of the association's work on the D-270 standard. By the fall of 2009, however, more than a year after the standard was unveiled by the CSA, and almost two years after the

BHS tragedy, Transport Canada had not even *begun the process* of adopting it into law. Officials at the department wouldn't explain why. One theory put forward by a member of the technical committee that created the standard for the CSA is that it wasn't worth the government's time or money. "Transport Canada didn't adopt it, because their crash statistics didn't show the value of it," says the vehicle expert, who was interviewed for this book but who requested anonymity. "In order for them to spend money on a new standard, they look for value, for cost-benefits." But in the government's view, he says, there weren't enough problems on the road with 15-passenger vans in Canada, not enough crash victims—even after the Bathurst tragedy—for them to want to spend money adopting and enforcing a new regulation for a safer school vehicle.

The U.S. government's repeated safety advisories on 15-seat vans also hadn't persuaded Ottawa to issue similar warnings of its own. In 2001, prompted by one of the NHTSA's first warnings, Transport Canada made an internal study, examining Ontario collision data in 1997 and 1998. The stats showed that 15-seat vans were involved in only four fatal collisions during those two years, out of 1,575 fatal collisions in Ontario overall. Transport Canada said those numbers did not warrant the issuing of a warning to Canadians.

When Isabelle and Marcella sat down with Godin in his office in September 2009, they asked if he could do anything to change Ottawa's mind, to get the CSA's MFAB standard adopted. They also wanted to know why, if the U.S. government had outlawed the sale of 15-seat vans to schools in that country, the Canadian government couldn't do the same thing here.

For nearly two years Isabelle had fought what she considered mostly a personal battle, seeking justice and accountability for Daniel, and trying to make his school and others like it in New Brunswick safer for other kids. But the more she learned about the 15-seat van issue, the more she believed there was a larger mission awaiting her, with far bigger stakes, and many more lives in the balance.

"When I learned that the CSA already had recommendations to have

MFAB standards, before the death of our children — every time I found out little things like that, it just made me more and more determined," she says. "It made me feel, 'There's no way I'm going to stop fighting for this. It's bigger than me. It's something that should have been done long ago for all children in Canada.'"

Godin was receptive. He asked his staff to examine the issue and figure out what might be done on the federal side to outlaw 15-seat vans. No doubt his political instincts told him it couldn't hurt, at the very least, to be seen to be helping these well-known, grieving, warrior moms, these courageous constituents of his. But he also genuinely admired what Isabelle and her allies had accomplished so far, and he shared their concerns.

"When the mothers came to me, they were well prepared," he says. "They had done some research and she explained to me the situation with the vans, and the situation in the States. Then I checked into it myself, and the more I got into it, the more I believed it was totally wrong for these vans to be used. You don't have to be a genius, it makes sense — the van was made for cargo, not for people.

"I lift my hat to those women. It's sad, they lost their children, and they could have sat on the sidelines and done nothing. I'm not judging anyone. Everybody, in the death of their children, takes a different path with their grief. Some want to be more private than others. But others say, 'I don't want my kid to have lost their life for nothing.' That's a decision those women took, they did what they felt was the right thing to do. I lift my hat to them."

...

On the far side of the country, another mother was watching, with interest and admiration, what Isabelle and Ana had accomplished. Stella Gurr, a fifty-nine-year-old former civil servant with the British Columbia government, had, like other Canadians, learned about the Bathurst tragedy in the winter of 2008, and had followed news of the hubbub surrounding 15-seat vans. The previous year, the van controversy had already surfaced in British

Columbia when three migrant farm workers were killed, and fourteen others injured, when a 15-seat van, stuffed with seventeen people, crashed on a highway near the town of Abbotsford.

"I had been fully aware of the problems with 15-passenger vans," says Stella. "I'd followed all the controversy. I notice stuff like that. I remember watching a *60 Minutes* program on it too. And then came the Bathurst thing. I just thought, 'Oh my god, this is so horrific.'"

Stella had grown up in Ontario, graduated from the University of Toronto, and moved to the West Coast in 1976. She lived in Nanaimo, on Vancouver Island, where she worked as a bureaucrat with the provincial Ministry of Social Services. Stella was a petite woman whose small size masked an iron will. She was plain-spoken, and didn't suffer fools gladly. Her twenty-six-year-old son, Michael, a former college football player, was the drummer for a Vancouver rock band called The Hotel Lobbyists. In the summer of 2008, only months after the awful news out of Bathurst, his band purchased a second-hand, 15-seat van for a cross-Canada summer performance tour. When Stella saw the van parked in her driveway before the start of the trip, she wasn't happy with the band's choice of vehicle.

"This is the van you guys are going to take?"

"Yeah," Michael said.

"You know the history behind these, don't you?"

"Don't worry, Mom. We've had it all checked out and maintained. We've put new tires on it. We'll be fine."

In September that year, as the group was driving west on the Trans-Canada Highway through Manitoba, the driver nodded off to sleep and woke up as the van's tires hit the gravel shoulder of the highway. When he tried to correct the steering, the van veered out of control and flipped several times on the road. Michael was killed. Another passenger was hospitalized with severe head injuries. The driver and two other passengers were not seriously hurt. The RCMP said there were no drugs or alcohol on board, that road conditions were good, and that the van was in good mechanical condition and was travelling under the speed limit. They blamed the crash on driver fatigue.

Stella thought differently: "That friggin' 15-passenger van."

She'd read and heard enough about those vans, including the one in the Bathurst crash, to believe that it wasn't only driver fatigue that killed her son—it was the van's design, its inherent dangers, that made it difficult to fix a steering error caused by a driver, the weather, or any other factor.

"The steering on those vans cannot be corrected once they go into a skid," she says. "Once you slide on black ice, or drive onto the gravel on the shoulder of the road, you're in serious trouble."

After coming through the numbing, initial weeks of shock and grief, and after coping with the myriad practical and legal details that must be attended to following the death of a loved one, Stella began thinking about the mothers in Bathurst. No longer were they just random women in a faraway news story from a distant province; they were now fellow travellers, wandering through thickets of sadness in a lonely world whose grey, never-ending wastes are known only to the heartbroken parents of dead children.

She wondered, "If the deaths of the Bathurst boys had created such a controversy about these vehicles eight months before Mike's death, why was my son able to buy one and drive in one? Why hadn't anything been done?"

Stella found Ana Acevedo's number, and Ana then put her in touch with Isabelle.

"I told Isabelle I was doing the same things she was doing," says Stella. "All the things I had come to query were the same things they were querying. I'd already started doing a lot of research. The more research I did, the more I was like, 'Something's got to be done.' I needed to do something about the vans. I also wanted the people responsible for the vans on the road to be held accountable."

Stella had already started a letter-writing campaign. She'd written to Boys and Girls clubs in B.C. and other organizations that used 15-seat vans, warning them about the vehicle's dangers. She'd also sent letters expressing her concerns to both the federal and British Columbia governments. The letters received polite responses, "But basically," says Stella, "nothing happened."

Isabelle was glad to hear from Stella and agreed to work with her in trying to get the vans outlawed in Canada. Their goals weren't identical: Isabelle wanted the vans banned for student travel, as they were in much of the United States. Stella wanted the vans off the road for everyone, adults and students alike. Still, the two women's causes were similar enough that it made sense to pool their resources. In the years to come Isabelle and Stella would become close allies and good friends, with much in common in terms of their sons.

"Isabelle and I each had two boys, and our boys were everything to us," says Stella. "She had spent tons of time with her boys, and I'd spent tons of time with mine. Daniel and Mike, their birthdays are both in January. They were both musicians, and they both played sports. They were both outgoing and popular, they were very similar.

"Isabelle and I, we went from being partners in a cause, to, over the years, becoming very good friends. I think we support each other."

Isabelle had also found a new source of support in the union that represented drivers of yellow school buses. The Canadian Union of Public Employees (CUPE) naturally wanted school bus drivers in New Brunswick to be tasked with driving students to extracurricular events. Isabelle had contacted the union several months earlier as she was preparing for the inquest, to learn more about the training that professional bus drivers received for their Class 2 licences. Delalene Harris Foran, president of the CUPE local that represented bus drivers in the New Brunswick school system, became a vocal supporter of Isabelle's efforts to have the inquest recommendations fully implemented, and to ban 15-seat vans.

Bryan Murphy, a CUPE member in British Columbia who was also a bus driver, mechanic, and licenced school bus inspector—and who had been working for years to have 15-seat vans replaced in B.C. schools—was also introduced to Isabelle and enlisted to add his voice to the women's new ban-the-vans campaign.

"Transport Canada has not issued any recommendations against using these vans," Murphy told Canwest News in September 2009. "They're passing responsibility to the provinces and the school districts, and I think that's short-sighted thinking. Transport Canada is negligent in not addressing this issue and bringing it to public attention."

CUPE made available to Isabelle its organizational muscle. It also contributed financially to her efforts, although not directly. Sometimes, if Isabelle travelled outside New Brunswick for her campaigns and Delalene Harris Foran went with her, they would share a hotel room on CUPE's tab. And when Isabelle travelled to Fredericton for television interviews, or to meet with politicians or bureaucrats, she was given a complimentary room at the Fredericton Inn by the inn's manager, a friend of CUPE's who sympathized with Isabelle's goals.

Isabelle was now surrounded by a small but deeply committed band of self-described Van Angels. She and Stella Gurr, as the two mothers in the group who had lost sons, became the faces and voices of a public campaign to bring attention to the dangers of 15-seat vans, and to have those vans banned for student travel and replaced by the newer minibus MFABs. The group had CUPE's moral support, network of contacts, and hard resources behind it, plus Melynda's organizational and media talents. But mostly it had Isabelle and Stella's personal stories and their determination to spur it on.

The group didn't have long to wait to hear from Yvon Godin. He called them in the fall of 2009, within weeks of his visit from Isabelle and Melynda, to confirm that he would be submitting a private member's bill in Parliament to take action against 15-seat vans. At first, it wasn't clear exactly how his bill would do this, or when the New Democratic Party leadership would allot Godin the precious time and space on the party's parliamentary schedule to bring his bill to the floor of the House of Commons. Those details were still to be worked out. No matter. Isabelle was thrilled that Godin and his party bosses wanted to help her ban the vans. And no sooner had she and Marcella heard back from Godin than they were suddenly immersed into the winter tires campaign, which would consume their attention and distract them from the van issue until well into the following year.

• • •

Seven months later, in May 2010, Godin telephoned Isabelle once again with urgent news. His private member's bill was ready and would be introduced in Parliament at the end of that month.

"Make sure you're in Ottawa," he told her. "Bring everyone on the team, all the mothers. You can be there with me, watching from the visitors' gallery, when I introduce the bill."

At the beginning of every new session of Parliament, the NDP typically drew names from a hat to decide which of its MPs, and which private members bills, would be introduced in that session. Not only had Godin's name come up in the most recent draw, but the party brass, including NDP leader Jack Layton, wholeheartedly supported his ban-the-van bill. Bill C-522, as the legislation was formally named — or "The Boys in Red Bill," as Godin called it — aimed to make it a criminal offence to transport students in 15-seat vans. It would also change the federal Motor Vehicle Safety Regulations, to limit the sale, importation, and interprovincial shipment of the vans. Since the federal government didn't have jurisdiction over the education system, these seemed like two alternate ways Ottawa could use federal power to remove the vans from Canadian schools.

Godin had talked about his proposed bill with John Baird, the Conservative government's transport minister, who didn't endorse the bill, but didn't oppose it either. The Conservatives at that time had a minority government in the House of Commons — the largest number of seats out of all the parties, but not an overall majority — making for an unstable and uncertain political environment. Godin knew that very few private members bills ever became law. Even if his bill had the support of enough MPs to eventually win passage through Parliament, there were no guarantees that the current session of Parliament would survive long enough to allow that to happen. If the government fell and Parliament was dissolved, all outstanding bills would dissolve with it.

Still, Isabelle couldn't quite believe that Godin was about to bring forward legislation to ban the vans like the one in which Daniel had died. Although still exhausted and recovering from the winter tires campaign, she booked two tickets, for herself and Melynda, to be in Ottawa on May 26. She wanted Marcella and Ana to come too, but they said no. They'd had enough campaigning and public activism to last them a lifetime. However, Delalene Harris Foran agreed to join Isabelle and Melynda in Ottawa, as did Bryan Murphy, the British Columbia CUPE official and school bus mechanic, and also Stella Gurr, whom Isabelle and the rest of the Van Angels group would meet in person for the first time.

Everyone gathered on the evening of May 26 in Ottawa at a welcome dinner, hosted by Godin at the parliamentary restaurant, a little-known, exclusive hideaway inside Parliament's Centre Block where MPs, political staffers, and members of the Press Gallery come to huddle, make deals and exchange gossip over prime rib, grilled salmon, and glasses of shiraz or chardonnay. Godin had told NDP leader Jack Layton that Isabelle and her friends would be there, and Layton stopped by their table briefly to shake hands and offer both his condolences and encouragement. The next afternoon the group returned to the Hill and were escorted through the grand, gothic hallways of the Centre Block, into the visitors' balcony overlooking the House of Commons chamber, with its ornately carved stone walls and soaring stained glass windows. Isabelle watched as MPs and cabinet ministers made speeches, passed notes, and shuffled about among the velvet green seats on the floor below. Transport Minister John Baird crossed the aisle from the government to the opposition seats to have a few words with Godin about his upcoming bill. When they were finished speaking Godin glanced up at Isabelle and her friends, gave them a thumbs-up sign, and then rose from his chair to address the House:

"Mr. Speaker, today I am pleased to introduce my Boys in Red bill," he said. "I named this in memory of the seven members of the Bathurst High School basketball team and their adult chaperone who were travelling in a 15-passenger van and lost their lives in a road accident near Bathurst, New Brunswick, in January 2008.

"At this time I would like to recognize Isabelle Hains, the mother of one of the students, who is on the Hill to see this bill introduced. Her work, along with the work of Mrs. Kelly and Mrs. Acevedo, two other mothers who lost their sons in the tragic Bathurst accident, has helped to ban these 15-passenger vans in New Brunswick.

"I hope that I will receive the support of members of the House for my bill."

Isabelle rose from her seat in the balcony as she was recognized by Godin. She stood there for a brief, shining moment inside Canada's most important national institution, the eyes of the country's politicians upon her. She had come a long way since 2008, transformed from a shy, naive, small-town citizen unsure how to create change in the world into a successful child-safety advocate, and a force to be reckoned with.

That afternoon Isabelle and her friends were swamped with national media obligations. Godin took them across the street from Parliament Hill to the National Press Theatre, where they held a news conference attended by about a dozen reporters. They carefully explained the differences between 15-seat vans and MFAB minibuses and discussed why they believed the vans should be outlawed. Isabelle and Godin were also interviewed on national television in the foyer of the House of Commons by Tom Clark for CTV News, and that evening she and Godin were invited into the CBC studios for another live national interview, with host Evan Solomon. It had been a busy and emotional day, and as Isabelle was having her TV-makeup applied in the CBC guest waiting room, only moments before going on the air, she was overcome by a sudden, uncontrollable bout of tears.

In two-and-a-half years of talking to reporters, appearing on television, and issuing public statements, Isabelle had become a polished interviewee and an experienced media source. With Melynda's coaching, she now knew what she needed to say, and how to say it with maximum effect for the eyes and ears of the media. Yet whatever "professionalism" she'd acquired in selling her message, in playing the forceful advocate, Isabelle was still a grieving mother at heart. Her love for Daniel and her determination to do right by his memory, and that of his friends, meant that she still carried with her, into every interview, into every meeting with every politician, a heavy emotional burden. Her sorrow was still close to the surface. It imbued Isabelle with authenticity — a rare and valuable commodity in Ottawa — yet it meant that her advocacy was still as heart-wrenching for her personally in 2010 as it had been in the months right after Daniel's death.

As the tears streamed down Isabelle's face in the CBC waiting room, her friends tried desperately to comfort her, to calm her down for the upcoming Evan Solomon interview.

"Melynda tried to give me one of her pep talks. She said, 'Isabelle, you're going to be fine, Daniel is proud of you.' I said, 'Stop saying that! You're only making it worse!' And Yvon was sitting there with Stella and everyone else, and they're all looking at me and wondering what to do with me. Well, I held it together for the broadcast, but I was emotionally drained and tired."

"I recognized the pain of another mother," says Stella. "This is all based on the love of a child, and the determination to make things right. No matter how hard it was for Isabelle, she was still willing to out there and talk and work and push her message. But the emotion is still raw. It never goes away."

The following day there were more meetings; with New Brunswick Senator Jim Munson, who offered whatever help he could, as well as with two senior political aides in the office of Transport Minister John Baird. The men were polite and sympathetic, as Isabelle and Stella explained their stories, but they made no guarantees that the government would support Godin's bill, or that Transport Canada would simply take it upon itself to change the regulations to limit the sale of 15-seat vans to schools.

As they were leaving Parliament Hill for the final time, walking in the spring sunshine down the long stone pathway that leads away from the Peace Tower, Isabelle, Stella, and Melynda noticed what looked like an MFAB parked at the entrance to the House of Commons. And as they looked closer, they realized that a number of other chauffeured MFABs — painted either dark green and labelled with the words "House of Commons of Canada" or painted white and labelled "Senate of Canada" — were in fact moving in stately fashion around the Hill, shuttling MPs and senators and other officials between the various parliamentary and government buildings in downtown Ottawa. These were the same vehicles the women wanted schools in New Brunswick, and across the country, to bring in as safe replacements for 15-seat vans.

"How about that!" Melynda told the others. "Our members of Parliament have the best vehicles to shuttle them around . . . we should make a video!"

So Melynda whipped out her video camera and Stella and Isabelle provided the impromptu commentary, and within hours the warrior moms had posted photos and videos of their discovery onto the Van Angels blog, pulling no punches in saying precisely what they thought.

"Parliamentarians use MFABs to shuttle around Parliament Hill," they said on the Web site. "The irony is that we are here in Ottawa trying to convince the same parliamentarians to ban 15-passenger vans for student use, and we are surrounded by MFABs. Rest assured that our politicians are safe when they travel around Parliament Hill. Don't you think our children deserve the same safe mode of travel?"

Every day in Ottawa, dozens of the country's most senior journalists, members of the Parliamentary Press Gallery, toil away in the hopes of holding national politicians to account, of unearthing examples of double-standard behaviour, hypocrisy, and undue privilege. Now, three visiting women had done the job all on their own, showing the disconnect between the political class and the needs of citizens, simply by asking the question: If our MPs have the best shuttles available, why can't our school kids have them too?

...

Yvon Godin says his bill created a minor stir in Ottawa, as any proposed legislation does that threatens to alter how society works, or to change, even in the slightest manner, the way established industries do business.

"When a bill like mine goes in the House, industry sends the lobbyists in," he says. "That bill was not welcome, for sure."

Although Godin himself wasn't personally lobbied, he says the auto industry dispatched its consultants to bend the ear of politicians and officials. Industry wasn't about to throw in the towel on 15-seat vans, which were still selling in Canada. But Isabelle and Stella were lobbying too, organizing a petition and a letter-writing campaign in support of Godin's bill. All through the spring and early summer of 2010 they sent petition pages and more than thirty letters to Transport Minister John Baird in Ottawa.

"We had to keep up the pressure on the government," says Isabelle, "to let them know we were not going away."

On June 25, Baird's office surprised the women by suddenly announcing an unprecedented federal review "of the safety standards applicable to 15-passenger vans." Transport Canada would begin testing and comparing the safety of 15-seat vans with MFABs, and it would open talks on the subject with provincial governments as well as with Yvon Godin, "who has proposed legislation on the issue," the government said. A week earlier Baird's office had also sent letters to his provincial and territorial counterparts, encouraging them to examine the kinds of vehicles used in extracurricular student travel.

"Extracurricular school activities are part of the fabric of Canadian society," said Baird in a public statement. "By launching this review, we can determine the best safety options for students during their trips and help prevent tragedies on our roads."

Isabelle was delighted. Once again, she and her allies had scored an impressive victory, or at least a tactical win in their battle against 15-seat vans. For more than two years in the wake of the Bathurst tragedy, the federal government had done its best not to get involved, refusing to fully examine the safety concerns surrounding 15-seat vans, or take action on the sale of the vehicles — or even issue safety advisories — the way the U.S. government had. From Ottawa's point of view, 15-seat vans were not inherently more dangerous than other large passenger vehicles, and the Bathurst High crash and its political fallout was a provincial matter and none of its concern. But thanks to the work of the Van Angels group, and the pressure brought to bear by the Boys in Red bill, Transport Canada was finally taking action, or at least entering the discussion, by embarking on a safety review and promising to raise the issue with the provinces, whose governments really held the power to outlaw 15-seat vans in schools.

Every year Canada's federal, provincial, and territorial transport ministers gather together for a two-day, closed-door summit, to compare notes and discuss developments on various transportation files. They were due to hold their 2010 meeting in September in Halifax, and thanks to Transport Canada, the safety of 15-seat vans was now an item on the agenda there. Isabelle, Stella, and Melynda decided they also needed to be in Halifax, to personally press their case for a van ban and for the adoption of the CSA's new minibus standard. They hadn't been invited to the summit, and had no idea whether their request for an audience with the transport ministers would be granted; yet they plowed ahead anyway and booked rooms for themselves and for their CUPE friends at the Marriott hotel, the same hotel on the Halifax waterfront where the transport ministers would be gathering.

In the weeks leading up to the meeting, Isabelle and her sister Linda carefully compiled a thick, one-hundred-page binder full of documents, photos, and press clippings explaining the history of the Bathurst High tragedy, the inquest evidence and its recommendations, and the technical arguments favouring Multi-Function Activity Buses over 15-seat vans. She paid a professional printer to churn out dozens of these binders, which she hoped to hand out to the news media and the transport ministers in Halifax, even though she had no idea whether the ministers would receive her. A week before the summit, however, Isabelle was called at home by a federal official with news that the ministers would set aside time to meet with her and her friends on September 30. Would they be available to join the summit at the end of that day, at 5:30 p.m.?

"YES!" Isabelle was thrilled. "We're going to get to talk to them! Our trip won't be for nothing."

The next week, Isabelle, Melynda, and Delalene Harris Foran drove to Halifax, where they rendezvoused once again with Stella Gurr and Bryan Murphy from B.C. The Van Angels had organized their own press conference on the first morning of the summit, booking space in a small public theatre down the street from their hotel, where they met a gaggle of reporters and explained why they'd come to Halifax. That evening the mothers' story and their demands were once again on the nightly news, and the next day, as they gathered around their summit conference table, the ministers were reading stories about Isabelle and Stella in the morning papers.

On the final day of the summit, the Van Angels team gathered inside Isabelle's hotel room to plan for its big moment with the ministers. The stakes were high. Perhaps never again would they have an opportunity like this, to put their concerns and wishes directly, face-to-face, to all of Canada's federal, provincial, and territorial transport ministers in one room. It was also their first chance to meet the newly installed federal transport minister, Chuck Strahl, who had replaced John Baird only weeks earlier in a cabinet shuffle. Although Strahl was a down-to-earth Westerner, a less partisan, more genial politician than Baird, Isabelle and her friends had no idea what his reaction would be to their demands. It was Baird, after all, who had witnessed the introduction of Yvon Godin's bill in the House of Commons; it was Baird's political aides who had met with the moms in Ottawa; and it was under Baird's watch that Transport Canada had agreed to launch a safety review of 15-seat vans. But now he was gone from the transport portfolio, replaced by an entirely different politician the moms knew very little about.

This was becoming a recurring irritation of Isabelle and the others. The quick and constant turnover of politicians in cabinet posts, in both the provincial and federal governments, simply added to the delays and frustrations of trying to lobby, pressure, and educate public officials to take action on any issue, whether it was holding an inquest, equipping MFAB's with winter tires, or taking action against 15-seat vans. Over the course of Isabelle's long campaign, she would experience not only the shuffling of several cabinet ministers — including five federal transport ministers in the five years following her son's death — but also elections, both provincially and federally, and a change of government in New Brunswick. Such constant flux and turmoil slowed down the already glacial decision-making process of government, and led Isabelle to believe that Canada's political and bureaucratic systems are so unresponsive to grassroots demands for change, so inflexible in adapting new ideas or even considering new policies, that governments may simply be incapable of serving their citizens well.

Stella and Isabelle sharing a moment during their trip to Halifax to
meet federal Transport Minister Chuck Strahl. (VanAngels.ca)

"I realize now that politicians have only four years in their mandate to
change something — and far less than that if a cabinet minister is shuffled
from post to post — which means that creating any kind of change in government is nearly impossible to do," she says. "I don't know how anything
gets done at that level. There's something wrong with our system. Four
years is not long enough."

Whatever Isabelle's frustrations, Chuck Strahl was now the man in the
minister's seat, and she and her colleagues were determined to get their
message through to him and not lose any of the ground they'd gained under
John Baird. Isabelle had invited two more experts to Halifax to offer advice
and support: Ron Campbell, the MFAB expert and salesman who had worked
with her on the tires campaign, and David White, a retired Nova Scotia
vehicle regulator who had helped bring about Nova Scotia's van ban in
1994. Both men had worked with the Canadian Standards Association on

its new, but unenforced, minibus standard. Both were keen for Ottawa to finally adopt the standard and recognize the MFAB as a new category of vehicle in federal law.

So White and Campbell joined Isabelle, Stella, and the rest of the Van Angels group in gathering with Canada's transport ministers in a hotel conference room at the conclusion of the ministers' Halifax summit. The Van Angels arrived first, and there was no one else in the cavernous room when they walked in — aside from one provincial minister, helping himself to a cupcake from a food table in a corner — so the group sat down at the vacant table and waited, with Isabelle and Stella choosing seats at the head of the table.

Eventually Chuck Strahl and the rest of the provincial ministers all filtered in, along with their political handlers and other aides. Strahl and his officials may have found it disconcerting to see their invited guests, the warrior moms, seated at the head of the table. But what irked them even more were copies of a single sheet of paper Melynda had placed at every seat around the table, listing the Van Angels' two key demands:

"We respectfully request that the Federal Minister of Transport" adopt the CSA standard on MFABs, and . . .

"We respectfully request that the Provincial Ministers take the necessary steps" to outlaw the use of 15-seat vans by schools, daycares, and youth groups.

However politely those demands may have been worded, Strahl's staff considered the one-pager, distributed to each minister, a breach of protocol. As the Van Angels would later find out, Strahl's top officials were quietly fuming as the meeting got underway. In their eyes, the Van Angels had acted unprofessionally in placing those demands so deliberately before Strahl and his counterparts. For the cautious bureaucrats, and the ultra-sensitive political aides, this was not how governments did business. Any demands or points of negotiation should have been cleared first, behind the scenes, before being presented to the ministers in a national meeting. It caught their staff flat-footed and — even more shocking! — put the politicians on the spot.

Still, Chuck Strahl was too polite, and too smooth an operator, to let protocol problems get in the way of a meeting with a pair of media-savvy, grieving mothers. On the surface at least, the mood in the room was friendly and welcoming. After everyone had been introduced, Isabelle and Stella each told their personal stories, and members of the Van Angels group then took turns explaining the problems with 15-seat vans, and making their pitch for a van ban and for the new MFAB standard. When they were finished, a few of the provincial ministers spoke briefly, but most of them simply listened to what the visitors had to say. Chuck Strahl finished the discussion by confirming, to the moms' delight, that Transport Canada would keep the matter on its agenda, and would carefully consider adopting the MFAB standard.

He then described some concrete details in the department's ongoing review of 15-seat van safety. A series of tests by federal government engineers were underway to compare the safety of vans and MFABs: "dynamic" tests, to measure vehicle handling and steering control, "static stability" tests to examine rollover risk, and most importantly for Isabelle, who had specifically asked for this, a "crashworthiness" test, complete with crash test dummies, to compare how passengers in the different vehicles would fare in a collision.

The Van Angels team was thrilled. There had been no promises by any of the provinces to take action against 15-seat vans, but on the federal side Strahl had confirmed and seemingly strengthened Transport Canada's commitment to fully review van safety. He had recommitted his department to consulting the provinces on the van question. He had accepted Isabelle's plea for a "crashworthiness" test. And he even promised to appoint a senior department official to liaise regularly with the Van Angels group, to consult and update them on the progress of the review. There was no hint, by the end of the meeting, of any missteps by the mothers, or bad blood between the officials and the Van Angels group due to breaches of protocol.

"When the meeting was finished, everyone came over to talk to us and to shake our hands," Isabelle says. "All the ministers and their officials, they gave Stella and I their condolences for our sons. They all made me feel like what we were doing was OK, that our campaign was not wrong, that we weren't just troublemakers. I got that feeling from them."

Strahl had a commercial flight to catch out of Halifax, and his aides were urging him to leave the meeting and make for the airport, but instead he ignored their anxious whispers and waited calmly and patiently in the room, smiling and chatting with Isabelle and Stella, as Melynda snapped everyone's pictures and took videos of the moment. When it was finally over and the ministers had all left, Dave White, the former Nova Scotia motor vehicle regulator who was advising the Van Angels, came up to Isabelle and gave her a congratulatory hug. White, a veteran former bureaucrat who understood how hard it was to force governments to take action, was amazed at what he had witnessed in the room — the moms' determination and fearlessness, Chuck Strahl's promises to push forward with a van review, the whole package of what the mothers had accomplished with Transport Canada in only a handful of months. He knew from long experience that just getting the federal government to the table, for a face-to-face meeting between the minister and a band of citizen-activists, was a remarkable achievement all its own.

"Your son," he told Isabelle, "would be so proud of you."

Nine

THE BARGAIN

WHAT WAS THE government up to? Why, after decades of near-silence on 15-seat vans, after years of ignoring the CSA's pleas for a new minibus standard and the safety issues raised by the Bathurst tragedy, were the bureaucrats at Transport Canada and their political masters suddenly so willing to cater to Isabelle Hains and her Van Angels? One answer, as stated by John Baird in 2010, is that Ottawa wanted to find "the best safety options for students" on extracurricular trips and "help prevent tragedies on our roads."

Another possible answer is fear.

Politics is largely an exercise in controlling public optics, maximizing the good publicity and minimizing the bad, and officials in Ottawa were likely afraid of becoming one of Isabelle's media targets. They knew how dangerous she could be, how relentlessly she and the other moms had pursued their goals in New Brunswick. They'd watched how eagerly the national news media had lapped up the mothers' visit to Ottawa and covered the tabling of the Boys in Red bill. They knew it was folly to face off in public against grieving moms who had lost their kids, something the New Brunswick government had learned the hard way — so federal officials decided instead to appease them.

In the months following the Halifax meeting, Isabelle and Stella had kept up the pressure on Transport Canada, sending letters to Chuck Strahl reminding him of his commitments to them there, and also sending a list of questions they wanted answered: What was happening with the van review? When would the test results be known? Would the government adopt the CSA standard on MFABs . . . and so on. All the correspondence was posted on the VanAngels.ca Web site for anyone to see, in the hopes of keeping Transport Canada on its toes.

Both the Boys in Red bill, and the demands placed before the federal minister in Halifax, had put Chuck Strahl and his predecessor John Baird "in a jam," according to one observer, a former civil servant who had closely followed events. "Isabelle wasn't going away," he says, "so they needed to keep these women out of the media."

The van review was indeed going ahead, but the whole process would take another two years. Meanwhile, the task of appeasement over that long period fell to a senior government official named Kash Ram, Transport Canada's director general of Road Safety and Motor Vehicle Regulation. In January 2011 Ram opened a series of regular, monthly teleconference calls with Isabelle, Melynda, and Stella to explain the progress of the review, answer their questions, and keep any disagreements with the government under control and out of the public eye. It was an assignment Ram surely didn't want. A career bureaucrat, Ram was an impeccable professional, a careful, diligent public servant who preferred working quietly in the background of government affairs. He had little desire to tangle publicly with these famous, blog-crazy warrior moms who, it appeared, would stop at nothing to get their way.

"When we first spoke to him, he said he was really nervous," says Isabelle. "He didn't know whether we would put everything he said on our Web site. He didn't know what we were going to do to him. But we told him, 'We know our limits.' We wanted to trust him and we wanted him to trust us. We said we wouldn't do anything to embarrass him.

"I believe they wanted to keep us quiet, and to keep a communication link open between us," Isabelle says. "If we didn't have that, we would have kept putting them out in the spotlight. Definitely we would have done that."

"I think they felt they should keep an eye on us," says Stella. "Overall, we were treated with respect, but in those conference calls I felt from day one that they were trying to guide us, to keep us out of the limelight."

Like Isabelle and Stella, Melynda doubted the government's sincerity, but the women all accepted this bargain. Ram would be their personal liaison with Transport Canada, offering detailed updates, guiding them through the sloth-like, labyrinthine process in which government undertakes studies, consults its provincial counterparts, and considers new regulation. In return for this quasi-insider access, the women would keep Ram's name and the content of their teleconferences (which often lasted several hours each month) out of the news media and off their blog. They traded their activism for the promise of partnership, in the dear hope that some kind of real and positive change might come from it all.

One thing they learned from Ram is that in the government's view, the women had acted unprofessionally in their meeting with Chuck Strahl and the transport ministers in Halifax. They had breached protocol — horror of horrors — by presenting their written demands at the meeting without prior negotiation or approval. They had, in effect, hijacked the minister's agenda.

For their part, the mothers chided Ram in their phone calls for Transport Canada's failure to even consider adopting the new CSA MFAB standard until the van review was launched in 2010. And they complained that he seemed to consistently advocate on behalf of 15-seat vans. As they told him in a 2011 letter, summing up their feelings from a series of teleconferences: "We sometimes feel during our phone conversations that you are defending 15-passenger vans because, as you say, they do meet the existing standards. But the fact is that the existing standards are not good enough."

Aside from these points of contention, however, and other occasional hiccups, their long, two-year relationship with Ram was mostly polite, friendly, and fruitful. Certainly Ram was impressed by the depth of their knowledge and the amount of homework Isabelle and Stella had done on these issues. Stella was particularly impressive, rattling off crash statistics and NHTSA studies, discussing "static stability features," "dynamic rollover resistance," and "National Safety Code standards" as if she had a degree in mechanical engineering.

"I warned the higher-ups," Ram once said, according to Isabelle. "I warned them that these ladies know their stuff. They don't have to be spoon-fed."

From Ram, the women learned that Transport Canada was proceeding with tests that would compare the safety and performance of vans, MFABs, and other similar vehicles. Ottawa was also handing off responsibility for acting on those test results to the Canadian Council of Motor Transport Administrators (CCMTA), a joint government body that co-ordinates road and vehicle policies between Ottawa and the provinces, and makes recommendations for change. While Ottawa would still decide whether to adopt the CSA minibus standard, it would be the CCMTA, not Transport Canada, that would ultimately choose whether to recommend a 15-seat van ban to its provincial and territorial members.

Meanwhile, Kash Ram kept the women informed and stickhandled their input. "We had our own agenda, and Kash had his," says Isabelle. "He asked us a lot of questions about the MFABs — how they're constructed, how the CSA standard was developed — and we'd get them answered by our experts Ron Campbell or Dave White, and we'd get back to him. We also had our own questions, and Kash would guide us through how Transport Canada works, and how codes for new vehicle types are created in Canada.

"Once Ron Campbell and officials from the Canadian Standards Association joined us on a call, and they explained the new MFAB standard to Kash. On every phone call, we'd press him on what was happening in the regulatory process for adopting the new CSA standard for MFABs."

As this was underway, political drama was unfolding in Ottawa. The Conservative government fell in the spring of 2011, prompting a federal election, the dissolution of the current Parliament, and the death of dozens of pieces of pending legislation on the House of Commons order paper, including Godin's Boys in Red bill. But far from being disappointed, Isabelle and her friends believed the bill had been a success. Although it never became law, it helped put their ban-the-van campaign in the national spotlight, and brought attention and pressure to bear on Transport Canada in a way the moms could never have done on their own.

"That bill helped us introduce the issue in a national political venue, right in Parliament," says Stella. "It made the politicians realize that we were serious, we were not going away, and that we needed to be addressed. That bill was sort of a trigger; it put us on the map, especially with Transport Canada."

Even if the bill hadn't died on the order paper, the government didn't want it and wouldn't have supported it. As Chuck Strahl told Isabelle in a letter in January, before Parliament dissolved: "While I sincerely appreciate that Mr. Godin has raised the profile of safety in this issue, I believe that the end result of improved safety can best be achieved through working with the provinces and the territories [through the Transport Canada-CCMTA van review]."

The spring election put the Conservatives back into power, this time with a majority, giving them a guaranteed four-to-five-year mandate, and giving the country a measure of political stability. Strahl, however, had left national politics. So once again there was a new minister appointed to the transport portfolio, this time a veteran Quebec Conservative named Denis Lebel. Yet again the Van Angels, having corresponded with Strahl and met him personally in Halifax, would now have to become familiar with another unknown quantity in the minister's chair.

Godin, however, was back for another term as the MP for Bathurst. He decided there was little point in reintroducing his bill once the election was over and he had been returned to Ottawa. "By that time the government was doing its tests on the vans, their review was well under way, and the mothers were being consulted. They were in the picture. So I thought things were going in the right direction," Godin says.

"That had been the whole original idea of bringing things to Parliament—to raise the profile of this issue and pressure the government, finally, to do the right thing."

...

Although Isabelle had immersed herself into her campaign with Transport Canada, and struck up a new alliance with Stella Gurr, she remained in touch with Ana, whose name and picture still graced the Van Angels Web site along with Marcella's and those of their sons. Ana was no longer in active campaign mode. She shared Isabelle's desire to see all the inquest recommendations adopted, especially the call for yellow school buses and professional drivers for extracurricular travel, but she no longer had the energy and the emotional willpower to be butting heads with governments, attending meetings, talking to reporters, and facing all the other demands of the activist life.

However, there was one final struggle Ana, Marcella, and Isabelle would embark on together in early 2011, before dispersing as a political trio. Soon after the three moms had returned home from Michigan following the winter tires campaign, they discovered that a Halifax-based film company wanted to make a fictionalized drama about their sons' crash and the subsequent rebirth of the Bathurst High basketball team. After losing almost all its players in January 2008, the Phantoms were re-established the following year and given permission to play in New Brunswick's AA basketball league, against smaller schools and at a lower level than the varsity (or AAA) league the school had played in before the tragedy. BHS went on in 2009 to crush the competition and win the provincial AA championships, led through the season by Bradd Arseneau, one of the survivors of the crash. The victory was seen by many as an inspiring story of a shell-shocked school, bravely and triumphantly raising its basketball program out of the ashes of disaster. When Dream Street Pictures set out to tell the story with actors on location in Bathurst, they were warmly welcomed by many families of the crash victims, and by municipal and school officials who gave the filmmakers access to city and school property, in return for promises of sporting equipment and other benefits for Bathurst High.

"There is a great potential for [the] community to benefit from this in terms of the economics of it all," wrote District 15 Superintendent John McLaughlin in an email to a senior provincial education official, correspondence that was later obtained by Isabelle.

"Our students will have an opportunity to be part of the process, acting, etc. Also [there might be] a legacy for the school in terms of sports equipment, etc."

McLaughlin knew the movie would upset some parents, particularly Isabelle and Ana, but he encouraged it anyway.

"We won't get unanimous support but if we get general consensus then we'll probably allow access," he wrote. "It is complex and complicated, but no more so than anything else we managed in this whole thing."

Ana, Isabelle, and Marcella objected fiercely to the movie, saying the 2009 Phantoms championship wouldn't have happened without their sons' deaths, and that Dream Street, a commercial company, was wrong to be trying to profit, even indirectly, from their grief. They also complained about the government tax credits that would flow to Dream Street through the project, arguing the money would be better spent on improvements to school transport safety. But mostly what offended the three moms was their sense that the movie was just another way for the school and the town to paint rosy pictures of the community and wash away the messy truth of the disaster. So incensed was Marcella by the movie that in the fall of 2011, as filming was under way outside a pharmacy in Bathurst, she protested by driving her car right into the midst of the film set, running over several orange pylons in the process. The police were called, but no charges were ever laid.

Despite the moms' protests and complaints, the filmmakers were undeterred. Dream Street finished making its movie, with the full support of other grieving parents, some of whom were offered small roles as "extras" in the film. In November 2012 *The Phantoms* was broadcast on CBC Television to mixed reviews. Many who saw it were supportive. Mike Ricketts, a BHS grad who had been friends with some of the Phantoms, told the *Aquinian*, the student newspaper at St. Thomas University in Fredericton where he was now studying, that the film likely helped friends and acquaintances of the victims find some measure of emotional "closure." Others were more critical. Tim Daley, who had survived the crash with Bradd Arseneau, and who later became a police officer, told a reporter that the film was a mistake.

"To me, this movie is fictional and I can't help but feel upset that it was made," he told the Campbellton *Tribune*, a North Shore newspaper. "My friends had to die for that [2009 championship] win to mean anything at all, and I can only hope that is not forgotten. They missed the real story and made a fictional story for financial gain."

...

The month before the movie's premiere, Isabelle, Melynda, and Stella Gurr all gathered in Fredericton for a private, face-to-face meeting with Kash Ram and federal Transport Minister Denis Lebel, who were in town for that year's edition of the federal-provincial transport ministers' meeting. By now the two moms were experienced players at these things. This would be their second visit to a national transport summit, and Lebel was the third federal minister they had lobbied in as many years. Gone were the shaky nerves and uncertainty they'd once felt as neophytes in the national political process, back when they'd travelled to Ottawa. They were now veteran campaigners, having seen their share of ministers and ministerial aides come and go. In fact whole governments had been changed, or dissolved and re-elected, in both New Brunswick and in Canada, but Isabelle and her allies were still fighting and campaigning, four years after the Bathurst tragedy.

In Fredericton they sat down privately with Ram, Lebel, and his deputy minister around a large table in a chandelier-filled ballroom at the city's Delta Hotel, where earlier that day all the nation's transport ministers had met behind closed doors. Stella had once again come all the way from British Columbia for the occasion. Although the Van Angels and Kash Ram knew each other well from their two-year marathon of phone calls and Skype conferences, they had never actually met in person before, and none of them had ever met Lebel. Through 2011 and most of 2012, the Van Angels had upheld their tacit promise to work as partners with the government, never publicly criticizing its van review or posting comments and questions about the process on their blog. Yet in this meeting Isabelle and Stella were playing it cool, aloof, unwilling to let their guard down with the minister and his senior officials. They had learned things in the previous months that had surprised and disappointed them, and their hopes for concrete action from the government on 15-seat vans had begun to wither. Where the mothers had once entered meetings like this feeling nervous and expectant, they were now skeptical, even suspicious, about the government's capacity and willingness for change. Kash Ram, however, was his usual well-mannered, professional self and he greeted the women warmly. Lebel, too, was friendly, encouraging, and down-to-earth.

"Look," he told them as soon as they'd shaken hands, "I may be a cabinet minister, but back in Quebec I've been involved in sports all my life. I'm a badminton coach. I have children. I have driven 15-passenger vans myself. I know exactly what you are talking about, where you're coming from on this issue."

That helped break the ice a little, and some of the tension melted away. But the women remained cautious. Was Lebel genuinely interested in improving student travel safety or was he just a smooth political operator? He and Ram then told the women that Transport Canada had, after two years, finished its 15-seat van review and was now making its own recommendations to the provincial governments — through the Canadian Council of Motor Transport Administrators (CCMTA) — about what, if any, changes provincial authorities should consider in terms of extracurricular travel. Ottawa had no power in this area to dictate policy, but Lebel made it clear that Transport Canada was issuing its own thoughts on the merits of a van ban and was hoping for a uniform provincial policy across the board.

Ottawa did have the authority, on its own, to adopt the CSA safety standard for MFABs, or to simply harmonize regulations with the United States by adopting the American version of the standard, which was essentially the same thing. Years earlier the U.S. had enacted a standard for what it called Multi Function *School* Activity Buses (MFSABs). If Ottawa chose the harmonization route and adopted MFSAB standard, there would exist a new class of vehicle in Canada, an MFAB built to the same tough safety standards as a yellow school bus, only it would be smaller and wouldn't have the flashing lights and traffic control devices of school buses. Isabelle and Stella's great hope was that the creation of such a vehicle class here would standardize production of school MFABs to a high quality and raise awareness about these minibuses among school boards. On top of that, a harmonized, cross-border standard would create a wider North American market for MFSAB vehicles with better economies of scale for manufacturers. That would lower their purchase price and make them more attractive as an alternative to 15-seat vans, which currently cost on average about $30,000 less than most MFAB models.

Exactly what Transport Canada would do regarding a new MFAB standard, however, and what recommendations it was making to the provinces on 15-seat vans, remained a secret. Ram told the women they would only learn the government's official position once final consultations with the provinces had wrapped up, sometime the following year.

But there was no secret about the findings of Transport Canada's two-year van testing program, and here the moms' campaign nearly ran aground on the shoals of doubt. In the months leading up to the Fredericton meeting, Isabelle, Stella, and Melynda had seen the results of those tests, and what they learned had dimmed their hopes for any real chance of a national van ban. All three women — convinced, like so many other critics, that 15-seat vans were technically inferior to the new MFABs — were astonished by the outcome.

The government had carried out a series of technical studies to compare the performance of various large passenger vehicles, including two, 15-seat vans and a 21-seat MFAB. On the first test, to measure "emergency stopping distance," the 15-seat vans actually braked more quickly than the MFAB, although the difference was relatively minor, a matter of only two-to-four metres. On "rollover risk" tests the 15-seat vans were again marginally superior, performing "as good as, or somewhat better, than the performance of the MFAB," according to Transport Canada.

Next came a series of "dynamic manoeuvre" tests to measure how well each vehicle responds to sudden steering inputs, such as abrupt lane changes or sharp turns to avoid obstacles on the road. Once again there was no difference between the performance of the 15-seat vans and the MFAB. Each vehicle tended to roll or spin out of control when faced with the same degrees of extreme steering. However, when the 15-seat vans were equipped with Electronic Steering Control (ESC), a recent technology now widely available on new vehicles, but not in place on the BHS van in 2008, the vans handled their extreme steering inputs much more safely. No similar ESC-equipped test was done on the MFAB, because ESC technology was not yet available for the minibus, making a true comparison difficult.

Only in the "crashworthiness" test did the MFAB perform better than the vans. The vehicles were loaded with crash test dummies and submitted to a high-speed, side-impact collision with a pickup truck. The MFAB protected its passengers better than the 15-seat vans: "The injury measures obtained from the dummies that were seated on the struck side of the [vans] were generally greater than for the same dummies seated in the MFAB," Transport Canada said. "Two of the three dummy heads were ejected from the window of the [van] while only an arm of the dummy seated in the rearmost row of the MFAB broke through the window."

Although the MFAB showed itself to be a safer vehicle in a side-impact collision, Transport Canada said the results of the crash test did "not lend themselves to generalization" on how those vehicles would behave in real-life collisions. To Isabelle and Stella's consternation, the government refused to make any formal comments about which was a better vehicle in terms of crash protection. "Transport Canada does not draw any general conclusions concerning the crashworthiness of 15 passenger vans nor the MFAB types of vehicles," the report said.

The tests were profoundly discouraging for Isabelle, Melynda, and Stella. For years the Van Angels group had been fighting for a national prohibition on 15-seat vans, explaining the vehicles' supposed design flaws and dangers, and begging schools, provinces, news reporters, and politicians of all stripes — anyone who would listen — to heed their warnings and outlaw the vans for student travel. Isabelle had been the driving force behind Yvon Godin's bill. Along with Stella, she had persuaded Transport

Canada to review 15-seat van safety—and that review had now produced little hard technical evidence to show that the vans were *comprehensively* inferior to the highly vaunted MFABs. At best, the comparison between the vans and MFABs was a wash, each with its own particular flaws or advantages. How could the moms now continue pressing their demands for a national van ban or for regulatory adoption of the MFAB standard? On what basis could they still argue that MFABs were superior to 15-seat vans?

"I was disappointed," said Isabelle, in a moment of understatement. "I was really upset."

Isabelle had won many battles in her long quest for accountability and her mission to make after-school travel safe for kids. She had succeeded in pushing and cajoling Transport Canada to examine an issue it had no appetite for at the start. She had shown her extraordinary mettle against legions of politicians and professional bureaucrats. But at the end of this process, unlike her previous campaigns, there was no sense of triumph, no moment of clarity in which the skeptics were silenced, no proof that she and her friends were right about 15-seat vans. What had happened?

Months later the moms wrote a letter to Girardin, the Quebec-based MFAB manufacturer who had supplied the vehicle for the Michigan winter tires test, and whose 2011 model MFAB had now been used in the disappointing Transport Canada tests. They asked the company why its vehicle didn't show better results against the 15-seat vans, especially in the extreme steering (or dynamic manoeuvring) tests. Girardin replied that the MFAB used by Transport Canada had only single rear wheels. If equipped with dual rear wheels, as are many MFABs operating in the real world, the vehicle would have been "more difficult to move or roll over," thereby improving its performance in the steering tests. In addition, Electronic Stability Control (ESC), which wasn't available for the 2011 MFAB test model, was now being supplied on all of Girardin's 2013 model MFABs.

"There is no doubt in our mind," wrote Girardin, "that our MFAB would have reacted much better than it did during these tests if it were equipped with the ESC standard."

As they pondered this information and digested Transport Canada's test results, Isabelle and Stella decided they should press on, holding fast to their conviction that 15-seat vans are a dangerous vehicle no child or student should ever ride in. After all, why else did the United States government make it illegal to sell 15-seat vans to schools or daycares? Why were the vans banned for student transport in at least forty American states? Why did Nova Scotia, New Brunswick, and Quebec each outlaw the vans from their schools? Why did the jury in the Bathurst inquest, after hearing all the evidence surrounding the death of Daniel and his friends, recommend a ban on 15-seat vans for schools across the country? Why, it seemed fair to ask, were members of Parliament shuttled around Ottawa in MFABs, not 15-seat vans? Isabelle says Transport Canada's "crashworthiness" test is proof that the vans offer virtually no injury protection to passengers during collisions or side intrusions. She says the government was wrong not to issue a conclusion in its report about the superior safety of an MFAB in a collision.

"In the end," she says, "the most important issue is passenger safety. When there's a collision or a crash, the passengers in those vans are just not safe."

Today, however, Transport Canada is sticking to its guns. In response to questions for this book, the government says it "has no evidence to suggest that Multi-Function Activity Buses are safer than 15-passenger vans. Results do not support allegations that 15-passenger vans are unsafe. Testing and findings indicated that *proper vehicle use and maintenance, rather than vehicle design, are the most important factors for the safe operation of these vehicles.* Large vans and buses do not handle like passenger cars. All school vehicles should be operated with care by experienced drivers." [Italics added.]

In there lies the nugget of truth. The real test of safety is not the way school vehicles are designed, but rather the way they are *operated*. In other words, it is the actions of human beings that keep children safe, more so than steel, chrome, rubber, and laminated glass. Technical tests on vehicle performance offer only a limited perspective. School vehicles aren't driven in a laboratory, after all, or on a test track by government engineers; they're operated in the real world by teachers and coaches, in changing weather conditions, and on real roads and highways. Transport Canada's tests don't say anything about the human factor in how those vehicles are used—how they're loaded with gear and people, how they're maintained, whether they're inspected before every trip, whether they have winter tires in winter and how properly those tires are inflated, how their drivers are trained and licensed, and whether those drivers are governed by hours-of-duty restrictions.

In its 2008 investigation into the causes of the Bathurst crash, Transport Canada said that weather and human factors were the main contributing causes of the disaster, not the BHS van's inherent design. Now, having carried out its technical tests, Transport Canada is still saying the same thing—that the way large passenger vehicles are operated is the key to their safety. And here's the rub: by almost any operational measure, 15-seat vans are entirely unsafe, because they are so often owned and operated in environments without rules or regulations, without well-enforced policies on how they're loaded, what kinds of tires they carry, how they're maintained, and who drives them. Perhaps because 15-seat vans don't look like buses at all—they *appear* simple enough, like larger versions of minivans—there is a tendency to use them casually, without the special cautions they require. Because they wouldn't look out of place in the driveway of a private home, 15-seat vans are treated like private vehicles. All across Canada, schools, daycares, church groups, and community organizations own them and drive children in them without giving much thought to the way those vans need to be operated. Their ease, accessibility, and simplicity invites carelessness and abuse.

Not so with MFABs. These small buses are unmistakeably commercial. No school would operate one, and no teacher or volunteer would climb into one, without knowing it was an entirely different class of vehicle, requiring careful stewardship and special user skills. Like yellow school buses, the advantage of MFABs is that they are commonly treated with the respect any large passenger vehicle deserves, and are usually put into service along with a whole infrastructure of rules and policies governing their operation and maintenance, rules that tend to be enforced. In New Brunswick in 2008, there were provincial guidelines in the Education Act governing how kids should travel to extracurricular events. Those guidelines applied to the 15-seat vans at Bathurst High, but they weren't widely promoted or enforced, and teachers, coaches, and officials weren't even fully aware of them. They drove their vans in a state of complacency and unwitting ignorance. Since the disaster, BHS operates MFABs for its students, and those vehicles are driven and maintained according to strict regulation.

The problem is that across much of Canada, few have learned the hard lessons of Bathurst. Consider one recent example. On March 5, 2013, a coach with Father Henry Carr high school in Toronto was driving a 15-seat van to a tournament in Windsor, Ontario, with twelve young basketball players in the back. The coach was pulled over by the Ontario Provincial Police (OPP) on Highway 401, the country's busiest roadway, after being clocked travelling at 146 kilometres per hour. Not only was he driving at that mind-boggling speed with a van full of kids, but the coach didn't have the special class of driver's licence he needed in Ontario to legally operate a vehicle of ten or more passengers.

"The OPP should be credited with saving the lives of those twelve students," said Brian Patterson, the president of the Ontario Safety League, speaking to the CBC. "Here's a teacher who has to take Physics 101: mass at that speed equals disaster if it hits anything."

But the teacher wasn't the only culprit. The van was a rental, and the coach's employer, the Toronto Catholic District School Board, had "no specific policy," according to its spokesman, on what kinds of vans could be used to transport its students to extracurricular events. Whatever policies did exist surrounding extracurricular travel, or the licensing and driver training of its coaches, the board obviously wasn't enforcing them—an astonishing fact, five years after the high-profile Bathurst High tragedy.

This sad episode reveals the ongoing casual attitudes of schools and school boards towards 15-seat vans, and how recklessly they are used and operated, not only in remote regions of the country, but in the heart of Canada's biggest and wealthiest cities. For Isabelle, it is further proof that little has been learned from the death of her son and his six friends.

Back in Fredericton in late 2012, at the end of their meeting with Kash Ram and federal Transport Minister Denis Lebel, Ram took out a pen and piece of paper and asked Isabelle and Stella what each of them thought would come of the government's van review. What kind of action did they think Transport Canada, or its federal–provincial partner, the CCMTA — who had weighed the issues and reviewed the vehicle testing — would now take? The mothers said they wished and hoped that Ottawa and the provinces would embark on a national strategy to at least phase out 15-seat vans in Canadian schools, and that Ottawa would adopt the CSA MFAB standard or the American version. But deep down, in conversations among themselves, the women were wary and skeptical. While they suspected Ottawa would enact the MFAB standard at some distant point in the future, they sensed there might well be no action on vans. They sensed the whole process with Transport Canada had been designed as just a way for them to let off steam, to keep the Van Angels under control, and to keep the federal government and the hot-button issue of 15-seat vans out of the media.

• • •

By the summer of 2013, Transport Canada still hadn't adopted the MFAB CSA standard, or the MFSAB standard from the U.S. However, the Van Angels believed change would come once the government's slow-moving regulation adoption process had ground its way through the bureaucratic maze. Isabelle and Stella believed this was purely a result of their lobbying, and the pressure brought to bear by the Boys in Red bill. They saw it as a significant achievement, with the potential to turn an MFAB minibus, with all the safety advantages of yellow school buses, into the vehicle of choice for extracurricular school travel in Canada.

Transport Canada was keeping its cards close to its chest. All it would publicly confirm by the spring is that it was "considering" the adoption of an MFAB standard. As for its position on 15-seat vans, Transport Canada handed over its test results, and also presumably its opinions, to the CCMTA, of which Kash Ram was a board member along with his counterparts in the provinces and territories.

The CCMTA quietly issued its own report, titled "Evaluation of 15-passenger Vans," in January 2013, without media coverage or fanfare. The seventy-seven-page document contained some interesting, previously unpublished data, including an inventory of all 15-seat vans registered in Canada as of 2008. Of the 27,674 registered vans, eighty per cent were not equipped with Electronic Stability Control, a feature that greatly improves the vans' emergency handling abilities. The inventory didn't specify who the owners of those nearly twenty-two thousand unequipped vans were, but it suggests that hundreds, perhaps even thousands of vans, are used by Canadian schools for transporting children, without ESC. In addition, the vast majority of all registered 15-seat vans were age models purchased between 1999 and 2004, a time when ESC was not being installed on these vehicles. Many would likely still be in service today.

The purpose of the CCMTA report was to make recommendations on van safety for the provinces and territories. It acknowledged the Bathurst High tragedy as a key reason for the study, and credited both Yvon Godin's bill and the Van Angels group for raising awareness about the vans among governments and the public. The report considered a variety of options, from doing nothing, to banning 15-seat vans for schools, to banning them outright for all Canadians. It settled in the end for the status quo, recommending against any prohibition on the basis that "research does not support" the need for a ban. Among other things, it said the financial cost of forcing schools to replace vans with MFABs would have far-reaching consequences for sports and other off-site activities.

"Despite school buses' excellent safety record, it may not be practical for all pupils in Canada to be transported to and from school on school buses," the report says. "Moreover, it may not be feasible to transport all pupils to and from extracurricular activities on multi-functional activity buses."

The report did say, however, that "Canada should develop harmonized [national] requirements for the safe transportation of pupils to and from [both] school and extracurricular activities for all vehicles used," and that "Canada should develop national guidelines to promote and educate users on how to safely operate a 15-passenger van." Those guidelines should "stress the importance" of monthly tire maintenance, proper loading of cargo and passengers, periodic and daily maintenance inspections, and proper driver licensing, including a requirement for Class 4 licences (for driving vehicles designed for ten or more passengers).

Having rejected a prohibition, the CCMTA instead focused on improving the human aspect, the way 15-seat vans are operated. Its call for a nationally implemented program to promote extracurricular safety awareness and careful van usage by schools, though less than what Isabelle and her friends had fought for, was a stark admission that problems existed: the vans were potentially dangerous vehicles requiring strict operating codes, as the Bathurst tragedy had proved.

The Van Angels may have lost the war, but they had won an important battle. Here was a joint government report recommending national action on policing the way vans are used. The report even contained a *six-page* set of "15-Passenger Van Safety Guidelines," neatly packaged into a slick brochure, advising schools on best practices for van use. At the end of the guidelines there were also a series of recommendations borrowed directly from the Bathurst coroner's inquest. Among them:

- "Weather should be monitored prior to travel, including the weather at the destination and projected weather for the trip home."
- "An itinerary of the trip should be made available to parents."
- "Development of contingency plans by each school board should be prepared for poor weather or other unplanned situations that require travel to be cancelled."

Isabelle, Melynda, and Stella believed, after reading the CCMTA report, that Transport Canada, or the CCMTA itself, would now embark on a project to mail out safety warnings to the tens of thousands of van owners across the country, and to ensure that all provinces adopted and enforced its six pages of recommended van guidelines in all their schools. This, they believed, would strike some sense into provincial education authorities and school administrators throughout Canada. It would save lives. It was a welcome consolation prize to their failed bid for a national van ban.

But even this was not to be. Transport Canada and the CCMTA were finished with their work on the file.

"With the exception of the [MFAB standard] issue," said Transport Canada following the publication of the CCMTA report, "our project is now complete and has been brought to a close."

"When we first read the report," says Isabelle, "we thought the guidelines would automatically be sent out. We thought that's the least the government and the CCMTA can do. But that's not how it works. Each government will choose how they will make this information public to van owners in their provinces, or if they will even make it public at all. We have no idea how or if the provinces will distribute the guidelines."

In the previous months, Transport Canada had posted "fact sheets" on its Web site, including a summary of its recent test results and a handful of safety advisories about 15-seat vans and how they should be operated. But there was no link to the CCMTA's report or its full list of guidelines. And little else was done on the federal side to educate the public.

"They never made any public announcements about all the work they did, or about the CCMTA's recommendations," says Stella. "They still do not want to draw any attention to this issue, or to us and what we're saying."

Isabelle and Stella, who had placed their highest hopes on Transport Canada's van review, now turned their attention to the provinces and territories. They sent a letter in April 2013 to every government, asking "when and how the Provincial and Territorial jurisdictions intend to inform the Canadian public, raise awareness, and implement an action plan" on 15-seat van use. They reminded governments that the CCMTA, their very own council, had in its report called for a national program to educate school administrators and teachers about safe after-school travel:

> We know that each Province and Territory has the power to initiate an information program that will include personally contacting all 15-passenger van owners as well as the Canadian public, establish new stricter policies and properly monitor and enforce current regulations. After the Bathurst tragedy in 2008 it was determined that policies and guidelines were in place but not followed. We are concerned that the CCMTA's non-binding recommendations and guidelines lack substance for effective, meaningful change.... Then and now the public do not seem to understand that this type of passenger vehicle is not just an "oversized van".... We are adamant that the use of just guidelines and recommendations will have no effect on driver behaviour if it is not backed up by regulation and enforcement.

The letter was more than just a plea for provincial action on 15-seat vans. Like every effort Isabelle had made since January 12, 2008 — all the phone calls, emails, and petitions, the news conferences, the media interviews, and the countless meetings with public officials — this letter was an expression of the pain of losing her son, and the conviction that Daniel and his friends did not have to die, should not have been robbed of the lives that stretched out before them in high school. Isabelle, Ana, Marcella, Stella, and their many supporters believed profoundly that the lives of more children could be spared if only public authorities, from the halls of Parliament to the offices of school principals across the land, would wake up to the inadequate, un-enforced, often non-existent safety regime that surrounds extracurricular school travel. Transport Canada and the CCMTA had finished their work, satisfied that the mere recommendation of "guidelines" was enough to protect schoolchildren. In New Brunswick in 2008 many of the same guidelines already existed in law. But because they weren't proactively pushed or enforced, the guidelines were useless in protecting a young basketball team when its players needed them most.

Isabelle knows from heartbreaking experience that if the CCMTA guidelines aren't promoted and enforced, "then all we'll have done is repeat the history of 2008."

Change takes time. It took thirty years of hard, incessant lobbying for yellow school buses to be adopted in every Canadian jurisdiction as the legally accepted standard for the transport of children between home and school. Getting there required decades of advocacy by volunteer activists and committed public officials. No one questions their fight today. Isabelle sees her mission in a similar light: because society chose to adopt strict standards for transporting kids to school, it will eventually see the necessity of applying those same high standards to after-school travel. After all, why would society choose to protect a child on their way to school, but not offer those same protections, to the very same child, on their way to a basketball game for the same school? Isabelle says she'll never give up fighting for that outcome.

"I can't stop now even if I wanted to," she says. "You can't just start something and not finish it. And this is way too important to let go. . . . If ever something happened at another school because of a 15-passenger van, or because there were no policies in that school to stop kids from being out in a winter storm like our boys were, if another child ever died . . . I would feel as much to blame as the school itself if I didn't do or say anything about it. I don't think I'd be able to live my life, because the boys would say, 'You didn't do your very best to honour us! You just let our death mean nothing.'"

Epilogue
THE PRICE OF COURAGE

ISABELLE AND ANA, with the help of their friends and allies, moved mountains. They forced a cozy, self-satisfied school establishment to rethink its policies and consider its responsibility in the deaths of its students. They cajoled a sleepy provincial government into investigating the causes of the tragedy, and then turned the screws on a mule-headed bureaucracy and political system, forcing it into submission over winter tires. Isabelle then brought the debate surrounding 15-seat vans to the nation's attention, and convinced Ottawa to consider the creation of a new, modern class of school vehicle. Most importantly, she and her allies raised awareness about the inexplicable gulf in safety standards between the way kids travel to school and the way they're taken to after-school activities.

Officials at Transport Canada didn't always see eye-to-eye with Isabelle and her friends, but the women earned their respect. "The Government of Canada applauds the Van Angels' continued efforts toward improving the safety of student transportation," a department spokeswoman said in answering questions for this book. "We also respect the substantial personal dedication of these individuals."

Ana and Isabelle showed that ordinary people, without status or fame or power, can accomplish extraordinary things if they set their mind to it. The mothers' greatest achievement was simply giving a voice to the dead, speaking out for their sons by questioning the conventional wisdom — that it was acceptable to put a bunch of school kids into a rundown van without winter tires, onto a dark, snowy highway in the late hours of the night, and that it was also okay to load the responsibility for getting everyone home safely onto the shoulders of a teacher who'd been on continuous duty for sixteen hours. This was the prevailing view, and it was a defeatist one. *That's how things had always worked at Bathurst High . . . we live in the snow . . . accidents can happen.* So said many people in the wake of the crash. Would this response satisfy the seven boys, now lying silenced in their graves? Ana and Isabelle thought not. So they challenged the prevailing view, they asked their questions, they reminded political leaders and bureaucrats that the disaster was not *a problem* to be expertly managed and then tucked away in a government file. No, this was a tragedy with an explicit warning about the safety of children on school trips, a warning made shockingly real by the extinguished lives of eight people.

Challenging the status quo, however, came at a price.

Isabelle always hated describing the moms' successes as "victories," and she routinely admonished Melynda for doing so. She knew that no "win" would ever bring Daniel back. No doubt she also understood that there was, for all the moms involved, a deep personal cost to their long, often lonely campaign for truth and change.

In Isabelle's case, her marriage was one of the main casualties. No married couple easily endures the loss of a child, but the thousands of miles between Isabelle and Allan, along with her activism, her obsessive pursuit of her campaign goals, made their married life even harder. When Allan came home to visit from his work in Alberta, or when the two shared an occasional holiday together, he was keen to let go of his grief and find a measure of happiness again. Isabelle couldn't let go, didn't want to "move on," and found it difficult to focus her attention on anything other than her newfound advocacy. In the years after the crash, the relationship fell steadily apart and they eventually separated.

The other casualty of the long campaign was Isabelle's own well-being.

"I worry about her," Ana would say. "She looks so fragile."

Isabelle poured so much of herself into honouring Daniel's memory through her activism, and became so emotionally depleted by the work, that for years she was unable to come to terms with the tragedy, the needless circumstances of her son's death. As she wrote in her diary in 2011:

"It's four years now since Dan passed away, and I've never taken the time just for him yet. I'm still thinking of all the things I need to do to prevent another tragedy. But I've never taken the time to grieve for Daniel."

Proof of that was her son's unfinished headstone, the incongruous, makeshift wooden cross that for years marked his grave in Holy Rosary Cemetery.

"I've said to her, 'Why don't you do the headstone?'" Ana once said. "It's not that she doesn't have the money, she does. But she tells me, 'I cannot accept that he's dead. I know he's dead, but I can't accept it.'"

In spite of such unyielding pain, Isabelle never forgot how to love, how to spread her legendary compassion. Just as she often did before Daniel died, she still offered shelter and hospitality to strangers in need, particularly young people such as the young, wayfaring woman whom Isabelle found cycling through Bathurst in the spring of 2012 with her little boy on the back of a bicycle. Isabelle stopped her car on the roadside, invited the pair home for several days, gave them food and beds, and did their laundry. After a week of rest and warm shelter, the mom and her boy thanked Isabelle for her kindness and continued on their bike journey around the province.

Ana also channelled her grief into the campaign for truth and accountability, determined that someone in authority should take responsibility for Javier's death, or at least learn from the mistakes of the tragedy. But she realized that activism was no substitute for personal healing. So Ana turned for help to community service studies at the New Brunswick Community College. The college and its teachers offered her understanding and comfort, and she earned a diploma in Human Services Counselling. But the diploma wasn't enough to find actual work in the field; she needed a university degree for that, a costly and time-consuming proposition. So Ana returned to Bathurst from Moncton, working again as a cook and hoping to pick up her journeyman cooking certificate, to perhaps one day be able to find a job at a professional kitchen in Ottawa, where she imagined she could go to escape Bathurst's unhappy memories, and at least be close to her eldest daughter Maria.

For Ana and Isabelle, grief was a Catch-22. Their pain fuelled their desire to force change on the system, but the activism itself only sharpened and prolonged the pain.

"Isabelle and I, we haven't grieved the way you are supposed to," Ana says. "We got involved in so many things, we were trying to do so much, we diverted our minds. We just kept busy.

"I've tried to heal, but it's hard, it takes time."

Healing, for Ana, meant ending her two-year streak of advocacy. Not only did she need a break from campaigning; she believed Isabelle was biting off too much, raising expectations too high in her work with Transport Canada and her search for a national van ban.

"With Stella on this campaign, they spend days and nights working," says Ana. "I know what they're doing is good, but come on, we have to be realistic too. Can we save the world? I told Isabelle she needs to take care of herself, take time for herself, but she said she can't. She said, 'When I'm done with the government, when I ban all those vans from Canada'... well, to me it sounds unrealistic."

At the same time, Ana was plagued by guilt that she never fulfilled her promise to Isabelle, made after their 2008 press conference in Fredericton, to stay with her friend and ally and keep fighting to the end.

"I feel bad. I feel sorry that I haven't stuck to my word," Ana told Isabelle personally, once the federal van review was under way. "We made a pact. We always said we'd go to the end. I feel a little bit ashamed of myself, like I let you down."

"No," said Isabelle, without a hint of resentment. "You did everything you could."

Another painful consequence of Ana and Isabelle's crusade was the rift that grew between themselves and the other grieving families in Bathurst. As disagreements emerged in the wake of the tragedy, so did hard feelings develop on both sides. In 2008, Isabelle became discouraged that more parents wouldn't join in the work she and Ana were doing, although she now believes it was the best outcome.

"We were a group of families that all lost our children together. But imagine how complicated it would have been if we'd all tried working together, fourteen parents, to lobby for an inquest or fight the government over winter tires. It would have been more difficult, because of all the little disagreements that would have come along. Maybe it was better that Ana and I, and then later Marcella, took this on by ourselves."

There were flashpoints throughout, but the divide between the families was most visibly expressed in the public dispute over whether Dream Street Pictures should be allowed to make a movie about the tragedy and the revival of the Phantoms. The views of many parents were sharply at odds. Some took comfort in a story that presented a happy ending for a school and a community so desperately in need of one. Others saw it as just another case of diverting attention from the real issues of the tragedy, of sidestepping accountability.

By the time the film made it to television screens, the real-life cast of teachers and school officials who were most closely involved with the BHS tragedy, or who had led the school through the crisis, had actually all moved on. Wayne Lord had departed his teaching job, and his beloved coaching duties, although he could sometimes still be seen attending Phantoms games, watching quietly from the stands. He still played golf in Bathurst with Mayor Stephen Brunet and other friends and former colleagues. Four years after losing his wife Beth, Lord married again. No doubt he continues to live with a heavy burden, as anyone would who endured what he did, although his precise feelings about the tragedy have never been revealed. Aside from his appearance at the coroner's inquest, Lord has vowed never to speak publicly about the disaster.

Bathurst High Principal Coleen Ramsay had also retired from her job by the time the movie was broadcast. So had Don McKay, the vice-principal who oversaw extracurricular activities at the school. In retirement, each remained a respected figure in Bathurst, active in the community, serving as volunteers or directors with local sports clubs and service organizations, including the Rotary Club, where Don McKay became president.

McKay's wife Nancy, a long-time organizer with the New Brunswick Progressive Conservative Party and a former political candidate in Bathurst, was appointed chief of staff to newly elected Premier David Alward when the Tories took power from the Liberals in 2010. And it wasn't long after Nancy had arrived in the premier's office that John McLaughlin, Don McKay's former boss, was called up to Fredericton too, promoted from his position as school superintendent on the North Shore, to assistant deputy minister at the Department of Education and later the deputy minister: the most senior English-language education official in the province.

. . .

There is no reliable guidebook on how to grieve the loss of a child. And there is no harder challenge. The only certainty is that every parent who goes through the ordeal does so in their own individual way. After losing their sons, Isabelle, Ana, and Marcella turned their heartache into public action. It was hard, thankless work. Public advocacy may not have been good for their souls, compounding their anguish, but their fighting spirits helped bring clarity and accountability to an unnecessary tragedy.

"We didn't achieve everything we wanted," says Ana. "Still, I think we have accomplished a lot. Changes have been made. I believe that if it wasn't for us — Isabelle, myself, Melynda, Marcella — nothing would have been done. If we didn't press for the coroner's inquest, if we didn't file our report to the police, many things we didn't know at the time, we would never have known."

"All I know," says Isabelle, "is that we did everything we possibly could to make student travel safer. . . . We made progress, and there is still more to do, but governments have seen and heard us. They know what they need to do to make the right changes for the needs of children."

On the fifth anniversary of the disaster, both women were finally also making progress with their personal grief. In the early years after Javier died, Ana refused to replace the calendar in her kitchen, which for years remained stuck on January 2008, when time, literally, began to stand still in her life. It made her daughters Carla and Maria crazy with frustration and worry that their mom was so beset by grief that she couldn't even bring something as ordinary as a new calendar into the house. But Ana has now let go of that, and for more than a year there's been an up-to-date calendar in Ana's kitchen in Beresford.

Ana's house is still adorned, in every room, with framed photographs of Javier — Javi playing soccer, Javi goofing around with his mom and sisters, Javi posing for his BHS yearbook photo. And some things Ana hasn't been able to let go: her son's bedroom down the hallway is still intact, filled with his things, the memories of his life.

At Isabelle's house on Lakeside Avenue, Daniel's bedroom is also un-changed, looking almost exactly as it did that Friday morning when Daniel left home for school, never to return. His quilt still covers his bed; his clothes still lie in his drawers; his electric guitar and a pair of boxing gloves sit in a corner of the room, along with a clutch of gold and silver athletic medals hanging from a hook on brightly coloured ribbons. On the walls there are posters of Jimi Hendrix, Sabian drum cymbals, and a guide to guitar chords. Isabelle can't say whether she'll ever bring herself to unpack her son's room and box up his things, or give them away.

"Today, I still have my electric candle lit in the living room window 24/7 for Daniel, and all my porch lights on, day and night, in memory of the boys. I never shut them off."

•••

In the waning days of summer 2013, long after the snow and ice had dis-appeared around Bathurst, replaced for a few, fleeting months by green grass and other signs of life springing from the ground at Holy Rosary Cemetery, so another welcome change appeared at the burial ground above town. Isabelle, finding a secure place in her heart for Daniel's memory, had finally OK'd the design on her son's headstone and arranged for it to be installed at his gravesite, alongside the headstones of his six friends. The monument was bigger and taller than the others, just like Daniel had been.

On the front there was a picture of Daniel, with his broad, reassuring smile, along with the sculpted outline of an electric guitar incorporated into one side of the headstone. On the back was a picture-postcard photograph of Tetagouche Falls — Daniel's favourite swimming hole, a summer hangout in the green verdant woods behind Bathurst — as well as this simple inscription:

"What we keep in memory is ours, unchanged forever."

Sources and
Acknowledgements

This book came to life because of the trust placed in me by Ana Acevedo and Isabelle Hains, who invited me into their lives and shared with me their stories. I didn't know it was physiologically possible, until our interviews, for human beings to produce so many tears. In the midst of their pain, Ana and Isabelle patiently answered my questions and tolerated my visits and phone calls over the course of many months, and for their honesty, courage, and co-operation I am profoundly grateful.

I'm equally thankful to Patrick Branch, Ginette Emond, Carla Johnstone, and Krista Quinn, who also lost loved ones in the Bathurst tragedy and agreed to share their thoughts and memories with me. My sympathies are with them and all of the families who still grieve the loss of eight precious people on January 12, 2008.

My thanks also to Stephen Brunet, Yvon Godin, Stella Gurr, and John Mahler for their invaluable interviews and perspectives. I am particularly indebted to Melynda Jarratt for her insights, intelligence, and encouragement throughout. I also wish to acknowledge the valuable briefings provided to me by current or former civil servants who played a role in this story, but who asked to remain anonymous.

A number of documents and digital sources were also useful, especially the collection of records, correspondence, media clippings, and private diary excerpts belonging to Isabelle Hains, as well as the hundreds of blog entries published on the Web site VanAngels.ca. Hours of video recordings made available to me by Melynda Jarratt and Charles LeBlanc were also helpful.

For different parts of the story, I relied heavily on the official transcript of the 2009 Coroner's Inquest of the Bathurst High School Van Collision, on the RCMP's Collision Reconstructionist Report into the 2008 collision on Highway 8, on Transport Canada's Technical Report into the collision, the Canadian Council of Motor Transport Administrator's

2013 Evaluation report on 15-passenger van safety, and the Transport Canada Web site on the same subject.

Also helpful were various media reports on the tragedy and its aftermath, published in print or online by the (Bathurst) *Northern Light*, the New Brunswick *Telegraph Journal*, CBC News, and Canwest News Service (now Postmedia News). Of particular help was the published work of reporters Kevin Bissett of the Canadian Press and Marty Klinkenberg of the *Telegraph Journal*. It was Klinkenberg who first revealed Marcella Kelly's extraordinary story of unease the morning before the crash. His account was published in a front-page story in the *Telegraph Journal* on January 10, 2009: "Heartache and healing; anniversary a year after the crash that killed seven high school boys and a teacher, the people of Bathurst try at once to remember, and forget."

The epigraph at the beginning of the book is taken from *The Sweet Hereafter* by Russell Banks, published in 1991 by McClelland & Stewart.

The baseball quote in the Introduction is taken from the 2011 film *Moneyball*, written by Steven Zaillian, Aaron Sorkin, and Stan Chervin. The film was based on the 2003 book by Michael Lewis, *Moneyball: The Art of Winning an Unfair Game*.

I am of course also grateful to the many people who encouraged me and assisted in the making of this book. At Goose Lane Editions in Fredericton, Susanne Alexander was an early believer who welcomed me into the world of non-fiction publishing; Colleen Kitts-Goguen was a steadfast champion who kept me on track; James Duplacey, John Sweet, and Patrick Flanagan were wise and patient editors; and Julie Scriver and Chris Tompkins designed the book with sensitivity and élan.

I am also indebted to the friends, colleagues, and family members who read the manuscript, accompanied me on my travels to Bathurst, tolerated my three-year fixation with this story, or in other ways provided advice and support, all of it deeply appreciated. Special thanks indeed to three people whose love means everything—Diane, Julia, and Jeremy.

Index

Richard Foot wrote about the tragic accident near Bathurst for Postmedia News, where he worked as senior staff writer for eight years. Before joining Postmedia, he was the Atlantic correspondent for the *National Post* and the Moncton bureau chief for the *Telegraph Journal*. He is now a Halifax-based freelance reporter and an editor with *The Canadian Encyclopedia*.